LORENE

Dear Vanada,
enjoy your trip
down memory lane with
Aunt Lorene. Love
Jan

LORENE

A DEEP SOUTH TURN OF THE CENTURY WOMAN

Lorene Hart Furney
and
Jan Furney Acompora

Copyright © 2012 by Lorene Hart Furney and Jan Furney Acompora.

Library of Congress Control Number: 2012912755
ISBN: Hardcover 978-1-4771-4502-9
Softcover 978-1-4771-4501-2
Ebook 978-1-4771-4503-6

All rights reserved. No part of this book may be reproduced or transmitted in any form or by any means, electronic or mechanical, including photocopying, recording, or by any information storage and retrieval system, without permission in writing from the copyright owner.

This book was printed in the United States of America.

To order additional copies of this book, contact:
Xlibris Corporation
1-888-795-4274
www.Xlibris.com
Orders@Xlibris.com

Contents

Preface 11
Acknowledgments 13

PART 1
The First Fifty

Lorene as a Child 17
Meeting the Furneys 20
Life with the Furneys 24
First Move, 1933: The Hart Homeplace,
  Tenant House by Hickory Tree 33
Second Move, 1934: The Devane Place 40
Third Move, 1934 and 1935: The Hart Homeplace,
  Tenant House 43
Fourth Move, 1935: The Old Griffin Place
  near the Howell Self Place 51
Fifth Move, 1936: Rock Hill, Our Own Place 52
Sixth Move, 1937: Hart Homeplace, Tenant House
  by Hickory Tree 54
Seventh Move, 1938: The Herrell Place 58
Eighth Move, 1939: The John Baker Place 60
Ninth Move, 1940: Kennedy Hill 67
Tenth Move, 1941: The George Mercer Farm 72
Eleventh Move, 1941: The Herrell Place 79
Twelfth Move, 1942: The Carl Bryant Place 80
Thirteenth Move, 1943: The Bell Farm 96
Fourteenth Move, 1943: Furney Farm
  (Old Jerry Wilkes's Place) 100

Fifteenth Move, 1944: Furney Family, Tenant House............. 104
Sixteenth Move, 1945: The Herrell Place (Again).................... 105
Seventeenth Move, 1945-1947: Brice's Plantation................... 110
Eighteenth Move, 1947: Durwood and Effie Crosby's Farm 117
Nineteenth Move, 1947: Guy Crosby's Farm 121
Twentieth Move, 1949:
    New Hart Place by Brice's Plantation 132
Twenty-First Move, 1951: The Mable Dill Place,
    behind Spence Field.. 138
Twenty-Second Move, 1951: The Watt Jenkins Farm 139
Twenty-Third Move, 1951 and 1952: Sunset Airstrip 146
Twenty-Fourth Move, 1952 and 1953: The Joel Clark Place 152
Twenty-Fifth Move, 1952: The Joel Clark Tenant House.........158
Twenty-Sixth Move, 1953: Laura and Ralph Crosby's
    Autreyville Place..161
Twenty-Seventh Move, 1954:
    Ralph and Laura's, near Moultrie....................................... 164
Our Twenty Eighth Move, 1954: The Jack Lewis House 172
Twenty-Ninth Move, 1954: Sambo Jenkins's House
    in New Elm Community 173
Thirtieth Move, 1954: House near Greenfield Church
    on Autreyville Road 174
Thirty-First Move, 1955: The Two-Story House
    on Old Adel Highway 177
Thirty-Second Move, 1955: Down the Street
    Next to Doc McCoy 184
Thirty-Third Move, 1956: Murphy House
    on Lower Meigs Road 188
Thirty-Forth Move, 1956: The Auger Place, off Meigs Road 191
Thirty-Fifth Move, 1956: Mayor Wither's Place
    beside the Pilco Creek 198
Thirty-Sixth Move, 1956: Jim MacOdom's Place 199

Thirty-Seventh Move, 1956 and 1957:
   The New Block House on Dad's Farm 203
Thirty-Eighth Move, 1957: West Palm Beach,
   Florida, High Ridge Road 208
Thirty-Ninth Move, 1958: Lucerne Avenue, by WPB Canal.....215

Part 2
Lorene Continues

Fortieth Move, 1960: Kinzy Apartments...................................223
Forty-First Move, 1960: Florida Drive, near Lake...................226
Forty-Second Move, 1960: Bermuda Road,
   Stucco House near County Barn...228
Forty-Third Move, 1961: Tradewind Apartments,
   near West Palm Beach Airport 230
Our Forty-fourth Move, 1962:
   Back to My Dad's Place in Georgia 233
Forty-Fifth Move 1963, Hypoluxo Road, West Palm Beach....235
Forty-Sixth Move, 1963 and 1964:
   Pine Drive, Gil's New Home 238
Forty-Seventh Move, 1965: Back to Kinzy Apartments...........242
Forty-Eighth Move, 1965: Mrs. Tiner's House 244
Forty-Ninth Move, 1966: High Ridge Road.............................248
Fiftieth Move, 1967 and 1968:
   Military Trail with Mae and JR and Children 253
Fifty-First Move, 1967 and 1968:
   Back to Tradewinds Apartments 254
Fifty-Second Move, 1972: Our Own Home
   by the Pecan Tree in Georgia 262

Dedication

This memoir is dedicated to my mother, Lorene Hart Furney, who left for all to enjoy her handwritten memoirs of the first fifty places she lived during her more-than-fifty years of marriage. She would like this book to be dedicated in memory of her loving parents, Jerry E. Hart and Eva May Croft Hart, and her eight children—Charles W. Furney, Gilbert L. Furney, Jeanette Veglia, Janice L. Acompora, Vernon C. Furney, Mavis A. Folsom, Melba Jean Deas, and Dennis Jerale Furney—without whom she would not have had the material or incentive to write.

Lorene noted a special thank-you to her husband, Webb, who (sometimes reluctantly) tolerated her love of books and writing through their many years of marriage until his death in 1989.

This book was compiled by me, Jan Furney Acompora, her fourth child. Part 1 of this book was from the handwritten memoirs of my mother, Lorene Hart Furney. Part 2 was written by me, Jan Furney Acompora. There may be some errors or omissions for which the writer apologizes. Note that from this point on, "I" refers to my mother speaking.

Preface

Lorene was born in Georgia in 1914, the beginning of the twentieth century. Her early life sounds like a hardship compared to today, but it was quite normal during her young years. With her stories, we have learned of the rich culture of rural America during the Depression years, World War II, and the progress afterward. As America moved forward, so did Lorene, to become an independent thinker and a liberated woman long before women's lib was popular. She was truly a woman of her time, leaving a legacy that will long be remembered.

This memoir will give insight to the level of poverty the people in America were born into during the first half of the twentieth century. If you were not born into the 10 percent of rich families, this is part of your history. It is not limited to the South, although the setting is in the South. A favorite aunt's, Rose, writing (born in 1908) about her life in the twenties in Long Island, New York, is the same, but in a different setting and culture. Lorene's history was an inheritance of women at work and juggling the demands of a very large family at home. Her day-to-day struggle highlights her grit and determination. Lorene was the oldest of twelve children.

I am Jan Furney Acompora, the fourth of Lorene's eight children, and we have heard all these stories as children growing up, not only with Lorene but with my grandmother as well. The ancestors in our family are great storytellers. Some keep logs when they travel, some are historians, but my mom always told us about the good old days and was glad they were of the past. Sometimes when writing, she tends to wander—she has so many stories to tell, but that is what makes her stories great, and they wouldn't be the same if she left out her Southern expressions. It has been my greatest pleasure to help leave this legacy of Lorene.

Acknowledgments

To all who helped me and those who provided their memories for this book

My daughter, Deborah A. Gerhardt, who encouraged me to publish my mom's memoirs and my granddaughter, Shawna Gerhardt, who scanned pictures and did computer input. Jeanette Veglia, Vernon Furney, Mavis Folsom, and Jerale Furney, who shared their pictures and memories with me.

Thank you.

PART 1

The First Fifty

The first fifty places I lived in my more-than-fifty years of marriage

The paragraphs, chapters, and sentences you are looking at is how two people's lives were completely changed and how the resulting lives of their eight children, who were very much involved in helping to live it, were also.

Lorene as a Child

On the twenty-ninth day of November 1914, I was born, Lorene Elvie Hart—oldest daughter of Jerry E. Hart and Eva Mae Croft Hart. Naturally, being the oldest had an influence on my disposition in a life yet to be lived.

First, being oldest, my parents had to learn to be parents and that they now had to share their life with another. More than that, I was their flesh and blood, produced by them, by God, our Holy Father.

Second, I learned I could not always get my own way as other brothers and sisters joined the family. A large family of twelve.

Third, I learned early to share all my small possessions. They had to be small as I was just a little girl. Little did I know this would last all these many years. Also I learned to love sharing no matter what; one does not enjoy being selfish and miserable.

I learned to be patient always, seemed like no matter what. My mama said, "Can't you wait a minute? I have other things to do" or "Just be patient. Your sister has a turn at this also," be it just looking at a book, drinking water, or getting dressed. I soon learned in such a short time I'd have the whole book to myself, or I'd get the last drink of cool water or cane juice. As to getting dressed, I learned to get dressed first because I was the oldest.

I learned to understand others at an early age because none of us can commune with small young children on an equal basis, so it was grunts, head nodding, yes or no. Then with grown-ups—no understanding meant your bottom gets a spank or a punch where it hurts.

I learned joy at our house by seeing others happy—my family, especially at Christmas or when there's a big watermelon to cut or a trip to our nearest city to the county fair at the fall of the year. All these added up to joy on most occasions.

Oh yes, peace—the precious quiet, and the joy of peace and love at evening time on an old porch, just after sundown. About three small children and our mom, in the twilight, singing the old songs. She sang alto when she was a young lady, before she was married. And to hear the whip-poor-wills singing "whip-poor-will" over and over again. Also, now and then, the squeaky shriek of a small night owl. There was an old omen that if it continued without being stopped, it would bring bad luck or death to the family it visited. To stop the bad luck, you would tie a knot in the corner of a handkerchief or a bed sheet. The screeching would stop almost at once! Everyone would be amazed at the silence in the early dusk of night.

Grandpa Babe Hart's log home built by Babe and sons, 1903

Grandpa Babe Hart's home

Meeting the Furneys

In the year 1929, early fall, William T. Furney (better known as Buster) and wife, Lucy D. Coley Furney, moved into our little community, or at least close by. The Furney family, like our own, was large enough—twelve children, I believe. They settled on the Turner Brice plantation, one of the largest farms in Brooks County, Georgia, and one of the oldest.

In no time at all, the Furney boys met the Hart girls. The boys were just a little older than the girls. This started lining things up in our corner right away. One of the boys, Cyrus Webster (better known as Webb), and me, Lorene Hart, hit it off right at once; we just liked the same things. A good time mostly. Going to the pond cuttings, the devil's hopper near Barwick, square dancing, and never getting tired. We enjoyed riding on the Hoover buggy and two-wheeled carts. A limousine would have been no better because we were young, happy and, later on, in love.

For four years we were very close to all the other young people, girls and boys. During that time we began to choose the company of each other most. Of course we partied and square danced in each other's homes. We would just take down an old bed, set up the music makers, and Webb would call the square dance. The square was called a set, which was an equal number of people following the calls. The calls were known as Ocean Wave, Bird in the Cage, Grapevine Swing, or River Bend. Also Willow Basket, Four Hands Around, or others.

There were two ponds in our community, Brice's and Melton's (now known as Nichol's Lake). Melton's pond had a grist mill where the water was used to turn the mill to grind corn into cornmeal and grits. Everyone brought corn to be ground. The force of the water made the mill wheel work. No electric power was used, and there was no heat from an engine. All of it was a cool operation, and many were the times I went to the mill at Melton's pond to get our cornmeal and grits made. While I'd wait, I would get a boat and take a ride over the deep smooth water.

The next most enjoyable time was fishing. There were two ponds, 1700 acres or more, with huge dams placed to catch the water. Every five years the dams would be broken by using shovels or dynamite to blast a large opening so the water could run out a screen fence or something else placed so the fish could not escape with the water. Now the pond would lower itself until one could wade all over it. It was well advertised, almost statewide. Everyone talked about the pond fishing for weeks. Then the day would finally come, usually in the fall, when it was really cool and there were crisp mornings.

At these pond fishings there was no more excitement anywhere than seeing men line up all around the pond near enough to hear the gun shoot at 8:00 AM on the appointed morning. Everyone would hit the water, fully dressed. Boots and all clothes were worn to protect the body from mosquitoes, snakes, and catfish fins. The men would fish most of the day. The wives helped clean the fish and cook on the hot coals fixed up to cook two pans at the time, and make coffee and cheese grits. Some people cooked in a wash pot (a large black wrought iron pot) and dipped out the fish when cooked with a pitchfork. Every family had their own special hush puppy recipe, and you never tasted such good homemade pound cake, a specialty also.

The men would come out of the pond at noon, like coming out of the fields from work. Stand around and warm up drinking hot coffee. They would really eat up the fried fish and hush puppies. Some would warm up with a few sips of White Lightning saved for such occasions.

Now the young ladies and a few musicians had a different good time. The music makers would look around; find a flat top stump where a tree had been cut down. They would sit there and play all the old songs requested while the young ladies showed off their lovely voices. Beautiful altos and sopranos pitched in on the old songs like those sung at the Grand Ole Opry. Some of these same people are the reason the Grand Ole Opry is the same today with country music. I saw a young boy of six years old playing a violin on the side of a flatbed truck, a natural musician, and he made it to Nashville's Grand Ole Opry. He later composed music for a group called the Beverly Hillbillies and also composed a famous song entitled "Come Morning." This song was sung many years later at his funeral. Ivy Bryant Jr.—we knew him as Boodle O. Bryant—was buried at the Pleasant Hill Church cemetery, and his headstone is a large guitar made of marble.

A nice fat prize was paid for the largest bass caught and weighed in, also the largest catfish. This was always so exciting to everyone. Sisters and brothers who had lived near the ponds as small children and had moved to other counties or to other states would just use this occasion as a homecoming. You have never heard such talking and handshaking politicians, singing and making merry for miles in all directions. Fires were built, and cooking places set up even out in the fields just so it was a sort of shady spot. Of course, in a few years, there was a concession stand with Cokes, gum, cigarettes, and candy bars. No hot dogs or hamburgers. You can't believe that? Well, the good fish just put a stop to such food should it have been available. Some of the girls would openly flirt with the most popular young men, and the steady girlfriends would really be jealous. You would soon know her temper when this happened. This was my first pond cutting.

While I've been thinking of the pond fishings and writing things down, I wonder why they couldn't do this in the summer when it was warmer! They waited until laying eggs and hatching little fish was over. Also, the fish caught would not spoil as fast if the weather was cold.

Brice's pond

Descendants of slaves home at Brice's

Life with the Furneys

The year is now 1933.

In the year Webb and Lorene were married, January 14, 1933, it was also Webb's father's birthday. Pa Furney was forty-seven years old, and my mother's last baby was twelve days old. Her name was Wilma Ruth Hart. I guess my mother felt like I let her down, come to think of it, after looking after me all those years. Like so many others, I did not think I'd need her too much more to help me. I was leaving the nest, I thought I could fly by myself and make my own decisions, do as I pleased. I left my sisters and brothers with my parents, who were just as reliable as I was.

Webb sold the cottonseed from a bale of cotton to buy our marriage license, and they cost three or four dollars, plus pay for the clerk who performed the ceremony in front of two witnesses. An old boyfriend of mine, John Griffin, the first one I had ever dated, was also Webb's friend. John used his car to take us down to Quitman to get married. We got married about 4:00 PM in Quitman, Georgia. I was a little scared because that was a very long step, but I was very trusting in Webb for the rest of my life. My vows were true and committed. I've never broken my marriage vows, and it is now fifty-one and a half years later, though many times I will admit I would have liked to. I was taught that when you made a statement to God, through man even, you lived by it come hell or high water, as the old saying goes. You make your bed yourself, and if it doesn't sleep good, turn over more often. Marriage is like a ship on an ocean: when it is calm, you sail, when it is rough, you hang on, and a captain does not abandon ship.

The first night, we ate our wedding supper at Aunt Mae and Uncle Shine Furney's. Webb's family had killed hogs (the weather was cold) for our year's supply of meat that day, and everyone was so tired. Little did I realize it then, I had thought hog killing was a picnic, though I was used to getting my hands into our butchering hogs. I was yet to learn a lot.

We never moved out into a home of our own until later that year, though I was told we would live with Webb's family a couple of weeks until a colored guy and his wife moved and we would get the house they were living in. Oh yes, I had no doubt that scalding water mixed with lye soap and good hot suds would make that house clean and livable, I was no highfalutin gal, I'll tell you. I did not mind working for better things, and I still had a lot to learn yet to be a member of the Furney family, to which I now had a lifetime commitment. Their ways of doing things were so different from my family. I helped milk cows, clean the house, and do fieldwork. I joined in everything. First I discovered a huge traveling trunk just, filled with new gingham and calico scraps and also some three-yard lengths, plenty big enough to make a small child a shirt or a cute little dress. Well, there was a simply wonderful sewing machine too! My sister-in-law Ethel got it all together. We heated those flatirons by the fire and pressed those scraps by the boxful, ready to cut out our favorite quilt patterns, of which I made good use.

You should have seen the lovely old quilts Ma Furney had, that her family made while she lived in Worth County. Her sisters and in-laws, especially Aunt Florence Coley, Aunt Sally Kerce and daughter Corrine, a great-aunt, Lizzie Slaughter, and Grandma Coley all busied themselves on long winter days and evenings, piecing tops and then quilting each into the intricate patterns: the maple leaf, double wedding ring, broken stone, bear tracks, drunkard's path, ocean wave, and bowtie. The older women of this time pieced by hand every tedious stitch, then the younger ladies stripped and sewed each square together until a double bed quilt was ready for the quilting frames. Each square was then hand stitched again to the inside filler and interior lining of the quilt. I loved this and made two complete quilts before my first child arrived on November 20, 1933.

This year on the Fourth of July, Pa Furney hosted a barbecue for family and friends. The pork was dressed and thoroughly baked on red-hot coals made from green oak poles cut right out of the woods. About ten AM the weather began to turn cool. By noon we drank coffee. We were cold enough without all the iced tea we had ready. Ma Furney made the best barbecue sauce and Brunswick stew you ever ate. This was one difference in our families. My dad would not have tolerated the idea of butchering, cooking, and eating a whole hog in two days, let alone in one day. We ate well in our home, but not like that. I could not help comparing Pa Furney to my dad. Oh yes, everyone went for a walk after dinner that day, and they all wore their winter coats too!

Pa Furney would often say, "All right, boys, we need some stove wood. Get the wagon, the axe, and the saw." At the end of the day enough nice-sawed split pinewood to last six months would be cut. Believe me; we used it too, as there was some cooking going on. Lucy D. was one good cook, and her daughters also became good cooks.

I still had a lot to learn. One day at noon, along in May, Webb came from out of the field with the horse they had been working. I walked to meet him, took the reins in my hand, and said I'd put him up for dinner. I took off all the gear, left on the bridle, led him out the gate, jumped on his back, and rode him about a half mile to the mailbox. He walked to the mailbox real nice, but on the return trip, all he could think of was his corn and hay for dinner, and he flew into a hard gallop. I was really enjoying the ride until I got into the house. Ma Furney just looked at me and said, "No more horse riding, Lorene. Do you realize you could lose your baby if you do things like that?" Words I was to hear many times during those nine months.

There was no seeing a doctor once a month, no prenatal care. We had to learn from older heads, mothers and mothers-in-law. Both of mine could not be beat, they were well experienced. Neither had gone through the change of life or menopause yet.

Ma Furney's last child, Marie, was six months old and my baby sister was twelve days old when Webb and I got married. My mother was yet to have one more child, a boy, Louis Virgil Hart. Of course there were the usual old wives' tales, but really, I did not always listen to them.

One of the things I became very familiar with the first thing was making soap using potash lye and a product from the hogs' fat that had been cut up and cooked until crispy and brown, usually in a big wash pot or kettle. The only bought soap at this time was Octagon soap and Gold Dust washing powder. Country stores didn't bother to carry fine imported French soaps.

The following was our recipe for homemade soap: Prepare 3 quarts (or 3 coffee cans) and good, fresh or well-taken-care-of cracklings, out of which all the rendered fat has been pressed. Place them in an iron wash pot with 2 quarts of water. Let boil ten or fifteen minutes. Add one can of lye. Pour out slowly (if you just dump it in, it will splatter. It can also be so very painful if it gets into your eye. You wash it quickly in cold water for fifteen minutes, so be careful). Then boil and stir until all pieces of the cooked meat are dissolved or have been eaten up by the lye. Then boil and stir gently with a wooden paddle (a long handle is best). Then when it boils up good, remove the fire by raking away all the hot coals. Let the soap cool. Make sure it is not going to rain and it is a full moon or a growing moon. Your pot of soap must not get rained on, and the right moon will keep it from shrinking. You may use some rosin and pine tar in the boiling to give a good clean pine scent in the finished product.

A nice bar of the soap was put away for Saturday night baths and to lay out when company dropped in for a meal. Then the company would wash hands and faces before coming to the table to eat. The soap was also good, softened and placed on sores and boils to heal them.

The pots or kettles were also used to cook the juice from sugarcane into rich red syrup for winter eating with good old buttermilk biscuits and sausage made at home from the big hog killings. The hog killings were usually once a year, generally on a very clear cold time of year. That is a thing of the past for all but a few families who butcher for year round use. Most just buy smoked meat and depend on freshly dressed pork all along as needed for farm families today, and bought at dear prices at the supermarkets now for most homes.

Another thing at the time was durable, beautiful, and strong almost-indestructible cotton. Cotton was selling for only four or five cents a pound, and cloth for sewing was only ten cents a yard. We were paid a penny a pound to pick the stuff. I could work my fingers to the bone and just got 150 pounds in a day. Sunup to sundown. My sister Leona was always better. She could shove two hundred pounds a day in her sack. I even picked cotton, and with me pretty well pregnant during the month of August, the year we got married, I never heard anyone say, "Lorene, you may hurt the baby." I guess the cotton had to be picked by everyone. Ma Furney did not pick. I wished I could sit on a porch in a rocking chair like her and swing my foot. Now me and Ethel still milked a bunch of cows and also cooked supper. Yes, I was still in the same house we started in, eight months later.

A new president came into office about this time, following Herbert Hoover, by the name of Franklin Delano Roosevelt. President Roosevelt did some strange things, as far as I was concerned. I never dreamed of such. He asked that all fertilizer, chicken feed, and bales of cotton be placed in cotton bags. White for guano fertilizer and prints for chicken feed. We already had our flour put in cotton bags. Bales of cotton at the gin were belted in cotton bagging. Now it is in plastic. Believe me, the chicken houses in the North Georgia mountains kept the southern part of Georgia well supplied with beautiful print sacks which, when washed, starched and ironed, and when made into a little girl's dress, it would bring a sparkle to her eyes. They were the prettiest dresses they had ever seen.

Until they were about nine or ten years old, my four little girls (and my sister Leona's four little girls) had not seen many store-bought dresses. Believe me; we racked our brains to make those dresses look as good as Sears & Roebuck's or Belk Hudson's. We ourselves had worn many a pair of flour-sack panties, but our mama bleached all the letters out. As is always the case, some mamas were not so careful, and the joke went around. When a round behind was seen with a flour-sack print on it that said "Self-rising is the very best!" everybody laughed.

For the first time in my life, I saw acres and acres of cotton plowed up right when grown boles were about ready to open up. As soon as it was cut under or cut up, the field would look like it had snowed in the summer. Now you can bet the farmers had taken a great step. They were paid a good price per acre to plow this cotton up, and thank God, we were not allowed to pick one sack full. The reason it looked so white was that the green leaves and stalks died and turned black, and they made a perfect background for the white cotton. There it stayed until the stalks were cut and the land measured. Then it was turned under for the crop coming up next year. The government paid for every acre destroyed.

We washed, soaked, then bleached in lye water overnight and washed again all the white sacks guano came in. Not one was thrown away, and we made pants or skirts, aprons and jackets with them. We also made hand towels. One sack made two towels. In the few years the Depression lasted, many homes did not have one terry-cloth towel in it. If they did, some righteous woman saved it for company that was very special, a dear friend maybe, and hoped they would never know it was her only one. Times were so tough here in the Deep South! Cotton prices soon made a difference in price. We were beginning to really think of all the good uses the government could put our cotton to besides borrowing money on it and filling warehouses until the prices went up.

Well, the crop we started in 1933 is nearly over. Fall is at hand. We have things ready for moving out of Pa Furney's home. We have settled our debts for the year, for Webb and me. All money we used for food we ate, and clothes and shoes which were charged to us. For the first time we were actually aware that it cost us to live. Thank goodness riding in a Hoover cart, driving old Bott the mule did not cost us a thing and we enjoyed riding through the pretty woods and country roads by the Okapilco Creek, a distance of about four miles "shortcut" to my mom and dad's. We just went about once a month. Was it ever a nice visit! We were always back at home Sunday night. The mules had to work.

So maybe you've already guessed. My dad had an empty house on his farm. We'd been with Webb's family for eight months. I know they needed our space. Come to think of it, there was a whole big bunch of us in a fairly small house. Ten in their family. Webb and I made it twelve. Can you believe? We had two big rooms, a fireplace in each, with one chimney in the center, and both smoked when heated up like a furnace, with a board over the opening. Then a room at the end of a porch built across the front of the two big rooms. Then two rooms on the other side with a small walkway between, leading to another two rooms along which was another porch reaching the walkway. This was the kitchen and dining room. That was five bedrooms, porch, dining room, and kitchen.

I don't know how we made it, but we all did fairly well. Webb blew his top once during this time. He made a resentful remark once because neither he nor I could stand okra cooked in peas. So we did not eat them. Well, it got to where it was, to eat or nothing. When Webb blew up, Pa heated up too and told Webb right quick what we could do. The first thing he said was not to say a thing about Lucy's cooking. He told Webb, "You married a gal, and it's a good time to let her do your cooking." "I like mine, and it's gonna stay that way." Today we both enjoy okra any way you cook it. Our taste changed with time.

Bill Furney left home, just walked out in 1933, at the end of the first year at Devane's. My brother J. E. Hart joined him when he left. The two walked and caught rides all the way to Plant City, Florida. Bill had an uncle whom he was on good terms with. Pa Furney's brother Barney Furney, who had sons the same age as Bill, had a small farm in Plant City. Bill and J. E. wore their shoes out walking. You just should have seen the roads in Florida then! I did not see them until years and years later, but when our brothers came back, we heard first thing. Miles and miles of dirt roads and sand ruts where the cars went into the dirt axle deep. No settlements or close towns. They slept in the woods at night and under bridges. They separated in Plant City, and my brother J. E. continued to travel south.

One night my brother caught some fish, cleaned them, and made a fire and baked them. After filling his stomach, he lay down under the dry end of the bridge and fell asleep. At about eleven PM, the place was surrounded by the police. A Negro girl going home from church had been stabbed and raped. They were beating the bushes, looking for the suspect, when they found my brother. He was grabbed up and taken to jail, searched, and fingerprinted. The knife he used to clean the fish had blood on it. He could not call Daddy, for he had no phone. J. E. thought the picture looked bad to him. The police kept looking for the right man and found him in a couple of days. They then let my brother go. He was on his way south again to Belle Glade and Okeechobee. He liked it there, and after moving around some, he settled there with his wife, Hattie Lee Anderson, and raised one boy and three girls. J. E. saw his baby girl graduate and marry before he was taken sick and died at forty-eight years of age. His pancreas ceased to work.

During this we are still at Webb's family's home. So we settled our debts when we got the money from two bales of cotton. The first bale belonged to the man who furnished the land, house, and mule we worked. This is called half cropping (or sharecropping).

Then we paid for half the guano, one half the seed of our bales of cotton, and that left us about $75.

Lorene and Webb Furney

First Move, 1933: The Hart Homeplace, Tenant House by Hickory Tree

We bought a complete bed. Ma Furney gave us a quilt, and my mom gave us a quilt. We bought us two chairs, just plain high-back cane-bottom ones. We used a four-eyed (burner) wood-burning stove, with an oven in the center, a door on each side. Did that thing cook! I'd make a pan of biscuit, put them in on the door on my side. Webb would stand on the other side, open the door, and take them out, brown and ready to eat. I had a dining table made by my grandpa Babe Hart with two benches and a large wooden box nailed to the wall about head high, two boards for a shelf to set bowls of food on. There was a drawstring curtain in front for a cover as a pie safe or food holder, and it worked out fine. We also bought our dishes and cutlery, with pots and pans all with that $75. After meals, all were washed, placed in a stack on our table, covered with a cloth, and used for the next meal.

Boy, we never had any idea how beautiful life could be. Just the two of us to talk, walk, sleep, and eat and clean yards. Why, we had never been alone in all our lives, and it was like a dream. We were afraid we'd wake up and be in a house with a big family. Webb did love to hunt, and that was about all he was really interested in. Oh yes, we did move a hen and twelve frying-size chickens to our new home. We set one of the hens on a nest at his mom's and got the chickens for a start of our own flock.

This was the last of August and the first of September 1933. We were glad to be near my mom now as I needed her to talk to, as I had begun to find I did not know very much! The water in my ocean was getting kind of "choppy." My pregnancy was very much in view, but I did go to the pond fishing for the second time in my life. Yes, the young people were still singing, flirting, eating fish, and really enjoying themselves. Me, I am in a different category.

I am married, expecting my first baby, and I can't get around too good now. I can eat only a little. There really doesn't seem like there is much room to put it. All my friends are speaking, asking how married life is. There isn't much to laugh about. I'm looking at more serious things now. I have not seen a doctor yet. Soon one must be posted so he will know I am expecting him when labor starts. Until then, I just wait, do my quilts, and sew little baby clothes. Thank God I did sew a fine seam. I made with my fingers every piece of clothes my baby would wear.

The middle of September is here. Webb goes back to his dad's to help break the corn and haul it to the barns. He sold our corn and bought some packs of gun shells. He gave a hog in exchange for a hunting dog. He had a gun when we got married, I think. Every afternoon he'd go off to Little Creek Swamp, fairly close to all kinds of wild game. Squirrel, opossums, coons, and birds. My dad even killed wild turkey down in the woods near the little creek. We only ate birds and squirrels. The fox were also plentiful. To get dogs together for a good hunt was a fine outdoor sport for hunting men.

Finally, Webb's vacation was over. We began to think of groceries, the kind you had to buy. There is no money. He is looking for work, any kind for the money. No luck. Then we heard of a new deal started by our new president. This was called Public Work Administration (PWA). The president promised jobs and better prices for products grown on the farms when he went into office. Well, Webb went for the job with dozens of friends and longtime buddies he had made since moving to Brooks County. At first he worked three days a week for one-dollar-a-day pay. The older men with children were suffering for jobs that would help. This was a nationwide program.

Flour, meal, grits, beans, and syrup were already a free commodity given out at a little country store nearby called Chitlin Switch. The people lined up, as did the people in the large cities, for this food in hopes that with jobs this could stop. Everyone was thankful for even three days' work a week. Some of the prices in the store were five pounds sugar, twenty-nine cents. Canned evaporated milk, five cents. Butter or margarine, twenty cents. Flour, twenty-four-pound bag, ninety-eight cents. Cornmeal, thirty-five cents a bag. Pork and beans, five cents. Salmon, fifteen cents. A dozen eggs, fifteen cents. Prince Albert tobacco, ten cents a can. Cloth bags of Golden Grain tobacco, ten cents. Everyone rolled their own smokes with OCB leaves. Boy, how times have changed. Gasoline was twenty-five cents a gallon. Syrup, fifty cents a gallon.

That year, my dad had a huge patch of POJ sugarcane full of good sweet juice to make syrup with. At this time, my mom was very active, and work could not go on without looking after things, like making syrup. The growing of sugarcane was a very necessary commodity as a farm product.

It provided very nutritious sweet syrup for eating with butter and hot biscuits. Brown sugar was used in the form of molasses and was rich in iron vitamins. The sugarcane juice was so good to drink.

Cane juice was extracted by pushing the cut stalks stripped of leaves, known as fodder, into huge iron rollers. These were turned as a long pole or board attached to the top of the rollers was being pulled by a mule that was hooked to the pole. The mule walked in a circle around the rollers all day. The length of the pole or board was determined to allow a space between the rollers and the mule for a person to manually feed the cane into the rollers. A small steady stream of the sickly green juice continues to pour out of a catch system into a fifty-gallon drum. The juice was collected and poured into a large iron kettle. The kettle is made stationary by using brick and cement to make a furnace underneath it large enough to place large pieces of wood for a fire to heat the juice. The juice is heated to boiling and cooked for about four to five hours until all impurities were skimmed off the boiling liquid and constantly stirred until thick syrup appeared. The syrup was then cooled and canned. There is a working cane grinder presently on a farm outside Berlin near my Cousin Mary Lee Norman's house. My children have enjoyed taking my grandchildren there.

Now Webb has a job. We have the groceries. He had worked one week when Uncle Lee Clark came calling one night to tell him that money was appropriated for five days work a week! Just think, five dollars for five days. People were actually joyful about this. On Monday, Webb took off to the job, which was near our home, between the Hart homeplace and the Little Creek Swamp, digging a huge ditch two miles long, five to ten-feet deep, three-feet wide, using a shovel all day for eight hours. Now good, well-thought-of people were in this ditch digging away. This ditch was to retard the breeding place of mosquitoes that brought on malaria fever from the stagnant pond water where they thrived and grew. To drain the water off the place would destroy the mosquito's breeding ground. All ponds were drained in the area by this type of government job.

Well, Monday morning after Webb left, a hawk disturbed my chickens under the little plum trees over a low fence that surrounded our house and yard. I went out, just clapping my hands, and stepped over the little fence and scared the hawk away. I walked back into the house and felt my first labor pain. There was no doubt in my mind it could be anything else. I was just so excited. I had to share the good news. Right away I walked down to my mom's, only to find her gone. I asked my little sister Sarah, who was out of school that day, to take a note that I was writing to my mom to the back side of the large farm. My mom, and others who were helping, was stripping and helping top the cane, ready for grinding to make the syrup before the frost and freeze of winter sets in. The quality of the juice is damaged if frost or freeze hits the cane before it is harvested.

My mama made good time and was home with me right away. That alone settled me down. She let me know it would be a while and we'd let Webb make his day if we could. So at about three thirty

PM, I walked back home and my little sister Sarah went home with me. My face was getting red as a beet with every contraction. They were stronger now, and she put me to bed, bathing my swollen feet and putting a cold cloth on my head. I began to vomit, and I hadn't expected this. My sister Leona got into my dad's truck and went to the old ditch they were digging in. It started near the old Storey place. Jim Sapp also lived there once. The ditch came out still further south near the old Johnson place, north from George Neurell's place on Sand Hill and Quitman highway. It was a very clay country road then, slick and muddy.

Mama came up, then Ma Furney and Webb arrived. The doctor came, but not the doctor I wanted. Old Dr. Fordham from Pavo came, and I expected Dr. Clower from Barney and Morven. Dr. Clower had started on another case, and he could not leave his patient. Well, around eleven PM on the twentieth of November, my first son, Charles W. Furney, arrived the very day he was expected, November 20, 1933. I did fine with no stitches, but my son might have done a lot better in a good medical center hospital. All babies then were born at home in their mother's own bed. I was put to sleep so as not to feel too much pain. Chloroform poured over a cup filled with cotton, held over my nose and provided by Ma Furney's hand, did the job. Crude in a way, yet I guess it was the best one could do then. Little did they know then that if a mother was asleep and couldn't push the baby out, the doctor had no choice but to assist with his instruments? Times changed.

Sarah and a neighbor must have thought things were not going well. They sat up right in the kitchen, along with my dad, and kept heating water to sterilize things, I suppose. They made coffee, and neither Webb nor I had ever drunk coffee. I was so sick smelling it, and the first thing they wanted me to have was a hot cup with cream and sugar in it.

My baby, Charles, had lacerations above and below his left eye, and the back of his neck looked bad. The doctor was glad it was no worse at the time, but one month later, he lost his sight in that eye due to infection, which set up from the use of the instruments used to bring him into the world. The doctor did not put nitrate of silver into his eyes, which was normally done to babies at that time. A very sad Christmas, 1933, Charles was only one-month-old. I had been home all the time. An old saying went "Don't carry your baby out until it's at least four weeks old." We spent Christmas at Webb's dad and mother's.

I'll never forget the nineteenth of January 1934. I thought it would be okay to go out of our house once again. It was Robert E. Lee's birthday. In Quitman it was celebrated with a street parade, barbecue, and bluegrass music. My son was two months old, and I could not go because he might take a cold.

Webb just walked and hunted every day and did not work at the time. I sat up nights with Charles, and then we both slept in the daytime. I never called on him to sit up with the baby. I guess I felt like taking care of babies was my job. Well, from doing about anything I wanted to, I really did my best to be a good wife and mother. Naturally, the thought of another baby scared me to death. Yes, before, I knew what made babies, but I was to learn more. I suppose I was to feel at least I was put to sleep so as not to feel too much.

David, Charlotte, Tommy, Shirley, Roy, Charles, and Roger Furney

Second Move, 1934: The Devane Place

In February 1934, we moved over to the Devane place on the Quitman Highway. We knew it as the Sheffield place. We sharecropped the farm there that year. Webb's dad traded for the place, and it had a nice big house on it, with a wide hall in the middle and a long front porch all the way across the front. It was so nice to sit on the porch and watch the cars go by. The local children went to school on the bus. We lived just below Webb's parents.

Those were hard times for everybody right on. There were many hitchhikers on the road. They even came in four to six to the bunch some time. I would get sick then, when they would all stop and just lay around. This was young people with no jobs and no place to go. There were no handouts from the government either. The people just walked the road. Sometimes they ask for a meal.

I remember we had a nice man who hauled fruit from Florida. He stopped by every two weeks to sell us oranges. That was welcome, for the people usually went to town to get their fruit. Webb's brother Iris and I would eat milk that was frozen. We would sweeten it with sugar, one-half milk, and one-half orange juice. It was quite a treat during the winter time. I had become very close with Webb's family as we had always lived near them. They were truly my family also.

That Fourth of July, we had the biggest barbeque yet. Margie Cribbs married Webb's brother Bill Furney near that time. (I know they were there by August.) Charles pulled up to a standing position for the first time. Boy was that encouraging. He was in a big wooden box so he would not crawl out the door and fall. Ma Furney would watch him for me. Sometimes she would put a quilt down on the floor, pull his little dress way out, and set the five-pound flatiron on it and he could sit up and not fall over. We all had a lot to celebrate.

During the year of 1934, Webb worked very hard every day on the farm. I always thought someone was just waiting to see me blow a fuse. Sometimes Webb's old girlfriends were mentioned. All things said were good. Worth County was a place they all really did enjoy living. Ma Furney's family was from there, and they all had such good memories of the place. The women up there were all the finest looking and the world's best cooks. You just ought to have seen how they could iron a starched white shirt. Ethel could do one proud. Me? Well, it took a long time. I'd never done up white shirts. I'd get a wrinkle here or a speck of smut or some spot. I'd have patience though and finally did a beautiful job. I got to meet most of the family from Worth County. All of Pa's family is from there too. To me they looked just like everybody else, and I treated them so too. Time seems to pass much faster now than it did then.

People of today can't imagine the work we people did back then. There was no such thing as Sanforized material. Everything had to be ironed to get the wrinkles out. Sheets, bonnets, everything. We had five or six flatirons, weighing three to five pounds each, Flat on the bottom with a handle from end to end, made of solid iron. Did they ever get hot! We used a double pot holder to grasp the handle. If your hand was not well protected, you could really get a blister. The irons were heated in the hearth in front of a hot fire, summer and winter.

We'd nearly roast but could get set up in a breezeway and get it done in half a day. All the best clothes were dipped in a starch solution and dried in the sun until stiff. They were brought inside and sprinkled with clear water, rolled up and placed in a bag and kept covered so they would be nice and damp when they were ready to be ironed. When the pile was finished, clothes looked like new and our feet and legs were given out. This went on in every home, and if a girl could not wash and iron clothes to look decent, she better have money and a good colored lady with a willing mind.

An incident occurred when Charles was eight months old. We were living on the Devane place or farm. The boys left the house on Sunday morning. I was making dinner at home and watching my little one. It was very hot weather, so the young men went over to another farm where a Negro lived. He had a thirty-gallon barrel of corn buck. A drink made from water, corn, and syrup or sugar, all fermented together, setting for a few days. The corn buck had about the same alcohol content as beer. Beer was not heard of at that time in our area. Well, Webb liked the stuff and had a few glasses. When they started home, he lay down in the wagon. The heat and the alcohol went to work on him, and when he got home he had to be carried out to the nice cool back porch, completely passed out. Then everyone wanted to see what Lorene was going to do with a husband who was drunk. So down to our house one of the boys came to tell me Webb wanted me. If I had known why, I wouldn't even have walked up there.

Charles and Shirley Whittington

Third Move, 1934 and 1935:
The Hart Homeplace, Tenant House

When we gathered cotton we paid our debts to the landowner, Mr. Devane, and had our corn left. We sold it when it was gathered and put in the barn. In October, we moved back to my dad's place, and it was so good to be near my mom and my sisters and brothers again. We were a very close family. Charles was now nearing one-year-old and this was hard for me to believe. That year made me a more patient, humble person. I learned of a race you can't win in farming. Also that year my prayers for Charles did not return his sight. What you can't change, one can learn to accept. I found out a man you go with and party with is a different person in lots of ways than the husband you marry and vow to live with "until death do you part."

The years were tough ones at the best, when Webb stopped working the government job and farmed at the Sheffield place. In October we sold our corn, and Webb bought us an older model car. He loved to hunt so good, and I always loved to grow chickens. Webb gave someone a bird dog puppy for some large Cornish game hens, all young. So we are now back at Dad's farmhouse up in the woods. It has a great old hickory tree in the yard.

In December 1934, Webb and several younger boys got together and coon hunted at night. They all lived nearby and enjoyed every minute of it, I'm sure. My husband was a real outdoors man. Oh, he was going to keep the animal furs and sell them and make money, but there was a catch. As it is in all schemes to make easy money. The animals must be skinned the right way, with no holes, and cured just right. There was no freezer to keep them in, and I could not be so sure a skin was perfect. Also he had to have a license to sell them. A lot of time was lost when Webb went hunting, but there were some good times along with the bad ones.

Often when Webb was hunting, a sister would come stay with me or I would go stay with Mom and the family. My dad thought my husband should pursue more serious things. I can see now what he meant.

One night Webb said, "Let's have an early supper tomorrow night, the boys and I are going coon hunting in Mule Creek," a very thick swamp. Well, I helped get him off. It was a real cool night in early fall. Bright blue skies and beautiful harvest moons. No one had gotten any wood in to build a fire, and just after supper I went for a bucket of water at the well. For lifting the water, a rope or chain was used and strung through a round wheel called a teacle. Before I got the bucket to the top, the rope broke and I nearly lost my breath as the bucket of water and one-half of the rope went plunging to the bottom of the well. I went into the house, reported the disaster, and was really downhearted, for we could not get any water until the next morning when we fished out the bucket and rope. Webb assured me not to worry, that he would get it out the next morning for sure, and away he went!

Little did I dream of the events that would take place. About eleven PM. I heard a little *putt, putt, putt* of a flatbed Ford truck the boys used to get them and the dogs to the woods where they were to hunt. It was coming up the little crooked road to our house. I got out of bed and called my sister to get up because someone was coming up to our house. Before I opened the door, I heard someone say, "Hold tight, we don't want to drop him. Hey, you can get a hold there, take my hand. All right, let's take him in the house."

Can you imagine the shock I got in when it was Webb they were bringing in? He had climbed a huge oak tree the coon had run up to escape the hound dogs. Someone would always climb the tree, shake the coon out, and that is when the dogs would grab the coon. Well, when Webb got about twenty feet up to the nearest limb, a cramp paralyzed him all the way down one side. He yelled, "I can't make it, boys!" By that time, after hugging the tree with all the strength he had, he hit the ground.

Both legs folded up, knees in, feet out. His eighteen-inch leather boots laced up good, kept his legs from breaking. (Forty-five years later, aggravation from having one knee knocked out of place caused him to retire with a complete disability.) When he was placed on the bed that night, his older brother J. B. went for a doctor and then his mom. The doctor said there were no bones broken, but the knee was out of place. His pain was something else.

For the next thirty days he couldn't do anything at all. The rest of December and middle of January he just stayed in bed. I begged him to just try to stand up. Finally, by sitting in one chair with his feet in another, I could move him. I got an old chair and cut the bottom out, put a bucket under it, and that was his commode. The doctor said to rub his legs with chloroform liniment. It put the pain to sleep. I ended up selling nearly all of my pretty hens to get money to buy the liniment. Christmas Day, or maybe Christmas Eve, my brothers took a rubber-tired wagon and we loaded Webb up, and we spent Christmas at Webb's mom and dad's.

He was so glad to get out of the house for a change. I would drag him from room to room in the chair, take care of my baby, cook, and wash our clothes. I have never been a quitter, though many times I would like to have quit. One morning I went down to the woods and found myself a small oak tree with a limb growing just right to make a crutch from. I cut and trimmed until I got it just right, padded it good, and tried to get Webb to use it. That day, a Sunday, Dad and Lon Rogers, a neighbor, sat a couple of hours with him while I got out of the house for a while. Webb talked some and dropped off to sleep.

When he awakened, he heard them talking real low, and he just listened. Lon said, "You know, Jerry, I don't believe he is ever going to walk again if we can't get him on his feet and out of that bed." Well, Webb moved an arm and let them know he was awake. When I came home he told me what he had heard. I told him they were right, that he needed to bend and move that leg. Right then he held on to the tall iron bed, and for the first time, he stood up. Next he tried the crutch and was so proud when he could move by himself. He had a hard time trying to walk and plow, but by holding the plow handles, he could walk. He did suffer. His knees would swell so badly. His coon hunting days were over. He walked with a limp always after that.

Daddy gave me a nice white spotted gilt pig, and in the spring of 1935, this hog had ten little pigs.

Along in April 1935, I found that I was once again to have another baby. The memories of my first little one were still fresh in my mind. Oh, how I dreaded another one. I'd learned my lesson. I'd never say I can't stand bearing a child, or whimper like a little girl. I said all along for the doctor not to take this one, and I would have no chloroform. I did cry a lot of silent tears (actually, I'm pretty sure they were real tears) because I was truly afraid I could not have a baby without help. I prayed and kept busy. When Webb and I talked, he wanted to choose the doctor and believed in a Dr. Austin in Pavo. He was known to be a man who drank too much and used drugs too. I'd argue and sometimes ask, "Who's having this baby, you or me?"

On September 27, 1935, about one AM, I woke Webb and told him I had started contractions. I progressed much better than the first time. When Webb went for Dr. Austin, he was not in, but he left word for him to come as soon as he returned. When Webb and his brother J. B. got home, I could not wait, so they rushed to get Dr. Clower, who came right away. My prayers were answered.

Now when one doctor was already on a case and the other doctor came, they would generally leave. Dr. Austin came, saw that everything was under control, and asked if he might lie down and sleep a bit. Just about eleven AM, I was having it tough, and Dr. Austin got up and asked if he might give me some medicine he had. It was all right with Dr. Clower, and in twenty minutes my little one arrived. Gilbert was a fine, healthy little boy. I was none the worse and was so happy. There were twenty-two months and seven days between the two boys. Charles could talk fairly good, and he named his brother by calling him Gilbert, after playing with a little boy whose name was Gilbert Houston near Pa Furney's home.

On the fifth day after Gilbert's birth, Webb butchered a hog. We had no refrigerators or home freezers, so we cut the meat up, boned it, fried it, and packed it in crocks of lard or fat that had been cooked out. Boy, did we work! Living back in the woods, we did not expect anyone to come visiting. On Sunday we cooked the meat, starting early while the little ones slept. I looked down the road from the porch, and a bunch of ladies were walking up to our house. My mom, Mrs. Rogers, Mrs. Myers (who later became my sister Eula Mae's mother-in-law), and Gertrude Croft, were all coming to see the new one and me. I pulled off my dress, got into a gown, and hopped into bed before they got to the door. Webb met them at the door and told them he was fixing dinner. I was so flushed and red in the face from so much rushing around, my mom felt my forehead to see if I had a fever.

We enjoyed living at my dad's place back in the woods. It was so nice to hear the whip-poor-wills at late evening, and on a moonlit night a great hoot owl or two would find their way to our grapevine. It sounded like they were talking to each other in their own language for sure. "Who, who, who?" They did make a fuss down in Little Creek, where they usually stayed, and we could hear them all the way to our house. Sometimes we walked down to the Little Creek fish hole and caught a whole mess of redeye fish. We would clean them and fry them, just a few bites each, but they were so good.

In the fall, we enjoyed good mullet from the Florida coast, St. Mark's or Steinhatchee. The mullet would be salted down, covered with water, and soaked overnight. The next morning some would be fried for breakfast in deep fat until golden brown and served with the new syrup and biscuits, a real treat. Also, new sweet potatoes might be on the menu.

Before the days of cars or trucks, a few men and their grown sons would make a three-or-four-day trip to the coast with big two-horse wagons. They would camp and cook out. The coast was a wilderness in the times when Dad was fifteen or sixteen years old (1904 or 1905), and this was something he did. They caught fish in nets, cleaned them for eating, and salted down the fish roe (this was the eggs), white or yellow, and packed them in barrels or baskets. These baskets were hand-woven from strips of white oak trees. These baskets were also used by the slaves (many of the slaves still lived on the farms where they were born) to put cotton in. The art of basket weaving was passed on to the next generation as well as home remedies for sickness and sprains, boils, or sores caused from numerous things. The slaves were the first to make the baskets, and this was quite an art. Some are still made today. I especially remember seeing Marion Hampton make these baskets for a good price from the local farmers to use in their corncribs.

When shucking corn to sell for making good water grist meal, one would pull the cover away, shucking, and then put the clean ear of corn in the basket. Later the ear of corn was put into a corn sheller, which was turned by hand, one ear at a time. The sheller had a mouth (or hopper) in which the corn was placed. The kernels were then placed in a clean white sack and carried to the grist mill to be made into fine cornmeal or grits. Grits are eaten today in most Southern homes either as cereal for breakfast with fried eggs, or supper with cheese melted in it, usually served with fried fish and hush puppies (small fried bits of cornmeal mixed with an egg, water, and cut-up onions).

The only chicken families ate were the fat, plump little fryers grown right on the farm. I was a grown girl, I guess, before I saw a ready-dressed chicken brought into our home, or a prepackaged loaf of bread. Some people probably had these things, but they bought them from a farmer.

Daddy would sell a fresh hog, dressed and ready to cut, to our doctor to help pay the doctor's bill. They were glad to buy the pork, and we were glad to sell it. Once, our doctor's little girl wanted to know what we did with the pig's tail. We took her into the smokehouse and showed her where a big ham was cut off each side of the pork. It left a nice chunk of lean meat and the end of the backbone all in one piece. The tail was still hanging on to it. She was surprised. Her name was Elizabeth Brannon. My brother, Brannon Ralph Hart, was named after her father who had delivered him. Dr. Cecil Brannon of Moultrie, Georgia. It was not unusual at that time for the doctors to have many children named after them.

Gilbert Furney's family: Laran, Betty, Gil, and Carrie

Laran, Carrie, and Gilbert

Fourth Move, 1935:
The Old Griffin Place near the Howell Self Place

In the fall of 1935, we moved out of the woods in the back of my dad's place. We had planted our field there that year, but we wanted to be nearer the main road, plus Dad wanted to remodel his old house. To remodel his house, Dad needed to live in our house. We moved into another house on John Griffin's place near the Howell Self place. This was close to Webb's brother J. B. Those brothers were so close, like twins almost. When it came time for fishing or hunting, J. B. could take care of his money better, with his mother-in-law buying his groceries; she was a little more affluent. We had very little money at any time, and our little family had grown into four. J. B. had no children at that time.

I'll never forget the bountiful supply of quail that fall. Webb and Ellis Copeland, my sister Leona's husband, would fill a hunting sack with the birds and use their pockets for the gun shells. Dad was never a hunter, but he would carry the hunting sack for them.

Fifth Move, 1936: Rock Hill, Our Own Place

In the spring of 1936, we were serious about getting a farm of our own. Webb and my dad bought two mules. Webb picked out one, and Dad took the other. My dad bought a little place for us near Rock Hill, close to a little town called Barney, Georgia. They built a little three-room house there, which had a front porch. This was in February of 1936. There was no well to get water from. We got our water from a Negro family across the road from us. I also took my laundry to their house to wash our clothes at their well. We always tried to be sure we had plenty of water in the house at night because it was a long way to the well if we needed a drink. I'll never forget when we had saltwater fish for supper one night and we forgot to bring in the water. My sister Sarah was spending the night with us, so she went with me late that night to get the water. We were not afraid. It was always such a job to have any of my family come visit us since we were quite a distance apart.

We did live within walking distance of Webb's mom and dad. Webb's sisters and brother—Ethel, Melvin, and Dick—were all grown up by this time and they often had a real slam-bang, swing-'em-around square dance. Pa Furney kept the crowd well entertained, and there were some troublemakers, but they did not dare go to his house. At some other dances a fight would break out and the party would scatter out. One night, Margie, Bill Furney's wife, had just taken a soiled diaper off her baby and was trying to quietly fold it so it would not be seen. A young man approached her asking her if she would be his partner for the next dance. Of course she stammered out that she didn't know how to square dance, that she would get lost and embarrass him to death. She then went to her room and got rid of the dirty diaper. Later, she giggled and said that girls must be scarce in the area for someone to ask her to dance. She looked as nice as any single girl there and had only been married for about three years. She did not let herself "go to the dogs," as the saying goes.

Melvin hated school, and we all tried to help her with her homework. During this time Marie, the baby girl, was getting ready for her first year in school. Ethel took a great interest in Marie and made some of the prettiest little dresses, all by store-bought patterns, complete with buttons, lace, and pretty wide sashes. All had to be starched and ironed, of course, along with Coley's and Iris's shirts. Coy had already started school, and I remember how he hated the short pants, even though they were really comfortable at the end of the summer when it was such hot weather. He finally refused to wear them, and Ma Furney let him wear long pants. Coy thought he was really grown up then.

Everyone was talking about war during this time. President Hoover went out of office, and Pa Furney and my parents often talked about another war. Pa took a daily paper called the *Macon Telegraph* and read every word from front to back. I was an avid reader, but I had no idea what a mess our nation was getting into. Coley was quite grown up at this time, and he worked at the little center store at Rock Hill, a job he loved. Iris kept up with the hunting and fishing and loved square dancing every Friday and Saturday night. Everyone was happy and busy.

When we gathered our corn and peanuts at the little Rock Hill place, we were sick and tired of the mule we ploughed. She was the slowest thing that ever crept, and Webb just could not stand her. A person had to like his farm animals to get along with them. This stubborn mule took the cake for being slow. Nothing on earth, not even a firecracker, could speed her up. In the end, we sold the mule, bought another, and tried again.

Sixth Move, 1937: Hart Homeplace, Tenant House by Hickory Tree

We have moved back into the woods behind Dad's house in the fall of 1936.

One Saturday night, in the fall of 1936, Gilbert was almost two years old by now. My two sisters brought us home from my dad's in their boyfriends' cars with the boys. Gilbert had to go to the bathroom really bad. When we got home, he hurried out behind the side of the house. There was a big tin tub, which I had used for washing clothes. You guessed it, he used the tub, and of course my sisters and their boyfriends could hear the tinkle of water hitting the tub. Were they ever embarrassed! Children will do the darndest things.

It's not long before I find out that I'm expecting another baby. So is Bill's wife, Margie. I was also hoping for a little girl this time, though I just prayed that it would be perfect regardless of the sex. The nine months passed quickly. After, I got over being so sick at first.

My brother J. E. Hart and his wife, Hattie Lee, lived nearby in the Carl Bryant house. We visited each other all along. Ma Furney and her children would take the wagon and come spend the day with us. Her boys could take care of her and the mules just fine by now. As it came nearer to the time for me to deliver my baby, I got things ready. I spoke to Dr. Clower in Morven and told him when to expect to hear from us. I also asked him to look at the broken veins that were now showing up in my lower legs and turning dark blue. He told me that pressure in the lower part of my body, on the main arteries, caused slow circulation problems. Years later, I had to have those veins repaired at Colquitt Memorial Hospital in Moultrie, Georgia.

My labor started one morning at dawn, on October 24, 1937. I woke up Webb since I had no clock, and I wanted to time my labor pains. We both went to Ma's and got her clock, leaving the boys asleep. It was about five-thirty in the morning. I thought I knew what to expect since I had already been through this twice. Just as the sun came up over the treetops to the east of our house that morning, a big red ball, our first little girl was born. Jeanette was the most perfect baby! Three-and-a half-hour labor wasn't much for someone so beautiful? My mom had come right after her breakfast that morning. Webb had walked to his brother J. B.'s and taken his car (he flew off like Moody's goose) to get Ma Furney. They got there at the same time the doctor came, and my daughter was practically peeping into the world by then. With her fat round pink face and bright red hair. She was named Jeanette by Ma Furney, after Bill Maxwell's daughter, who went to school with Webb's sister Laura and whom Laura talked about all the time.

It is fall of the year once again. Big harvest moons, possum hunting, pond cuttings, and cane stripping time! Also square dancing time. Webb and I both loved it. When Jeanette was about two months old, we got my mom to keep the boys one night for us to go to the dance. It was cold, but there were clear skies. I think everyone I ever knew was there, and it had been so long since I had been anywhere that I thought I had molded. I had bought myself a new dress for the occasion, a hunter's green (to bring out the green in my eyes). My sister Effie's new dress was a rust color. I was told I looked like a teenager, but after four-plus years of marriage I thought I must have looked much older. We stayed at the dance until two o'clock in the morning that night and lost one of the baby's shoes, which we never found!

By this time I had learned what it meant to sit by a little one's bed all night long trying to cool their fever from a cold. We had no telephone to call a doctor nor a car to go after one. We made our own home remedies, and when applied in time, and vigorously enough, it always worked.

One remedy for colds was a tar jacket. The tar jacket was made with a soft flannel piece of cloth, like an undershirt with no sleeves. The tar was puree sweated out of really fat or rich pinewood, mostly from pine stumps. A smart person would fill a fifty-pound lard can with small pieces of wood (splints) packed tightly, secure the lid, then turn the top side down on an old iron disc that had a hole in the center. No air could be allowed to get in the can. A small can could be placed under the iron disc to catch the tar. A fire would then be built, with the burning wood on the top and around the sides of the can. The tar caught this way would be used in the tar jacket. Two teaspoons of tar, two teaspoons of tallow, one teaspoon of Vicks salve. This was melted in a pan on low heat, and the cloth was dipped into it, squeezed out, and cooled. Then it was placed next to the chest and back, right over the lungs. Right away, usually in three hours, the bad cough would stop. Then castoria or castor oil was used to keep the bowels open.

Within two days the child would be all ready to take another cold! I made my own tar. It was good for everything but childbirth, nothing helped that. The tar-tallow mixture was used on hogs when they were castrated and for cuts and bruises or collar wounds on the horses. There were no drugs on the market back then for pneumonia or malaria fever. A tea made from a bush that grew in the woods, called bone set, would take care of malaria fever. Quinine also helped for malaria. This medicine really worked too.

Charles is now growing up to be a cute young one, really smart. I could depend on him so much. Gilbert walked right in his footsteps as they got older. No one ever said to me that I couldn't do this or I couldn't do that. We just tried to do the best we could with our knowledge. My children were taught the same way. They did like their toys, whether they were trucks or baby rattles. If it jingled, those two boys had to see what made the noise. Whenever they got quiet, I'd know to check things out. I read a lot when nursing my babies. I read over four hundred pages of *Gone with the Wind* once. I had gotten it from a traveling bookmobile.

People talked to one another during this time. No television, no radio, no home freezers or refrigerators. The men went hunting while the women cleaned house, quilted, embroidered, or cleaned yards. Oh yes, wood had to be cut for the fireplace or wood-burning stove. No one was bored for lack of something to do. I guess that is why the children were two years apart. Once in a while they were born just sixteen to eighteen months apart. When it rained, if the children would be quiet or go to sleep, the parents went to bed too.

When Jeanette was born, we lived in the woods in the back of my dad's house, the same house in which Charles and Gilbert were born. She stayed right up with the boys as she grew up. She might have been a little more spoiled. Webb took care of the boys, but I took care of my daughter. She even slept at my feet when the next baby came along.

Seventh Move, 1938: The Herrell Place

For the first time we had truly moved away from the family, his and mine. Mr. Baker had a sawmill and Webb got a job there, along with his brother Dick. Everybody had to work all the time, no time to hunt or fish much. I learned to walk two miles to Mom and Dad's. We were still deep in the Depression, and there were just no jobs to get easily and the ones you got paid very little money. Fat hogs were sold for five cents or ten cents per pound, right out of the field. Corn sold for fifty cents a bushel. Wages were two or three dollars a day. I remember thinking we would never get snap beans, okra, or butter beans ready to eat that year.

Dick Furney and my cousin Hubert Hart helped spoil Jeanette some, as she sat in their lap every night and repeated every word they said. She was learning to talk, and they thought she was just a doll. Her aunt Ethel took every scrap of cloth left over from Marie's little dresses or Laura's 4-H Club projects and home economics classes and made them into lovely little dresses for Jeanette. Four or five at a time.

Josh, Corey, Al, Pat Gassaway, Jeanette, Dianne, and Jerry Veglia

Eighth Move, 1939: The John Baker Place

We lived in the Howell Self place until the first of the next year. We then moved to the John Baker place, while Webb worked at the sawmill. He traded with Mr. Baker to farm that year, and our house was next door to Dad's brother, Uncle Dink Hart's son Everett, and his wife, Virginia Hart. Everett's brother Hubert lived with them.

All this time trouble was brewing overseas. People talked a lot of war. We had a few daily papers, but older heads could see a little further than we could. They said we were headed for war for certain. In worldly times, of course, young people just thought there was no use to worry until the time gets here. Later on so many of our young boys, now men lost their lives in that war. Jewish people were wiped out by families in Germany, under Hitler's rule. It was truly a holocaust for them.

Franklin D. Roosevelt was still president of the United States and very well-liked by the majority of the people. A young man, Adolph Hitler, somehow became the ruler in Germany and was heartless. One of the worst. So many lives were lost, and barbarous things were planned and carried out. Our fathers and mothers talked a lot about the suffering and lives uselessly lost in World War I, but nothing equaled World War II. Prisons and concentration camps, all the nations finally got involved in the war.

As long winter months stretched into short summer nights, we made a bountiful crop. Including okra, butter beans, string beans, and peas. We also had corn, sugarcane, tobacco, peanuts, and hogs. I did enjoy working in the tobacco harvest with Mayro and Elizabeth Baker. Everyone who could pick up a leaf was needed. Webb really enjoyed working with my cousin Everett Hart that year. His wife, Virginia, had a little boy who was born early in the Spring. Everett sold his fine milk cow to get money to pay Dr. Daniel for delivering the baby. She had a hard time, it was her first child. Everett kept Webb up all night when Virginia's labor pains went from sundown to sunup that night. Early that evening when the labor started, Dr. Daniel left Virginia a painkiller and went home. Each of the four times they would go to Pavo to tell Dr. Daniel he'd better come on out, he would just give her more painkillers.

Just at sunrise, at about six AM when the baby was born, only Ma Furney and Virginia's mom, Mrs. Shepard, were present. She had given birth to her son, Gaynor, and he weighed close to ten pounds. All during this time she had not slept, but after Gaynor was born, she went directly to sleep, just passed out from all the medicine. Dr. Daniel finally came about an hour later! Everett was furious with the doctor letting him down. He had paid him for his service two months before.

At the Baker place we finally had plenty of fresh peas, okra, butter beans, squash, and string beans, along with watermelons. All I could do was watch the children. Another one was on the way. I had been married six years and had three children, but I felt good. Webb's brother Dick Furney was living in a room we furnished him. He was near his work, and we were glad to have him to talk to. Mom and Dad had a radio. There wasn't much news. Then people enjoyed talking, walking, and hard work. I cut okra, pickled beans, or washed clothes at a well, which was way out in the field. We absolutely never slept late. Time wasted was considered the height of laziness. Even the baby was up before sunup.

The lifestyle I was now leading was no different from when I grew up at home. My sister and I arose early and milked four cows. Mom then strained the milk through cheesecloth and put it away for drinking and making butter. We then turned them into the pasture or field. Sometimes we had to fill a huge water trough, which had to be filled from a hand-operated pump. My skinny arms really grew tired, but my mind was sharp. I learned that if two of the boys and I grasped the pump handle, we could make play out of the work and share the chore.

As my pregnancy progressed at the John Baker place, I soon found out that my sister Leona was also expecting one of the little bundles of joy right along with me. She already had two beautiful little red-haired girls. Also, Mr. and Mrs. Baker's daughter Earnestine Williams was expecting a baby. She already had two little girls and really wanted a little boy. I remember Earnestine craving the most unusual things, like chicken salad. She would also have her mom cook bacon in a frying pan over the coals in the fireplace along with scrambled eggs. Recalling her family's trips to Panacea, Florida, cooking outside on an open fire. Her mom petted her to death. Her son, Johnny Mitchell Williams Jr., came after my baby was born. After we finished the farming and gave Mr. Baker his half of everything, Webb kept waiting around for me to have the baby. Charles would be six years old this year, and I could have started him to school but I had not because he was blind in one eye.

Exactly one week before Janice was born, my sister Leona sent me a letter on the same mail route that her baby had arrived. A cute little girl named Velma, born November 3, 1939. When I got her postcard, I put my hat on, took my little girl and the two boys, and walked to my mom's house.

That morning in November, I awoke with a backache and fixed breakfast for Webb and packed him a lunch for work. I told Webb to go on to work, not knowing I was in labor. After the school bus passed, I took the children and started walking down to Everett Hart's house. I saw the postman coming, and I got a postcard from him. I wrote my mom to come, that my labor had started and I was alone. In the meantime, I walked on to get Virginia. By the time I got home, Mom and Dad had come in some kind of tractor. Everett had gone for Webb, but before he got to the sawmill, he had a tire go flat. When he got to the sawmill, Webb had gone to look at more timber with Mr. Baker. Finally, at about one-thirty PM, they started home and stopped to get the doctor. The doctor was already out seeing another patient. They made it home finally. Of course, babies don't wait for us, so when my little girl Janice was born, Mom was with me alone. She must have been worried though because she had sent Charles to get Mrs. Baker. It was November 10, 1939, about noon, when she was born. The postman had just passed on his way back from his route. Mom and Mrs. Baker took care of the baby and me, doing all the things a doctor should do. We were all settled and none the worse when Webb finally got home. When the doctor finally came by, he was stopped and asked to give us a looking over. We were fine.

Dick Furney had moved out several months before, after giving my family the measles. We really had a time with them, and I was worried because I was pregnant. Janice was not very large because of my having had the measles, but she was healthy. I felt like I

Pat, Shawna, Debbie, Brian, and Jan Acompora

was really tough by then, like being a boy in girls' clothes. I had loaded big trucks of hay weighing seventy-five or eighty pounds each when I was growing up. I rode the mules. Once I even tried one, which had never been ridden before, but he threw me over his head. When Dad saw what was happening, he started running toward me but stopped when he saw I was all right then went back to work, and I climbed trees.

I really did love climbing trees. Once I saw a nice vine of grapes just twined and twisted, all in the top and around the trunk. I had nothing to put the grapes in, but I had on a good shirt. I just tied it tight around my waist, real snug, and up the tree I went, vines and all. I got lots of beautiful black grapes. I just unbuttoned my shirt a couple of buttons and filled my shirt up. Talking about scratches! When I got back down out of that tree, I looked like I'd had a fight with a wildcat. When I got home, I unloaded the grapes. I'd already started breaking out in a red rash. Of course, I bathed, and then I did look bad. Half the vines on that tree were poisonous, called cow itch vine, which is a close cousin to the sumac vine. Well, I got the regular hot salty water patted on well, and it really burned. I then added a good coat of black stuff made from gunpowder and cream. In twenty-four hours, I was good as new. For a while I really looked like a barbarian had given me the whipping of my life. I was about sixteen years old then. We did have a huge white grapevine on a trellis in our backyard then, but even though they had a delicious taste, they weren't colored like the red grape juice the black ones give you.

My boys loved to visit my mom. They played with my brothers Paul and Louis and my sister Wilma. There was plenty of white sand and cool shade from the giant oak trees growing in the yards at our old homeplace. We still get a real treat at seeing the old place where Leona and I turned into our teens, had our first boyfriends, who always happened to be hanging around when we were doing our yard cleaning on Saturdays. We had asked Mom to tell Dad it was very necessary not to ask us to help in the fields on Saturday so we could rake the leaves. We'd never burn them up and make a black spot in those beautiful white yards. We'd just take them up and carry them off. Those were glorious days. We had beautiful pots of geraniums, red and white, pink and rose, sitting all around the edge of our porch. That was where both of us learned to set rose cuttings and geranium cuttings. Mrs. Oliver Hulett taught us how to root them. She said you had to have the right soil, the right pot, and a green thumb, plus plenty of water and sunshine. We learned lots, never many idle moments. "Lost time is never regained" was one thing we learned. Also, "Idle hands get into much mischief" and "Love your brother or sister as yourself." We learned this before we knew what neighbors were. We were taught to never take or say God's name in vain, which we understood very well. Never call a brother or sister a fool, for the one doing the calling was himself in danger of hell fire. I got a good switching once for calling my sister a liar. I'd heard someone say, "That's a black lie." Well, I couldn't wait to use that phrase. My mom did not spare the switch that time, but she never had to use it again for that, at least.

Years earlier, when I was about ten years old, Mom had done the washing. She was very pregnant, but I did not realize how tired she must have been with four little ones already. She asked Leona and me to take the tub of clothes and hang them on the barbed-wire fence. Well, I hung a few clothes then found one of Mama's dresses. I hung it with a sleeve on each side, the whole length of her dress. It was kind of comical looking, and I said, "That should be Mama hanging there like that." Well, Leona ran and told Mom what I said. I couldn't deny it, for there hung the dress as proof. I think Mom got the switch out of her yard broom, and I got a good switching on my legs and behind.

Once in each month we'd go into the woods and gather green gall berry bushes. We would beat the leaves off each long switchy-looking bush then take about six of the switches, tie them together, and make a broom to sweep the whole yard. We would take a hoe and dig up every sprig of grass, leaving a beautiful well-swept yard of white sand. Having nice yards was like keeping clean floors with no rugs. It was considered good housekeeping. We also gathered broom sedge in early fall to make old-fashioned brooms for sweeping floors and cleaning little spider webs out of the houses. I was a grown girl before I saw a stick-handle, store-bought broom. About the only way we could get out of work was to grab a Sears & Roebuck catalog and run to the outhouse, flip the door shut, and sit and read until someone found us. And they always did.

Ninth Move, 1940: Kennedy Hill

We had some nice hogs that year and sold them to make our profit that year at five to fifteen cents a pound. We were already looking for a place to move as there was no wood for fires on the Baker place, and our little ones had to be kept warm. We got a house from Newt Kennedy, right in front of Jay and Corrine Kennedy's and moved again just before Christmas.

The house was in the edge of a big pecan grove that belonged to the Kennedy family, Hogue and Newt, together. We enjoyed living there. We were near their sister Margie Hires. Jay and Corrine's, Hogue and Beatrice's children were small. I picked five-gallon buckets of blackberries for Beatrice to make jelly and jam. She paid me for every bucket I carried her and also bought the pretty blue huckleberries we picked. Corrine also bought berries from me. We would work while it was cooler in the fields then leave the children for Charles to look after while we went to the Pilco Creek to pick the berries.

Mrs. Kennedy and I would go fishing sometimes. If I got a bite or two first, she was ready to go home, but if she got a bite first, she wanted to stay a while. I had a nursing baby now, so I couldn't stay long.

We did have a few really good square dances while we lived there. My younger sisters, Webb's brother Dick, the Furney girls, Durwood Crosby, and my sister Effie led the bunch. Also Christine and Geraldine Alderman as well as Margie Kennedy Hires did love square dancing. One night in early spring, we had a dance and stopped long enough to go serenade Newt and Louvenia, who lived just around the big livestock barn. Everyone got something to make a noise and circled the house about midnight. They had just gotten married that day. He got his gun and started shooting.

Believe me, the bunch scattered, but it was fun just to think of disturbing them.

We also helped gather pecans that fall. There must have been twenty acres of trees, most full of delicious nuts. We were paid three cents a pound for picking them up. In September that year, Charles started to school. Calvin Willis drove the school bus. My sister Wilma and brother Louis also rode the bus. I was so excited. Now I really had something to rise and shine for. Charles would be seven years old on November twentieth. He loved carrying his lunch.

My dad was pretty smart politically. Nothing passed by him. He was the justice of the peace for Brooks County for sixteen years. He was the trustee for the school board in the Tallokas school district. Sand Hill had not yet started a cafeteria, but it did the year after Charles started school. When the Sand Hill School was started, we had no school bus. Well, my dad put one together for our community, and guess who he let drive the bus around those muddy country roads? That was a good guess, I was only thirteen years old, but I drove around and picked the kids up for school and delivered them home after school.

Our governor of Georgia, Ed Rivers, as I well remember, decided one reason for lack of education in rural South Georgia was a lack of books. A parent had to find out what was needed then go out and buy the items from a central location at the county seat. The books—along with supplemental workbooks, color crayons, scissors, and glue plus a notebook—were hard to come by for people in times that were really tough with the Depression slowly strangling families.

Children in large families walked miles to attend high school. Two boys our age walked to Pavo every morning (about five miles,) and back each day to attend high school. They worked their way through college, and both became lawyers. Where there were two or three grown boys, one would stay home while another attended school. Then the next year another would stay home and work.

Ed Rivers changed all of that. A law was passed, that all children must attend school until at least sixteen years old. No children could take a job until they were sixteen. Also, books were given to the parents of schoolchildren. The books were to be taken good care of. No writing in them or leaving them at home.

They were used for teaching the three Rs: reading, writing, and arithmetic. All was fine until the teacher decided a child needed a supplement to these books. Clothes, coats, and shoes were the number-one reason I never finished school. I, like many other children, dreamed of graduating and going to college. I even ordered literature from Bessie Tift, Mount Berry, and Norman Junior College. It was exciting to even get that close, but there were a number of children younger than me at our house who also needed things. Also by this time, Leona proved herself smarter than me by advancing right up to me in grades. I missed passing in the seventh grade, so she caught me in the ninth and left me in the tenth. She went on to the eleventh grade. By then all we could hear was, war, war, war!

Every little country overseas was already involved, and we were to join if we were pushed a little farther, of which we most certainly were. Hitler and Germany became bywords in the homes of the people of the United States because we all dreaded war and lost lives, like in World War I. You should have heard the experiences of our moms and dads of that time. We heard plenty. Now this was 1940, and the rumors were now to become realities. The next thing, we were involved. Inside every home it was felt.

I guess I could write a book about the worldwide revolution that drew action from every country and every nation, but I will be brief. I will say, two of my brothers were drafted, Wayne A. Hart in the army and Brannon R. Hart in the navy. Webb had two brothers drafted into training, Jim Coley Furney (Coley) in the army and Iris Furney in the navy. They left our families and, after eight weeks' training, went right into action. I never realized until years later what a short period of training these poor boys had.

There was heartbreak in every home. Webb's sisters were married to young men in the service. All young men newly married or thinking about it had to say good-bye to loved ones and family. My sister Eula Mae had to say good-bye to Tony Myers. The long train that they were on had many coaches, and alongside the tracks, the walks were filled with girlfriends, sisters, brothers, moms, and dads. All with handkerchiefs in their hands, smiling through their tears, waving until they were out of sight.

I hope, as these few words are read, you can really feel the fear that must have been in the bosom of these brave young men, the cream of our generation. The sad part I had never thought about is that at least half of those boys barely had a fourth—or fifth-grade education. In the navy, they were handed a comic book to study characters of which they were to identify for the game they played in the real navy combat. Brant (Brannon) still remembers the names of the characters they were quizzed and graded on. The answers determined their ability to fit into an area where the navy would use them in the war. Some of those guys were sent home for lack of simple reading skills and poor coordination. How sad but true. They knew nothing of geography as they had never studied it. They also could not read instructions as to details or on a map. Some could learn if given half a chance, and they were taken into the navy.

The whole United States really learned something about poor education of the young people of that time. That is about when school became mandatory, isn't it a blessing? Then a young boy who had to plow a mule or work in a factory, of which many did, ten or twelve hours a day. By age fourteen, they were so discouraged at trying to go to school, they thought they knew enough to get by and just quit! They left school and just went to work! There was even a law in effect to keep people from working or giving jobs to children under sixteen years old or working more than eight hours a day. I mean, things were cruel before these laws were passed.

In large families in the cities that had factories, like cotton mills and shoe factories, a child was often put to work at twelve years old, twelve hours a day. Poor lighting conditions, little food, and no rest. Some parents then, as now, literally failed as parents and only wanted the small amount of money these children made. Tuberculosis was prevalent, many died young for lack of fresh air and sunshine. The children got the poorest of education. Well, in the country it was just as bad. If a child showed ambition or interest in books and figures, they were sent to school to help them learn more. But thanks be to God, and legislation, after a few years and laws passed, all people now have an equal right to a good education. It really makes me sick to see the young ones today try so hard to throw their lives away and completely destroy their hardworking parents, who at such a cost and much sacrifice for their children give their all.

Okay, so much for that. We had some good times and bad times at the Kennedy Place. Webb and Hogue turned about twenty head of hogs out from the pecan groves, drove them down the road, opened the gate, and put them in Newt Kennedy's corn patch with peanuts and cotton. He blew a fuse when that was done because they would not keep the hogs in a pen or the farm lot. Hogue was mad, Newt was fighting mad, and Webb got the worst! He and Newt tied up over his part in the squabble and passed a few licks with their fists. Naturally we made plans to get away from so much friction. I was constantly afraid they would go at it again.

Tenth Move, 1941: The George Mercer Farm

Webb was now going over to Rock Hill where his dad lived. He really liked it over there. You see, the Okapilco Creek was between us and the Furneys, which put us seven or eight miles away by country roads but half the distance walking through the woods. It was also near where we all lived the first year we were married. Quite naturally, by now, the Furneys knew everybody around Rock Hill, so Webb worked up a deal with George Mercer while over at the store at Rock Hill. When he got home that day he told me we would soon be leaving Kennedy Hill and would be farming at Mary and George Mercer's.

While this was going on, my two brothers went into training. Brant was in Virginia and Wayne in Camp Hood, Texas. Wayne said if he ever got home again, he would like to go there on a sightseeing trip. Hopes were high. With the fighting going strong, both boys went into action. Wayne received two injuries, one in the upper arm and one in the hand, while he was on the front lines. His hand was hit first. He said it was a bright moonlit night and the visibility was good. When he was hit, he received first aid. He then walked two miles and carried another badly injured soldier on his shoulders to the camp behind the lines.

Wayne was badly shaken up and had appendicitis immediately from the strain. He was walking the day after the appendectomy. There was no time to recuperate and no one to give assistance to a weak person, just care for the really serious injuries. He wrote Mom all about it and was thankful for a few days off the front line. He received the Purple Heart award for bravery, uncalled for in the line of duty. All of us would have cherished this Medal of Honor if it was given to us, but his wife, Mary, many years later left it with odds and ends of junk in cleaning house, and it was carelessly mistaken for junk and thrown out. I was so sorry to hear of the loss of it, as it followed a very bitter tragedy that was to hurt our families more than I can describe.

The year we moved to the Mercer place, Coley went into service. A few months later Iris, then six months or so, Ethel's husband, J. W. McCullar, and Melvin's husband, Roy Deloach. Laura had grown up and graduated from school then married Ralph Crosby, who right away was taken intoservice. Now my sister Eula Mae also finished school and married Tony Meyers, who was immediately called into service. It was really a time!

All factories were now turned into services for making clothes, food, boots, guns, and ammunition for our boys overseas and servicemen. Civilians could hardly get five yards of cloth. Sewing thread and canned goods were no longer on the grocery store shelves. Sugar, meat, cigarettes, lard, cooking oil was nonexistent or they were rationed. Can you imagine one pound of shortening or five pounds of sugar, a few pounds of meat? For this, one used coupons, which were issued once a month and no more!

If a few bolts of cloth arrived in a store, like JCPenney's or Belk Hudson's, just a few people found out and the store clerks called all their close friends. By ten or eleven o'clock in the morning it was done gone. I could get enough denim to make my boys overalls, thank goodness I had learned how to sew, but sheets and pillowcase materials would be gone as soon as it came in. Some people bought yards of cloth and stacked it up; knowing good and well they would never make a thing out of it. I knew this and bitterly hated to see it done. That was one reason we bought up all the print feed sacks we could get. Until now they were using cotton by the tons to make cloth and using it as fast as it was made.

Now going back to the price of cotton, it was now thirty-nine cents a pound, three cents a pound just to pick fresh open cotton by hand. Meat prices rose to an all-time high. City people had to eat canned meat, salmon, and sardines. Gas prices were out of sight. Instead of new cars coming off the lines, now it was ships, airplanes, and tanks as we had to have them. It really was a time, and you won't realize this until we are at war again. Of course, we won't have to ration things in America again, just up the price and they will ration themselves. Everything worked around the clock like every day was the last.

I have written about Webb's brother Coley as you have read. While we lived at George Mercer's, he managed the store at Rock Hill. There never was a better-hearted person in the world. When my little girl Janice got sick with whooping cough, every day he would send her a cup of ice cream and she would eat every bite. As I mentioned earlier, this was my tiniest baby, and at eighteen months old, she had no fat to spare. She had good use of herself and, at nine months old, was walking everywhere. She made you think of a little bird. She made little noise and hardly ever cried.

She also started talking early too. Now she had gotten whooping cough from my healthy brother Louis. Mama said she knew he had it, for he was making a whooping sound and coughing. This always starts in the third week, and right away, my little girl had it too. Mama had been keeping her for me to make a little money tying tobacco. Again the whole crop was harvested by hand. Every leaf personally handed to one person to be tied on to sticks and loaded in the barn on tiered poles. This was a real day's work for about fourteen people.

I was only nine or ten years old when my dad announced we would all be learning some new things! Which did prove correct? This new thing has lasted some good sixty or sixty-five years since the day my dad said, "We, as farmers, are desperate for new beginnings." We first had a different kind of tobacco, from the early farmers who grew some for their own use, before I came along. It was cut down by the plant and shade cured.

This new stuff was called flue-cured tobacco. Farmers grew their own tobacco plants. This was accomplished by sterilizing the ground before seeding the plant bed. The seeds were planted the day after Christmas and covered with cheesecloth, to avoid contamination of outside weeds and for protection from the cold and frost. In the early spring, when the plants were three to five inches tall, they were planted into the fields. As they matured, the leaves were gathered when they began a slight yellowing and tied on to sticks, which would be hung inside a barn for curing.

Everyone had to build special barns to cure it from green leaf to dry foliage. The barns had to be tight enough to hold heat at a 280-degree level. This was done by a very large flue, or metal set of pipes laid out in a square all around the inside of the barn. This was usually covered by a wire cage. Chicken wire or large mesh, because when tobacco leaves had been dried out sufficiently, they just might fall on a pipe. The falling of leaves, or tobacco sticks, which were layered and hung three feet above flue pipes to the top of the barn, could cause disastrous combustion and the farmer would lose his barn as well as the crop on the inside.

Of course this required someone to stay with the barn to keep the heat at certain levels and make sure there were no flare-ups inside. Also there were sometimes flare-ups outside. The women whose husbands stayed up all night to watch the barns were called tobacco widows. Of course no good man who had to watch a barn, and had friends to keep him company, would plan to be alone. Sometimes there would be a little sipping of alcoholic beverage, and then you would see the tobacco widow's temper flare hotter than the barn. She only saw her husband at mealtime, and she felt completely forgotten.

A smart woman would see to getting her family fed early and get the kids off to bed. When the house became quiet with sleep, a man's loving wife, who had begun to feel like a poor widow, would ease out of the house and go to the barn. Her husband usually had a bunk or nap-taking place, convenient for him to rest and work. He usually stayed till the barn was done. She would share her thoughts, reassure him on his efforts for a better life for the family and that he was greatly appreciated by one and all. I know there were many tobacco widows. In time we all learned to make play of it by having chicken fries, peanut boiling, and just anything else nice to do to be together. I did love to tie tobacco though.

So much for the tobacco. Well, I had the sickest little girl I had ever seen. If my mom and Ma Furney had not been good at taking care of sick little ones, she would never have pulled through. It was God's will truly that she lived. I prayed to keep her and realized you don't make bargains with God. You can beg all you please to no avail; he knows what is in your heart. Well, I ended up giving her back to God, whom she belonged to in the beginning. I right away sensed the difference in my prayer approach. Really, death was on my daughter. Her fever was high, way too high, her eyes set in one position, and rubbing your hands over them made no difference. Ma Furney laid her arm around my shoulder and said, "Lorene, Janice can't last through the day, just try to hold up." Now I knew something they did not know. The lump in my breast had quit hurting because God, I know, had given her back to me.

Since I talked with God, I realized neither me, man, nor our mamas could give life—only God. Now he knew what was in my heart this time, trust and compassion. Oh yes, I had always talked to God in secret places. I thought I could not pray in the presence of others, but when I knelt by the bedside of my little girl, I truly had a talk with God. Ma Furney was on one side and Mary Mercer on the other. They just bowed their heads.

The next day, I knew she looked sicker, but if she was to die, why had the awful pain in my chest gone? I alone knew why God had given me courage to hope, something I could depend on. I fixed the water for an enema to use on her for cooling the fever. I just kept making ready. We inserted the half gallon of water in that tiny little stomach and intestines. Well, neither the water nor anything else came back. I was beside myself. I sent Webb for the doctor. He told us to stand her in a tub of warm water with wet towels and lift them up, dripping the water around her then rub them down again. We did this. One person held her up while the rest worked. We placed her back on the bed, and in a very few minutes, the water came running out with lumps as hard as rocks also. They must have been the last food she had eaten five days earlier, because she had eaten nothing since, just sipped a bit of juice and liquids. Well, her fever cooled right away, and the next day, the doctor came out and said things looked good. There was very little fever, and the pneumonia in both lungs was gone, with still some cough but not as bad. My other three children also had whooping cough, but we barely noticed as it was so much milder than what Jan had. I was so glad. After seven days of grief and sitting up nights, I'd forgotten how a good night's sleep felt.

Now while this was going on, my sister Leona had just given birth to one more little girl on August 9, 1941, Vanada. She was named with a *V* to match the other three *V*s—Vara, Vivian, and Velma. Ellis and John Allen came over to sit with us one night and said Leona would love to come, but due to the new baby and taking care of her own health, she couldn't. Women knew in those days you had better take care of yourself or pay the price of poor health if you didn't.

My daughter made a recovery but was so very weak, it took a long time. She had to learn to walk all over again. I held my arms up beside her to hold her to take those first steps. I had lost so much weight. I must have weighed a hundred pounds at the most.

All was improved, and Charles started to a new school in Barney, Georgia. Gilbert started to school that year with his big brother, Charles, who was now in the second grade. He and Charles were two close little boys. When one got into something, both were into it. Webb's youngest brother Coy was already in school in Barney. They both thought he was a really big boy and they both looked up to him.

Webb had now finished our crop and had gotten a job in construction. His family was getting bigger with another mouth to feed. Webb got a job at Spence Field. They were laying out a big airport for training men to fly airplanes in the Air Force. It was also a place to keep German prisoners of war. He loved his job, and times looked a little better for us. We bought a refrigerator and a car.

George Mercer, the landowner, got a couple of men and broke our corn and took it to his barn, not ours. He said he thought Webb was finished. Webb was waiting for the cooler weather and frost to kill some of the weeds and grass before harvesting the corn. When sharecropping, you saved the corn for the end of the year so when it was sold there was money available for the winter months when there were no other farm crops to sell. So the men had a falling out. That went on so often when you farmed with someone else.

Eleventh Move, 1941: The Herrell Place

We moved again to the Herrell place, near Little River Creek. Very close to my mom and dad's. Webb continued to work at Spence Field, but we didn't stay long at the Herrell place. There was no water there. We had to haul or bring it from Dad's.

Twelfth Move, 1942: The Carl Bryant Place

We moved again even closer to my mom and dad's, this time to the Carl Bryant place, within a hundred yards of their house. I know they must have gotten mighty tired of my family being so close. There were some good things to remember along with the bad though. I helped Mama make chicken coops. I learned to saw and drive nails helping Dad build tobacco barns. We built two new barns before I married. I had some experience. I even helped roof them and build the furnace of brick and cement so they could be fired up to heat the barn to cook out the tobacco. We really did enjoy cooking out at the barn while setting up nights. We mostly were frying chicken and boiling peanuts.

I awoke one morning, after getting moved again, to a very sick stomach. Oh, oh, not again, I prayed. It was no use, I was pregnant again. We were not careful after Janice's illness. We had been apart for a while, and what do you know. We only thought of ourselves, not our future. We were pretty good at controlling the baby business until then.

On the long winter days Mama would start a new quilt she had stitched, and we would talk and listen to the radio while our fingers flew to get as much done as we could before the school bus brought the children home. We then put the quilt away until the next day and then start again.

Dad had acres of turnips, collard greens, and mustard greens as well as rutabagas. Now my little Janice took to those greens like they were pudding. She really liked them. I'll always know they gave her a lot of vitamins. Daddy asked Webb why he didn't get into the farm and home administration like he and Ellis had done. We thought a person had to own or be paying for a farm. We asked about it and found out the government would even rent you a farm if you planned to buy it. Land was cheap then, so we got right with it, signed up ready for business. After Christmas, we were all settled in and I went to Mom's every day. I guess just because she was within walking distance. Now Jan is still improving. My little one's growing right along, mean as ever, like all other little ones. Gilbert and Louis are near the same size but a year difference in age. All boys then had homemade slingshots, mine too.

One day Mama said we are going to kill this old rooster, a great, big red one. The boys, Gilbert and Louis, took this in. Mama said we will do this on Easter Sunday. We'll make chicken dressing and have an egg hunt later in the afternoon. This must have been about the first of April. As soon as everyone scattered out and left Louis and Gilbert alone, they were doing some shooting with their slingshots, rocks at the old rooster. Dad walked up just in time to save the rooster, and gave the boys a good spank on the behind that broke their hearts. They tearfully told him that they were going to kill the rooster for Mama, for Easter Sunday (almost two weeks away). Little did they realize the trouble if they did kill the rooster. What would they do with him until Easter? I was so mad at Dad for spanking them; I would not even speak to him for a week. I was mad because he took it on himself to spank Gilbert, but Gilbert knew better than to shoot chickens any time after that.

Our Farm & Home loan went through okay. Money to really go into farming. We bought a high-stepping mule that Webb had to run to keep up with, also a Jersey milk cow, and one hundred baby chicks and a brooder for raising them. There was money for feed and everything a farmer could use. A home demonstration representative came and helped me plan to can vegetables and fruit, also a pressure canner to cook them in and how to save meat by canning in jars, because we had no freezers back then. So an order for two hundred quart jars was placed. My baby was due around May twentieth. Farm & Home sent me a beautiful baby bed and playpen combination. No flies or mosquitoes could get in that baby tender. A godsent blessing, I was to find out, as the mosquitoes were so bad and we had no screen windows—as a matter of fact, no glass windows either. We had wood-shuttered windows. I had a frame built over every bed in our house and mosquito nets stretched over them. It was a really wet spring that year that made them so bad. I don't know how we stood the heat then, as compared to the cool air-conditioning and paddle fans of today almost fifty years later. I often think of this when I hear someone complain of the hot weather. We also had a stove for cooking our meals three times a day that burned wood to heat it. Remember, we did not have electricity on the farm, had not so far even dreamed of it.

Now Coley, Webb's brother, was being trained in the army, first in one base and then another. All training bases near us were finished now. A man was really lucky to get a full-time job helping at the bases. A lot of men did get jobs. Local men too, some to spot planes, others to run mess halls, some to drive generals around, just to name a few, but Webb just stuck with the farm. Things did look much brighter for all of us that year. Of course, the war was going strong.

There was talk and radio news of invading Germany on a full-scale takeover, but that was a tough little country. Every day the newspapers were full of this news and the cruel treatment of all prisoners, and Jewish people were punished unmercifully as hundreds were put to death. A bulldozer made a long trench in the earth, the bodies were thrown in, and then the machine covered the hole up with bodies and all. Wounded boys were now being sent home, and the tales they told were grizzly and sickening. About this time in the year of 1942, Coley came home from camp for thirty days before leaving the United States for England. A place he said where thousands of soldiers would be gathered for a mass invasion at the nearest point, so the waiting was like waiting for a keg of powder to explode or dynamite to blow up. Only this had to be planned to perfection, no mistakes. The best of our boys were poised for the time to get across the English Channel. On this particular morning, Coley came, we were all so glad to see him.

I kept in touch with letters at each place he was stationed. Coley was our go-between when Webb and I were going together. He was the only one we could trust to carry our love letters. Oh, he was like maybe nine years old, and a really quiet little guy. At school I'd write two or three pages, fold them up, write Webb's name on it, ease around to Coley, give it to him, and he would zip it up in his little overalls. When he got home, he'd ease out to where Webb was or walk to the field where he was plowing. When Webb saw him coming, he knew Lorene had slipped him a note then he'd know what was going on at school and across the creek in general. The dances or peanut shelling or wood sawing, all these things had their rewards of nice refreshments, tea, coffee, or lemonade and meeting the newest girls and boys who had moved into our community. Can you think of a better, quicker way if there is no telephone? Well, I can't!

We were all sad to see Coley go this time, for he had a good chance of being killed or wounded. There is a huge bulletin board that was put up at our County seat in Quitman, Georgia, that has every boy's name in Brooks County who lost his life during that war. Believe me, we knew lots of them and we never saw them again. I hope those who read this will know those were some heartbreaking times.

About this time, Aunt Rosa Herndon's sister, Ira Mathis's wife, had a fine little boy about five in the morning. The doctor had been there all night waiting for the baby. After the baby was delivered, she also seemed to be doing fine. He went home, and two hours later she was dead. No one knew what caused her death. My sister Effie Crosby lived nearby. Her baby Dorothy was only three or four days old, so the ideal person to help take the place of the little one's mother would be a nursing mom, Effie. I know she did all she could until the right person took the job of raising the little one. So Aunt Rosa became the foster mother of her sister's baby, little France Mathis. Someone asked her a few weeks later how she was doing, and she said, "By golly, it will sure keep you out of the road."

Now that news made me a little less secure when I heard it because I already had two boys and two girls someone would have to bring up if this should just happen to me. It sounds like I might not care, but I loved my little ones with my life. I thought no one could do what I could do for them, and I'd die trying to do my best.

On the morning of May 21, 1942, I awoke bright and early, fed my chickens, got Webb off to work, fed the four children breakfast, and here I go again. I am having my first contractions by nine AM. I know before many hours there will be a new one at our house. There would be two-and-a-half years between Jan and Vernon; this was our best spacing yet. Yes, one is never the most secure in the world when you walk alone through the valley of the shadow of death.

I had planned not to use a doctor this time, just have my mom and Webb's mom, and should I not get along all right, I'd then get the doctor. Well, I tied my apron around me and walked half a mile to the back of our field to the patch of green beans that was hanging full of beans, ready to pick right then. I couldn't wait to start canning in those new jars. I picked my apron full of beans and slowly walked the path back home, my contractions coming every few minutes. I made dinner then made ready for the baby which would arrive in the night for sure. Both of our parents were there now; ready to help when I needed them.

Well, Vernon arrived at about eleven PM, a very large red-haired little boy. Two days later I weighed him, and he weighed ten pounds, no less. We both did fine, so did our mothers, they were proud of themselves. I had plenty of pretty bought baby clothes as my neighbors had given me my first baby shower. Showers were the latest thing those days. It was a great help as well as a morale booster. People in a community enjoyed seeing the expectant mother so happy, and I certainly was.

Quite naturally I was soon my very own self again, and about the seventh day, me and the boys walked down the fence to the farm of Calvin Willis and picked a gallon of the prettiest ripe yellow plums. It was a treat for them. I knew they were just ripe for the picking, you see. That morning I gave my little son his bath. He was so big it was a joy to bathe him, put him in his nice screened-in baby bed, where he would lay and sleep most of the day. I would feed him every three or four hours. I had plenty of milk, so the new baby was no problem.

We had a good name for him, Vernon Carlos Furney, born May 21, 1942. Vernon is such a fine healthy baby. Ma Furney said he looked like Turner Brice. Turner was a very fine-looking man of that time, six feet tall, wide shoulders, big landowner, and a real go-getter. Most people in the area looked up to Turner Brice. He owned Brice's Pond, where we all fished, and a huge plantation. Well, it made me feel good for her to say that, for as a usual thing she found something to cut me short about. Especially my canning and quilting. I also had a yard full of chickens. We were really doing well, and she must have been proud of us. We certainly paddled our own little boat.

Christopher, Todd Gaines, Nichole, Vernon, and Cynthia Furney

Grandchildren McKenna, Emerson, and Sutton
with Cyndi and Vernon Furney

I wrote Coley all about it. By June 20, I was helping gather tobacco again. Tying or handing whichever needed to be done, and Charles looking after the children. He was so good with them. He just left Vernon in the bed, and I'd know right when to go feed the baby. The rest of the children played outside. Although we lived in a wooded area, they would never leave the yard. Somehow we never worried about snakes or such. I know they were around because I was chased by a black snake once. I guess he was trying to get some little birds out of a nest in a little scrub oak tree about as high as my head when I came up on him. He just started running all over the little trees, and he dropped onto the ground, and boy, I flew down that path I was walking in and left the snake way behind me. I had never heard of a black snake being mean until then.

Believe me, being in the woods, there were a lot of things one could be afraid of. Such as weird noises from sundown till daybreak. A person from the country learns to live with noise, and soon, one knows the difference in a noise of danger and just the regular noises. So many people today make a big fuss about roaches and just one housefly in the house. They spray and put out bug bombs, and still one can be seen occasionally and a little tiny mouse. At the time this little one was born, as I have said, the windows were wooden shutters and very few people had screen doors or windows. Now mosquitoes were one of our worst enemies. The bite of the female *Anopheles* mosquito could carry malaria fever to a whole family. That was something to fear.

They were very small and usually traveled after sundown. Many times I took an old washbasin or a gallon syrup can, packed rags, and dusted a powder called sulfur all in the rags then set it on fire late in the evening. We would burn trash from raking yards or cleaning up the scraps from the woodpile. We'd set this on fire also, about eight thirty or nine PM. All flying insects, inside or outside, would be gone. Now all could sleep well. We knew nothing at all about the lovely air-conditioning we have today. To cool off sometimes, we'd get out our gallon ice cream maker and make delicious peach, chocolate, or vanilla ice cream. Really, our wants were few, but people are never completely happy with what they have. Plans were being made every day to bring more luxury to our life.

Now I'd lived in a time when the coolest thing we ever had to drink was good spring water from a surface well in the heat of the day. For an extra treat, a quart jar was filled with this cool water and a few teaspoons of good cane syrup stirred or shook up in it. Now that was a cool thirst-quenching drink at the end of a long row of cotton while hoeing or suckering and topping tobacco. It helped cool a person as well as tide you over until ago, got you to the supper table at night. One worked until the sun set and started at sunrise. If we wanted to finish a job really bad, we'd start before sunrise.

No wonder our inner timer is set for six AM. We are still awake at this hour, Leona and me. There is no way I can lie in that bed until nine AM. I can get up at my regular time, and at about nine AM, I can go back to bed if I stayed up late the night before. My regular hours are from six AM to nine PM. It's automatic. Our parents were like that also. Many rural people were amazed when they started working off the farm and were told a "workday" was eight hours. Now only a few let the farmers know a workday was eight hours.

You may have a time believing this, but that is why there was such a thing as a sharecropper or half cropper. A landowner made the plans, and some of them would drive up to the farm one hour before sunup, just sit down on their usually new car, horn and blow it until someone came out then say, "I didn't know you were not up. I just can't sleep late." Now if a family wanted to put up with that, they would say nothing. If they felt it their right to get up when they wanted, it was just a matter of saying, "Now look, I don't have to be gotten out of bed so you can save yourself the trouble of waking me up." I am serious when I say that is why a lot of farm owners had the upper hand. They lived by the older ones' slogan: "Early to bed, early to rise makes a man healthy, wealthy, and wise." Sharecroppers were treated only a little better than slaves, actually.

Now getting up to go to work was one thing. Staying healthy was another. Being lazy hurt the whole family. A landowner would spot a good family that had grown boys and girls big enough to work, at least eight to ten years old was plenty big enough to start. The sharecropper always looked forward to hitting a big streak of luck, one in a thousand did. The rest just existed from year to year. The Bible states the poor will always be among us, so make plans to care for them too, also those who really don't know how to make plans for themselves.

I was so glad to make four dollars a day tying tobacco or shaking peanuts. At least one got their money at the end of the day. The time put in was sunup to sundown. Now this was not one hundred years ago. It was right here in my lifetime. A farmer could get a truckload of cotton pickers in the black quarters in town. All lived in little shacks close together. The men usually had regular jobs at big sawmills or worked at turpentine stills, taking the sap (or juice) from pine trees by chipping the trees then placing a cuplike box under the gash to catch the raw tar that constantly ran out, a tiny bit at a time.

Some worked directly at the distillery, and some worked in the woods gathering and emptying each box on each tree. You know how pine tar sticks, I guess. Well, this was real hard work, but it had to be done and these people had children and they all had to eat, so as soon as one got big enough, he learned to work. Two cents a pound was paid for picking cotton. A really good picker could gather two hundred pounds, which is not hard to figure, four dollars a day. That is hard to believe, but it is true, one could buy a lot more with a dollar then. You could also get forty or fifty people on a truck to go out to the farms to work. A bale of cotton a day or sometimes two a day could be picked. No one got on a truck that did not plan to work hard all day.

Those were the days, but good cotton, ready to make into cloth, as I said before, was so cheap, now this was before the war I've just written about, during the four or five years while we were in the struggle supporting the same president, Franklin Delano Roosevelt. He did work very hard to relieve the poverty of this kind of working people. All these things brought on work by the hour. A salary was negotiated then a person would go to work. The next thing people did was fight for a minimum wage to be law, and it happened. People couldn't believe this was happening until then. Workers would work all day for one dollar a day.

The thing needed most was a minimum wage per hour then decide how many hours was a day, and it all came out. Eight hours was a day. Now a boom came when people began getting jobs. That is when one started to work, he first had to have a card issued to him, and this nearly drove people crazy. If you worked, you had to get a card. A record was made of it in Washington and kept at that time. As soon as you got an application to fill out for work, you were asked for your Social Security number. Now a small amount of your paycheck was taken out every payday and saved for a person and was placed in an escrow account for the purpose of helping you later on, and giving our then-elderly people a small amount of money to buy the little necessities they needed, like better food and clothes. This helped relieve the children of the elderly ones of expenses. Older children were taking care of them now as some required looking after like babies. I mean, you could not forget them. They were to be bathed, dressed, and fed just like a child. Lots of old people lived to be very old.

My dad's mother received a Social Security check for sixteen dollars per month, like a gift from heaven. She had grown quite old by now, worked and raised a family, a large family of eight boys and two girls. She also now was left a widow as her husband of many years had passed away. My dad said, "I'll add a nice little room with a good fireplace to my home if you will just come make your home with me, and it will be yours, all yours." Until then she lived alone in our tenant house up in the woods where three of my babies were born. Grandma was fairly active, kept her one old cow and some chickens. She milked her cow and made good rich butter, yellow as gold, no color added.

She also gathered green feed out of the woods and field, tied it in a big tobacco sheet, lifted it to her shoulders by herself, and carried it up a little hill and put it in front of her cow so she could eat every bit. Now the serious part comes in. My sister Leona or I had to eat our supper and hurry up to spend the night at Grandma's. She really was a sweet old lady with lots of hard years of work, of housekeeping, and bringing up her ten children. The real reason for her being alone was her stubborn independence. People with a purpose in life, and some being stubborn too, helped them live longer and healthier lives, I guess. She had it all. It would have been easier for her to stay in our house with us than for us to go stay with her. Even then, Dad showed his respect for her. He did not tell her what to do, at least not yet.

Leona, I'll admit, spent most of the nights with Grandma in that old house. I started driving the school bus and had to leave early to pick up the children. I was only thirteen, but one night, my turn came and I could not get out of it, so here I go off to stay with Grandma. She sits by the dull red coals of oak wood until sort of late, just looking at the fire. She is a little short old grandma, rocking away in her bonnet made of fine brown-and-white checked gingham. She has a kerosene lamp on a nearby table for light. She does not talk very much, that little old grandma of mine. Until this day, I wonder what kind of thoughts traveled through her mind. As I lay down in her big high feather bed that night, I was very aware of sleeping with this little old lady, I surely slept on the far side of the bed.

She was so old and brown and wrinkled, I thought to myself, "What in the world could I do if she should die way in the middle of the night?" There she lay in a long flannel gown, pale blue, I think it was. She had a small nightcap with a little ruffle around her head, her glasses by the bedside, on a table where she placed the lamp just before she knelt to thank the Lord for that day and her health, and thank him for his mercy and love. Me, I just lie down in that soft feather bed and said my prayers to God and myself. Grandma blew out the flame on the lamp, and everything was so dark.

You could hear sounds—crickets chirping, a lone hoot owl now and then, a cow lowing for her calf who had wandered off a piece from its mother. So with Grandma going off to sleep, I couldn't be more awake, and all at once, she started to make this little noise. I wiggled and turned over. It was louder! I knew she didn't have any teeth in her mouth. The noise got louder now. She was really asleep. She wasn't snoring, just making little puffing sounds—*poof, poof, poof, poof.* Unless you saw this, you'd never believe it. She drew in air through her nose, made a little O with her mouth, and let the air out with a puff. These noises went on and on until I rose up and took a good look as I had gotten used to the dark and could see her face making all those little *poof, poof* sounds. I don't think I slept an hour that night. I thought of Little Red Riding Hood's grandma, and the big bad wolf and a thousand other things along with it. That was my last night with Grandma in her bed.

Daddy finally talked her into selling her cow, was I ever glad! Later she had to be totally cared for, even fed by someone the last week she lived. My mom really did look after her good but only as she would let her at first. Leona and I were married by now, and the next two girls had their turn helping out as they got to be grown girls. Grandma got feebler soon. If her bed was discovered to be wet, she would say when she tried to make it up, "Mae, will you come here and look? It rained last night and has leaked on my good feather mattress." My mom just picked it up and carried the mattress out to be washed, and into the sun to air and dry it out.

Later in the day my mom got her dressed for the day. It consisted of two petticoats, snow-white lace around the bottom tied with a drawstring around the waist, a camisole over the upper part of the body, a pair of cotton stockings and high-top soft leather shoes, then a fine tiny print dress with a full-gathered skirt joined together to the waist, and then she is completely dressed. Now after having dressed twelve children, one may wonder how could anyone think she would have the patience to care so much for the elderly, not even her own mother, just a mother-in-law.

Well, my mom was a Christian woman, reared by Christian grandparents who truly believed in God, his blessings and patience, his miracles and love. Mom's parents, Thadeaus and Sarah Malissa Croft, along with their son Walter, lost their lives in a fierce epidemic of typhoid fever in 1902. Somehow this was very plain to be seen, as one looked at the six little girls and one small boy left, they took into their home at a very early age.

The youngest was one and a half years old, and the oldest was sixteen. The grandparents also brought up another three children who survived with only one parent left. I still say the children reared by them have had a beautiful experience in loving, giving happiness, joy, and peace and sharing of which I think love was the greatest. These girls and one boy never forgot their love for each other. They also were very generous with their love and patience with all who knew them. They had time for the old and the sick in their communities, wherever they lived. Mom's Grandma Betty's father donated the property for Pleasant Hill Church.

Well, as soon as Grandma got dressed, many were the times she had accidents that called for a complete bath again—clothes changed, stockings and also shoes. The big tin tub was brought in, and warm water taken out of the warming tank on the stove then poured into the tub. Now this is where my younger two sisters learned a lot in many ways. After finally showing Grandma she had to be changed, first as Mama pulled one side of her clothes off, Grandma would pull them back on. Oh, she would get so mad but never used dirty talk, just said, "Stop! Let me alone! Do you hear me?" But with Mom on one side and Effie on the other taking those clothes and stockings off, in spite of her fuss, she would step into the water then start crying, "Lord, come get me!" When it was done, all were calmed down, but no one knows how often or how many times a day this went on. At least a year or two, I know.

My mom had the first washing machine in the Sand Hill community. She had a Maytag with a gas motor. It was started up like a push lawn mower. Daddy said, "If you have to wash so much, maybe this will help you." That thing was a miracle. Leona introduced us to Clorox bleach. You should have seen us all standing around a machine that could really wash clothes. A thing that today's girls have no idea what it was like then? No standing in the cold anymore, truly a miracle to our family.

Grandma grew weaker and weaker, then just slept away, first until nine AM then eleven AM, finally until noon. On Sunday I fed her lunch for Mama to go to the all-day sing at our church. She just slept after that, and the doctor who was called in said no serious ailment in particular, just affirmatives of old age. She passed away on Thursday afternoon in May 1939. She was eighty-four years old. This was the year my Janice was born in 1939. Grandpa Babe preceded her a few years earlier, in May of 1935. He was buried on the same day Leona and Ellis got married. They would not change the wedding date. It was thought to bring bad luck if you changed your wedding date.

Now as I have gotten carried away again, I'll go back a little. Charles was then, as now, a very dependable child and to be sure he did what he was told to do. He never hurt his brother or sisters. He knew right from wrong amazingly, for one so young. This year my number-two son had to spend a few days in a hospital. Gilbert nearly choked to death with a throat infection similar to diphtheria, only this was a croup that caused the throat muscles to tighten up very badly and cause a hoarse, rasping noise. He came out just fine with proper medication.

School was to start again, and now I have another son Gilbert in school. I'll never forget his first day. Mrs. Lila Shrivers (Guy Crosby's oldest daughter) was his teacher. Would you believe his very first day at school, all in the room were given paper and a pencil then told to write their names? Well, Gilbert had never tried to write his name even at home. So there he sat, afraid to move. The teacher came over and said, "What is your trouble, young man? Don't you want to write your name for me?" He said, "I don't know how to write." She said, "Get that pencil going. Try! Try!" He just sat there, stunned. He really did not even try, so she just jerked him out of his seat and spanked him good. When he came home that day, I, of course, asked him how his day was. My mouth just dropped open when he said he had gotten a good spanking. I asked for goodness' sake why? When he told me because he couldn't write his name, I thought that was ridiculous, the very first day of school. Well, he really started trying for the first time to really write his name.

Thirteenth Move, 1943: The Bell Farm

This fall, of course, we were planning now to move again. To a much better house with plenty of room, nice glass windows, a good roof that doesn't leak, some flowers in a big fenced-in yard. We had a nice barn for the cows and mule and those chickens. Well, we were just thrilled to death to have a nice place like that. We couldn't wait to pack up and go. It was a bigger job than usual with all those fruit jars and canned foods to move without getting those jars broken.

In the year of 1943 we moved to this new place. It must have been during the old twelve days after Christmas, for our two little boys were so excited about living near Pavo. They could walk to Sand Hill School, which they had been attending. Gilbert just loved Mrs. Ernestine Baker Williams. She would put on a play and used everyone in the class. It made each child feel so important. Everyone in our community enjoyed the plays Ernestine Williams put on with those little ones. Charles was already having a time getting homework done as his eyes were acting up. Such poor light, just a kerosene lamp or fire light to see by. We also had a very active PTA at that time. Oh yes, Sand Hill was going strong. My youngest sister, Wilma, and Webb's youngest sister, Marie, were both in school there also Margie Gays' children and the Touchton girls. I mean, they all seemed so happy and were looking forward to Barwick High School to finish them up.

The worst thing a girl could do then was smoke cigarettes or slip around with a boyfriend and get pregnant. No drugs or pills or booze to get hooked on. Some did get pregnant, and some did learn to smoke. Those were the good old days that I remember so well. We did have a world war going on, but the children did not feel the strain so much.

While living at this nice farm place that was for rent, we made good on our crops, and we bought more cows and hogs and thoroughly enjoyed the harvest. Some people don't enjoy farm work, but Webb and I both did. We grew tomatoes, squash, string beans, butter beans, and cucumbers for pickles. I filled up those jars again with everything that grew on the farm and also helped Webb farm. We started out with one mule, also planted the crop with one mule.

One plow hooked to the other and one mule pulled them both. Charles was tickled pink he could help his dad and I could take care of the children. He was little but a willing one to learn, and I was so glad. Oh yes, about this time, I noticed every time I cooked okra or cabbage, I turned deathly sick. Oh yes, I would like to call it anything else, but I knew the symptoms. Sick stomach and dizzy headed as soon as my feet hit the floor. Yes, it certainly took the wind out of my sails. In spite of everything else that year, I would have another baby in the spring of 1944.

We bought clothes for the children to start school with in the fall, also a perm for Jeanette as she would start school in September. Now this year the three children started school in Pavo. The school bus came right by the gate. None of the children liked Pavo school. The big boys tried to smash my two little boys, and Jeanette was in tears every day when she got off the bus. Now I was looking after the children and our frying-size chickens. We turned the mules and cows in the field after the corn was hauled in. Webb would walk from the Bell farm to Rock Hill almost every weekend, and me and the children stayed home.

He also helped Pa Furney break his corn and make hay then helped J. B. gather his. They did a little drinking of alcohol. Both Webb and J. B. carried their money in their pockets, and I was afraid Webb would lose ours. Not a lot, but when you carry money with you, it sure does get away easily. I felt I had my hands full taking care of the children, cooking, washing, and ironing, also starching all those pretty little dresses I made for Jeanette and the shirts for the boys. It looked as if there was no end to it. Many are the times I would have been glad to exchange places with just about anyone. Thank God for a Christian life at home and parents who did not quit when the going got tough. I know there must have been times when I was sorely tempted to walk out. Then what would become of my little children? I loved all of them. I would not let anyone bring up a single one or two of them, so I just prayed for strength to go on and the knowledge to do the right thing.

This business of having a baby every two years caused me many bitter tears. I cried all alone, for when you smile, the world smiles with you, but when you cry, you cry all alone. Yes, I heard many phrases from my mom and his to give me strength. Little did I know that right then all my troubles were little ones. As the children grow bigger, your troubles get bigger also. So I said if Mama did for her children so can I. Thank God I did realize my job was no greater than my parents' job with twelve children to care for.

Now the military bases and training fields are built, there are people everywhere who are possibly able, doing their jobs. Yes, all our young manpower is fighting every day in the Pacific, Japan, Germany, Italy, and in the Mediterranean. Believe me, it was fierce. You see more young men were "coming of age," and they also packed a bag and joined the others. So many had been wounded, some just worn out and needed a rest stateside. Coley was sending money home to pay for himself a farm place when he did get back. Also my brother Wayne was doing the same. Then Iris had to go. Coley had been gone for three years. They were so close and wanted to see each other so bad. Then my brother Brant went in. He got the Pacific, and Wayne got Italy and the Mediterranean.

People dreaded to see a strange car drive up, afraid of a telegram saying, "I am sorry, but I have to tell you" and on and on. The mothers were so nervous, and the young daughters with babies in their arms who never saw their dad. It was really a bad time. Webb and Ellis Copeland were just a little too old and had too many children. Roy and Johnnie P. Copeland both went in and came home. Webb's brother met one of them coming home. One was just getting there. Coley's commander made a short trip in a very important jeep just so Coley could be with Iris for one night before shipping out.

Well, Pa Furney traded with a man for a place that was up for sale. The owner had died, and it was a very big farm. Coley came home and helped out, but by now, Pa was much older to take on a farm that big. Right away things were planned for Webb and the family to move into the tenant house at the foot of the hill near the little Negro church, where the only water was from a well across the road. We packed our things and made ready to move again. This was around November. We had wanted to rent this place again, but a very smart black man went and paid cash rent in advance before Webb had a chance to give it much thought. While he was riding with J. B., this smart man just went right under us. I just cried as I did not really want to live right beside of Pa's family. It was nice to go visit them, but to live on their place was another thing! We did move there in the fall of 1943.

Fourteenth Move, 1943:
Furney Farm (Old Jerry Wilkes's Place)

I had no building to put my nice canning jars in. No chicken house, no outdoor toilet. We just plain had a house, nothing else. Our cows were put in Pa's barn until we could build a pen, and as usual, Webb just took his easy time. Well, by now Dick and Wilma knew they were expecting a little bundle of joy. J. B. and Evelyn were also expecting one. Me, I had so many little ones, just one more was no excitement at all. I'd probably wake up in the middle of the night and get J. B. to carry me to the hospital. I would have a girl or boy, stay a few days, and come home just like nothing happened. It did turn out a little different as Vernon, my least one, played out in the spring like weather in a freshly ploughed field and was already hoarse by suppertime. I had a time now looking after the children.

Cooking, washing, and carrying water from across the road, and my time so near. Well, I stood over Vernon's bed most of the night because he had a bad spell of the croup, a bad hoarseness that tightened the bronchial tubes, making it very hard to breathe, making the child very frightened of losing his breath. When I did get a chance to go to sleep, my labor started. Well, this time it was planned for me to go to the hospital in Quitman. The money was available, so here we go. Webb, J. B., and me. J. B. drove so fast, I wondered if we would make a safe trip. I stayed the day and came home as I never did get contractions sufficient to bring the baby. Dr. Smith said it just wasn't time. One week later I went into the hospital. I had a little trouble. I was frightened as it was the first hospital I had ever been in.

A young girl who lived next door to my sister Leona, by the name of Lillian Wade, was there working. Her face looked like an angel to me that morning, I was so glad I knew someone there. I was placed in a hallway next to the delivery room. There had been a bad fire, and several rooms were burned out completely since I was there before. Now there was just one delivery and emergency room together. Yes, I had my baby this time, a fine little girl, so round faced and loved to eat from the very first. If she was not placed in my arms when she got hungry, she just scratched her face with both hands. The nurses got a real laugh at her. If my dinner came at the same time, I had to eat first. Well, she would pitch a fit. She grew fast and was one pretty baby with little blond curls. We named her Mavis after a new face powder and a little girl who attended school with Webb's sister in Barney, Adonis Gamble, who was her friend at school. She was named Mavis Adonis Furney, born February 9, 1944.

Michael Vanacore Jr., Mike III, and Mae

We lived at Pa Furney's on the old Jerry Wilkes farm. A small little church just across the road was very exciting, and we enjoyed watching the black people dedicate themselves to worshipping God on Sundays. Their movements, their clothes, only the best—oh, it is so hard to picture this. Most of the people walked to this little church, but the main thing was their devotion together, and to talk and how they live their lives.

We all enjoyed ourselves, going to Webb's home so much. Ma Furney believed in cooking three good meals a day, and I learned a lot of good things from Webb's family. One thing I won't forget: somehow Webb's name was on the registry in Quitman for the draft. Now Webb and I, with six children, could not believe our eyes when Webb got his letter of greetings from our president, saying he should be in Quitman on a specified date. He should be prepared for induction into the armed forces. First of all, we thought he was just too old to make a soldier. Next, he had six children and he had tried to enter the service as a young man but was declined because of a bad foot and leg. He had failed the test. Well, we knew for sure if things were that critical we would never win the war. Our best men were there. If they were killed, someone had to take their place. I knew Webb would never pass a physical now. I was not really worried a lot when the letter came. He did have to go before the draft board that day.

It was a gut feeling and a very sad feeling for his parents at their age. They expected anything. I remember I was picking butter beans most of the day, thinking what I would do with six children to feed. Me, with no training of any kind to work, I just knew how to take care of my house and children. Of course everyone else had figured out my income for a husband in the army and six children at home to care for. I would get more money if he did pass the physical than I had ever had in my life. Well, it didn't happen.

So the hard work kept going on and a bumper crop of cotton to pick. Of course we hired some help to get it done. My older children had to look after the smaller ones. Leona and Ellis helped us some. Vivian, Jeanette, Jan and Velma were the babysitters. Of course my daughter Jeanette had to show off. She told Vivian she could sew then sat down at the sewing machine, gave the wheel a turn, and promptly ran a needle through her finger. Webb went to get some water from the house, and one of the children told him what had happened. Well, he just got the pliers, got a hold of what he could see, and pulled it right out. She never even cried, but it was a while before she tried any sewing again. I nearly fainted just to think of how it must have hurt. We did enjoy swapping work with Ellis and Leona, even if it was cotton picking, tobacco work, or shaking peanuts, or killing hogs for our winter meat supply. There was a lot of working and talking going on. This is still 1944.

At the end of this year, a few things had happened. Iris had gone into the navy, and Laura Bell graduated from Barney High School. She was a smart young lady. Now Ma and Pa Furney had three grown girls at home. Then two of his sons-in-law, J. W. McCullar and Jimmy Roy Deloach, were in the service. Laura met Ralph Crosby, and they were married. Those days, when a boy liked a girl, they made up their mind right away if they wanted to get married. You would be here today and gone tomorrow. Yes, you guessed, Ralph could not spend a lot of time with Laura; he had to join the other boys. Some went to the Pacific, some Germany, and others to Italy and the blue Mediterranean. Melvin's husband was in Italy as was my brother Wayne and Ellis Copeland's brother Roy, also Ellis's younger brother Johnnie P. Copeland. It was really sad to know so many gone away, and just as seriously, many never saw their families again.

Fifteenth Move, 1944: Furney Family, Tenant House

Okay, we never got rich that year farming. We moved to the other empty house on the farm where it was not so wet or close to the woods, however it was near Webb's dad's house. Moving meant using a wheelbarrow to carry our belongings for the small stuff and a sled for the larger items, like the stove. There was no place to put my nice canning jars but under the house. There was no shade there. None of us liked this move. The year was soon to end. We did get us a car, a convertible of all things. With six children, there was no room for all of us to fit and go somewhere at the same time. When the crops were in, Webb went to Moultrie and got a job at Swift's Packing Company. He rented a room in town, which did not cost as much as going back and forth as well as the getting out in the wee hours of the morning way back on those dark country roads. Yes, he did at least make money for groceries and weekly expenses, which was very good as there was no money left over from farming that year. We now needed more food for eight people and school clothes for three children and lunches to pay for. While staying in Moultrie, he came home on Wednesday night and back on Friday nights for the weekend. Jan started school that fall as she would be six years old in November. They were not so strict on six-year-olds then.

Well, it was time to move on again. We packed up, and Webb had rented us a much-better house to live in. Mr. Cecil Hobbs from Pavo had bought the Harrell Place. There was no water there but plenty of wood for firewood.

Sixteenth Move, 1945: The Herrell Place (Again)

We had all started going to Pleasant Hill Church before we left the place over by Webb's dad's. We continued going to the Pleasant Hill Church, which I had a fond closeness for. My great-grandfather had donated the property in the eighteen hundreds where Pleasant Hill stands on today. Webb sold the convertible and bought a new Ford car, which we could fit into comfortably. He was still working at Swift's through the fall and Christmas holidays. I made a big square Japanese fruitcake for Christmas that year. Now don't ask me why it was called Japanese, because I sure don't know. One thing I do know is when baked about three weeks before Christmas and set up to get mellow, it seemed to take on moisture while setting up, yum, yum. It was a Furney tradition. If you did not have this fruitcake, well, you just missed the boat, that's all.

Early in the winter, Webb was talking to Cecil Hobbs and found out no one was living at the Herrell Place, and here we go again. This time around we will be doing the farming. The well had been cleaned out and dug deeper, so now we will have water. The other time we had lived there we had to haul the water in barrels, lots of work.

The war was still going strong. Meat, lard, and sugar were rationed, and one could only get a small amount of each. We never used all our sugar stamps. Our children drank milk and very little iced tea. We gave our extra sugar stamps to Ma Furney. We did use all our ration stamps allotted. A forty-five can of lard made from pork meat cost a fortune but was sold on the black market, as many things were during these times. There was so much of this going on. Some farmers made enough of these things for themselves, but the war hurt them in other ways. It really touched all Americans.

You cannot believe some of the most outstanding things that did take place that year. My dad sold our old Hart homeplace to Mr. Ashley Williams, a nice family. But he could not sell our memories of a lot of interesting happenings as well as the dreams for all my brothers and sisters. Our family, as is the usual, was now getting married and leaving the nest. The only ones left at home now are Eula Mae, Wilma, and Louis. Paul followed my brother J. E. to Belle Glade, Florida. Eula Mae was a senior in high school. Wilma and Louis were still in school also.

We planted, ploughed, and worked corn, tobacco, and peanuts for Mr. Hobbs. We then planted cabbage at our neighbor's, Mr. Williams. We also helped Mr. Williams plant his tobacco. When we were finished in the afternoons, we all went to the Downing Bridge and built a big bonfire for the young ones and cooked a big super of mullet fish, potato salad, and hush puppies. We fished in the nearby Okapilco Creek until eleven PM, packed up, and came home. Now our children were fast learning to work doing regular chores, feeding the mules, milking cows, and getting wood—just about everything that needed to be done on a farm though they were still small. As I said before, people did not wait till they were grown up. We started learning young, and so did our kids. Charles turned over all our land with a plow that year.

One day in February, near Valentine's Day, I'd bought the boys and the girls their Valentine cards. All of them were busy writing names of their classmates on each one. I noticed Gilbert had finished very fast. I thought, *that was quick*, when I asked about his speedy job, he laughed and said, "Well, I made mine easy. I just wrote the whole bunch out to Barbara Ruth Mitchell, and I'll just put them in her mailbox on that day." Of course I told him that was no way to do the job. He must give all of his friends one. He thought she was the only friend that counted.

Another time, when he finished a real hard day's work, while walking home out of the field, he said, "You know something? I am not gonna work like this always!" We asked him what he planned to do. He promptly replied, "When I get grown, I am going to marry Barbara Ruth Mitchell and quit work." We all had a big laugh. One day Webb, Gilbert, and I were hauling corn to the corncrib. Gilbert hopped off the wagon and was gone only a minute, with no noise, and he was right back on the wagon again. He had shot a big fat bobwhite quail. He was learning to be a good shot with his homemade slingshot, which he carried in his pocket or about his neck all the time.

Most of the children learned to swim that year, in a hole of water at the Little Creek Bridge. Our sons were dependable at that age. When we went away for a trip to town, to church, or to Pa Furney's, Webb told the boys, "No swimming till I get home," and they didn't. Someone said, "Don't you know, those boys will sneak in swimming anyway." They never did. Most children would have, but ours didn't.

My brother Wayne was injured in the spring of the year and finally made it home for a visit. We were all so glad to see him, even with a badly injured arm. The upper part, which was hit with shrapnel, was almost gone. He received the Purple Heart award for that.

In the summer of 1945, we wanted to celebrate our finished tobacco crop, so we and the Lon Rogers family wanted fish to eat. Well, as I said before, shortening was hard to get, so Opralee, Lon's wife, and me drove all the way to Quitman. We had heard of a store there that always had lard, which one could buy. Just a little to everyone. Believe it or not, with a family of eight, I was issued one pint and she was issued one pint. It took both pints to fry all our fish and we had driven thirty miles to get it. People who could killed a pork early and cut it up into small pieces and cooked it all at one time to get the lard and meat to eat. Killing pork in summer was a no-no because we only had ice to keep it cold and it would spoil if not cooked thoroughly.

In late summer and early fall, no matter what, everything I ate or drank was making me sick again, especially in the morning. I found out that I was once again to have another little one. Mavis was walking everywhere, a real smart baby, trying to talk, does have a teething problem though. Soon that will be over.

It was now the fall and the boys were raking up all the leaves in the yard and burning them. My daughter Jan had forgotten the fire was there, and it even looked cool. She went to jump over the pile and stepped into it. The ashes were real hot, and she burned her foot really bad. It took a good while to get it well. She also had pneumonia in the fall. We had her in the hospital for a week. We brought her home, and in two weeks, she had it again. This time I did the nursing. The doctor said they could not have done better in the hospital.

We made no money that year at the Harrell place. Just broke even, though we still had our car. Webb went to work at Swift's again, and at least it provided clothes, shoes, and some of the best bacon I ever ate. We were visiting my mom and dad who live near Leona's at the very end of Brice's plantation, where Daddy had now bought another new farm. The property had not been cleared, it was all woods. The German prisoners of war who were kept in the base at Spence Field were allowed to come to help clear all the new ground. They really enjoyed being able to work outside in the fresh air and enjoyed our family and my mama's cooking. The few who spoke English would translate for us.

Webb liked Turner Brice as a young man and had worked many days with him. It did not surprise me when he told me he had traded for a crop that year with Mr. Brice. That was the man my dad bought his farm from. Really just a piece of woodland, grass, and pine trees with low wet places, but my dad knew land and no job was too big to undertake. He was happy to get a house started and get Mama settled near her churches. When she married Dad in 1914, she and Daddy joined the Missionary Baptist Church at Pine Grove near Uncle Bob Hart's where Myron, his son, is a deacon at the present time.

It was like going home, to Mom. She was within sight of Wesley Chapel Church, a Methodist, and one she became a very dedicated member of at about nine years old. At the church's one-hundred-year centennial celebration, Leona and I saw our mom's name on the church records with other family members. She attended Wesley Chapel all of her single days. Pleasant Hill Church was only a couple of miles from Wesley Chapel. Mom's granddad gave the land for Pleasant Hill Baptist Church and Cemetery in the 1800s, which she went to again when she moved to the property bought from Brice's.

Seventeenth Move, 1945-1947: Brice's Plantation

Now with Webb making plans to farm with Turner Brice, we were so glad to live near Leona and Ellis. Mom and Dad came by our house if they had to go to Quitman for anything. I really think we all enjoyed living there. Leona and I were real go-getters those days. They had a pickup truck, and believe it or not, she and I and our children moved all our household items and furniture in a couple of days to the Brice house. Of course, what really kept our steam up was knowing we could visit and go to PTA meetings (our mom was president of the Sand Hill PTA when we went to school there) and go to church together with our families.

We loved for the men to go fishing. Brice's Pond was right behind our house. Leona and I would talk while our children played. We didn't grow any cotton at Brice's, but we caught our share of fish. Webb placed a big steel barrel in the pond. The barrel had small holes in it, so the water filled the drum and it was the same temperature as the pond water. When Webb caught a big haul of fish, he would turn them loose in the drum, so they just kept swimming. When someone wanted a mess of fish, Webb just put his hand down in that drum and got out what he wanted.

Oh, I forgot to tell you how we got our boat when we first moved to Brice's. Webb and I would walk down to the landing near our house. He'd look across the pond and say he wished he had a boat. I mean, every few days he would say this, so in February one day, the wind had blown all night from a little winter storm and had blown us a nice boat. From all the way across the pond. It was really cold that day though, and the boat was like fifty yards from shore, up against some logs that were floating. Well, we wished again, but the only way to get that boat was to jump in and swim to it and paddle it to shore. We built a big brush fire to keep warm after getting wet. Charles had come over to where we were, and he said, "I'll go get it, Dad." So he threw off his clothes, walked as far as he could on those logs as naked as he was born. I couldn't help but laugh, then he was ready to jump into the water, but he let out a yell and said this water was cold as ice! He swam a little distance then pulled out of the water on a log and said, "Doggone it; I am so cold I can't swim, Daddy." He came out to that warm fire and got his clothes on in a big hurry.

Now it was Webb's time to see if he could stand the cold water. While we watched, off came his clothes (no, not his underwear). He jumped in with his underwear still on. This time he got the boat. He was freezing, his teeth just chattering, so off came the underwear this time. I had his shirt and overalls warm, and in less than a minute, he was dressed and laughing and planning to go fishing.

Mr. Enoch Hires, who ran the landing on the other side of the pond, never asked about the boat even once. He liked Webb a lot. Believe it or not, he talked me into getting in that old rickety boat and paddling for him to put out some nets he had. Fish ran and played at certain times of the year, and into the net they went. To tell the truth, I was afraid the wood bottom in that old boat might just fall through, with me, into the pond. I went that very afternoon, and by dark, we had already caught a nice bunch of fish in those nets and also the next morning again. I was so large with my seventh child I looked like a blimp. I was afraid I might be having twins. Yes, times have changed. I now am going to Dr. Smith in Quitman for my prenatal care, although I did have five children before I could say the word *prenatal*. I am sure it is good to have in case something goes wrong, also makes for better health for both mother and child.

Now Webb had to have someone to row the boat while he put out the nets. He chose Gilbert, our second son, because Charles was more reliable to feed the cows and mules. Gilbert would forget to, but in the boat with Webb, he did not forget to paddle the boat and soon could do a good job. Now it was fun, but the more Webb caught fish, the more he wanted to fish. Soon he got a line to tie from one stump to another with short lines and good hooks in between. Now each hook must be baited with large worms or meat from freshly killed birds or liver. Now this was a new kind of fishing. One usually caught catfish or bream. He would start out in the pond at about four in the morning, put out the nets then bait the lines (called a trotline). He was now selling fish on weekends. He could not catch enough fish to supply the demand. Yes, Gilbert was known as the Little Fisherman, and he was good. At this time, he had never earned any money for work other than farming. Way on in the late spring, Dr. Tuck from Thomasville, Georgia, came to the boat landing to fish way out in the pond for bass. No one was around to row his boat, so Mr. Enoch Hires said, "C. C., this little boy living on the other side of the pond is a fine little fisherman, go get him.

He can really row a boat." Now remember he was just ten years old and was quite shy with a strange man. When Dr. Tuck got to our house, I was washing clothes. Gilbert had on cutoff overalls, and he wanted his long ones and went into the house to get a pair that was in the dirty clothes. I was really embarrassed as this doctor went right into our house with him to help him get his overalls. Well, he found them and went on. They fished for about three hours and caught a few. He brought Gilbert home and gave him five dollars Now Gilbert really thought he was a good fisherman, for he only got five dollars for working all the day in the fields.

Ethel had her little son Rodney about six weeks before Melba was born. She and her little girl Arlene, the new baby, and her husband, J. W. McCullar, who was now out of the service, came by to see us. J. W. had always wanted to go fishing in the pond. We had a boat and could go anytime, but he never got to go that year at all. He was so busy driving his big truck and working on other trucks he just could not make it.

Now my little girls had been a little smarter. I had washed all my baby dresses, wraps, and diapers to get them soft and fresh for the new baby. I was at Mama's that afternoon when my children came home from school. Another woman who did the wash left all the baby clothes on the line. So the little girls got busy, took them in off the line, folded them all very nicely, and packed my suitcase full. When I got home, they met me at the door with eyes bright and round and said, "Mama, we have everything ready." They were holding the suitcase. I said, "Ready for what?" They said, "Well, aren't you having another baby?" I could have flipped! I had no idea they even suspected a new baby. I said, "Thank you both, I'm sure I'll need this done." Well, that just proved they were smarter than you think.

Talking about farming and fishing. We really did our thing! We made lots of tobacco, corn, and peanuts too. Also our baby came before Easter Sunday, on Wednesday morning. My brother Brant took me to the hospital. He left me his wristwatch so I could see the time, and it came in handy, timing contractions. Melba Jean was born April 17, 1946. This little one was no trouble, another little red head full of curls, with large brown eyes, a real good and beautiful baby. Oh yes, on the coldest Easter Sunday, I came out of the hospital. The nurses never let me even sit up in bed, and I was carried to the car on a stretcher where a complete stranger just picked me up in his arms like a baby and laid me in the backseat of my sister Eula Mae's car.

I felt really out of place. My sister and her mother-in-law came and got me. I didn't understand why Webb hadn't come to get me. Later he explained, "Lorene, where would they have put you if I had come too? They took up the front seat and you were in the back," then I understood. As soon as I got home, I got dressed, went into the kitchen, and made some good biscuits for Webb and the children. They hadn't had any since I left.

On Monday I cooked dinner for everyone who could help us pick a snap bean. We really worked hard that summer, all of us. That year, our boys were allowed to crop tobacco as regular helpers. When we got our barn full, they could help our neighbors. This did really please them, for they made some extra money. We let them trust their judgment in buying their own clothes. They tried them on for size and choosing the style and color. I'll never forget the look on Webb's face the first Saturday I let them go to town by themselves. Ellis Copeland's brother Roy had made his time in service and came home. He and my sister Sarah were going together right along, so I felt I could trust the boys with Roy. He let them catch a ride to Quitman on Saturday with him.

They would have twelve or sixteen dollars each to spend. They were different then from most boys as they would buy shirts and blue jeans. Charles liked khaki pants instead of the blue jeans Gilbert liked, but they were told by me to put their money to good use, and they did. Oh, Webb thought they would just throw it away on drinks, candy, and junk. Later, I was to see these same boys go to Pavo on Saturday afternoon and never buy ice cream or drinks. They would go to the movies for fifteen cents. They were still small. Charles was twelve years old and Gilbert was ten. Believe me, those kids worked ten hard hours a day and were so tickled to go to town with Roy and buy school clothes.

We really did enjoy living at Brice's. We had what is called a surface well for our water supply. It was a big five-foot square well with a wooden curb around it. We lived near the pond, so it stayed full of water, and was it not a bad job to draw water out with a chain and bucket. One day we came home from my sister's to find the two ducks gone. They usually came to meet us when we came home, but this time, they were not to be seen. When we went for water, there were the ducks floating around in our well, just like they were happy as could be. I promptly hooked a chain to a bean hamper, let it down beside the ducks, got it under the ducks, and the ducks came up in the hamper. Now this works well with ducks, but don't let any cats get in your well as they can only swim a few minutes before they drown. That would be bad as you have to drain the whole well one bucket at a time.

We all worked, the tobacco did real well. It may be years later, right now as I am writing this; I still think how nice it was to get things ready for work. Eula Mae would come along in her pretty car. I'd have already cooked our dinner, all but the corn bread. I just set it aside, take my baby bed, and put it in the shade at the tobacco barn and tie tobacco like mad until noontime. I then fed the crew and got back to the barn to get it finished. It was so nice to ride around the big pond every morning. So nice and cool just as the sun is peeking over the trees in the east, looking at a thousand beautiful pond lilies, just like little bouquets, now in bloom with white and yellow on green leaves. Listening to the radio's snappy tunes. We all loved to hear the music. There was no television, and this little break started my day right. This was where Mavis walked under the mules' feet to watch them eat. She was really small, and we got her out in a hurry.

In July, I had tobacco all over the house. That was where we removed the tied leaves from the sticks, graded it for color, and then packed it in big sheets made out of burlap. We put one tied-up sheet on top of the other in a stack until we could reach no higher, and then start another pile. We had one of the downstairs rooms of our house stacked to the ceiling with cured tobacco. I mean, all our time was spent working, no fishing now!

On the first day of the tobacco sale, the load we had carried in brought us one thousand dollars. Webb went off on Friday night with my sister's husband, Tony, and Hubert Hart. They bought a fifth of whiskey and got drunk as a skunk and stayed out all night. He said they were at the boat landing, but when men do that, the truth is not in them. From then on, I saw to it that the boys got every penny they worked for with others to buy what they wanted and needed. I did not think Webb was capable of taking care of their money for them as he did not feel too bad spending what he and I and the boys worked so hard for. Oh yes, we did clear some money that year, but with a family that size and school clothes for four and three babies at home to keep warm and feed, it really took some money to keep us going.

In the early fall and winter, Webb and all of us did enjoy fishing once again. Also that year every rural family paid a small fee of five dollars to get a hook up to the electric lines that were being built by the REA. Everyone was truly excited as we would have wonderful lights, running water, electric irons, and all the other things gradually came into the homes, like washing machines, dryers, and refrigerators to make ice and keep things cold. President Roosevelt had said all homes would have electric lights. Now the next thing was whose farm had lights and whose did not. I really think the night the lights came on was the greatest thing that ever happened to farming families. Work was so hard, and with no lights to see by, one can't imagine it.

Melba, Little Sandy, and Stacey Deas

Eighteenth Move, 1947:
Durwood and Effie Crosby's Farm

About this time, my sister Effie and her husband, Durwood Crosby, who lived near Quitman, Georgia, were working with a construction company that was moving up around Atlanta, Georgia. They wanted to move up there, rent a place, and work. They needed someone to live in their house and care for chickens, mules, and cows. They had a big beautiful home close to Quitman. Well, it looked like we were the right ones to live there and work on his farm while he worked in Atlanta. So there we went again, this time in a real nice house.

We spent a good Christmas while we were at Effie and Durwood's. The children all got presents, and we had fireworks. The little ones were all playing with sparklers and, as usual, were running all over the place. Jan quietly lit her sparkler from the fireplace and forgot to watch where she held it. The front of her pretty Christmas dress was burned, but she wasn't.

We used wood fires for heat and woodstoves for cooking, but we had electricity and a good school at Morven for the children. Vernon had not yet started school. Mavis was about three years old, and Melba, the one born at Brice's, was nine months old. Poor Jeanette was her second mama, and carried her every step she went. I had to have help, and she was a smart little girl, had never missed a day in school, and was learning to cook a little. One Friday, she came home with chicken pox and was beside herself. She just knew she would miss a day of school now. Well, Monday she felt fine, and her chicken pox was drying in. She caught them at school, and she went right back to school that Monday morning like nothing was wrong.

We did some hard work there. The boys working our tobacco, and two days a week, they worked with Walt Eatman's boys nearby. They did like our boys to help them. Jeanette also had learned to tie tobacco or hand the leaves to the tier as she was now ten years old.

Webb won a pair of turkeys at a turkey shoot, and that got us started, trying our hand at raising turkeys, and we had a nice bunch of guineas as well as chickens. We really gave ourselves a good chance at farming. Oh, those peanuts were so hard to gather. Ten acres and no power tools or machines, just plain backbreaking work, and we had to do it.

Oh yes, you might believe it, my sister and her husband stayed on that job for about three months and came home. We gave them their home back, and we moved into their tenant house near the pond. Our ducks did love the water, and every morning, the old mama duck would take her dozen babies to the pond right across the big road in front of our house. One little duck right behind the other, led by the old duck. Even the cars would stop and let them go down the road.

Gilbert was now twelve and learning to hunt, and he wanted to catch a raccoon! There were so many little tracks on the sand beside the water of the little stream that ran into the pond of water across the road from our house. He tried all kinds of bait but no raccoon. Nothing touched the traps, and still plenty of tracks. He could not figure why. One day, one of the men he had helped gather tobacco for found out he wanted to catch a raccoon, and he told him how. Use sardines from a can to bait the steel trap then take a stick (do not put hands near the trap), gently rake leaves over the trap when set and tied good to a tree, then let it stay till the next morning.

Well, this little boy was so excited he slept very little that night. He was so sure he would catch a coon. Bright and early the next morning, just at daylight, we were disturbed from our sleep by the most ferocious barking of our two dogs and Durwood's German shepherd, Josie. Gilbert was leading the bunch bringing in the full-grown raccoon. The coon was in so much pain with his little foot caught in that horrible trap's claws. He knew nothing but to fight and bite. Gilbert was hunting for his dad to help him free the coon. We were shocked he finally caught one as he must have come home twenty times before with nothing. We had a large wire cage on legs, so we put the coon in there to calm him down then we all went into the house for a good breakfast.

Later that day, when this animal had rested and everyone left him alone, he made his escape from that little prison with only three legs to carry himself. He had already bitten his leg nearly off to escape the captors' hands. Gilbert found trapping animals was cruel and such bad suffering for the animal that he never set another trap, and he loves hunting, but I've never known him to hunt the little raccoon again. He likes bird hunting and deer hunting and a squirrel if he sees one.

I've never seen Charles carry a gun, even a half day till this day, fifty years later. He loves to go fishing, so does Gilbert. There never were two brothers closer. Though as is the case, I think all brothers argue and pass licks once in a while. I think it is the usual in growing up. Most of the time, they agreed on the things they were doing.

We just broke even this year some corn to move and money to buy school clothes. School had started, and we were looking for another campground as Webb thinks Durwood wants to get rich first. We have no car, just a big family. Now when we start looking, it must be for a larger house, for we now have seven children to eat, sleep, and work with. I did learn some new things this year. If you are buying turkeys to eat, they cost a lot of money, but if you have a dozen to sell, it's another story. We just could not sell ours, at a turkey shoot even. They were so fat and pretty, we both were disgusted. We had a bunch of turkeys to start the next season with. Those things were a hard job to dress out for eating. As usual, the male turkey was a mean old bird. He would run after any child till he fell down then flog him with his wings till someone ran him away. So we ate a lot of turkey and sold the gobbler to the furniture salesman. We took our young turkeys to a turkey shoot near Valdosta. Because we did not post our number of turkeys to be shot off, they did not get to ours, so that was why we ate a lot of turkeys.

Well, this is another year gone. Much of the time we spent at Effie and Durwood's was alone, just me and the children. I think Webb must be discouraged with everything. Making babies, being married, farming and oh, just about everything. Our separating was never mentioned, but he did not marry a quitter. If he fell short, I was able to keep things together. Oh yes, he found him a buddy with a car. All he had to do to get to town was just get dressed, walk out to the road, and Cleo Culpepper would be by our house soon. He and his wife had separated, so he kept the road hot and drank too. So Webb went off too. I had so much to do I never missed him too bad. I did argue some when he came home in the wee hours of the morning or had spent the night someplace. All he had to do was say "I met my brother and went to Ma's and spent the night." *Yes,* I thought. *Is this really all married life is about?*

He met Mr. Guy Crosby (Durwood's cousin) somewhere in his rounds. His plans were soon made to get us moved again, to Mr. Guy Crosby's farm on exactly the opposite side of Brice's Pond from where we lived when we worked for Turner Brice in 1946. Now it is fall of the year 1947. You see most people are looking for a good family to work the coming year, so from September to January or February, one gets the plans made for the coming year. So we made our plan to leave Quitman and go back to the Brice pond near Pavo on the Guy Crosby farm. He was also my mama's cousin. My grandma Betty had a sister, Alice Cooper, who married Paul Crosby. She always said Uncle Paul and Aunt Alice, Guy Crosby was their son. We never spoke of our little bit of kin.

Nineteenth Move, 1947: Guy Crosby's Farm

OK, we have moved back near Leona and Ellis and their children. We are overjoyed! The girls love each other so much. My two girls and Leona's, Vivian and Velma, are almost like twins. The older two were redheads, and from a short distance you could not tell them apart especially if their backs were turned to you. They occasionally got into trouble, which the other one had made. Once, one got a smack on the behind by mistake when caught in the act with their backs to one of us. I remember it being holding on to a car just after it was moving off.

This was dangerous, as my brother Louis had found out. He tried something like it when my Uncle Jim Hart came by my dad's place in a big truck loaded with trees, all cut and trimmed to make lumber with. Uncle Jim had a long trailer hooked to the truck for hauling logs. Louis thought it might be fun to put his finger in the hole on a hook in the back of the trailer and it would be no trouble to chase along behind when Uncle Jim took off. Louis was only about eight years old and was not aware the rig was too long for Uncle Jim to see anyone running behind him. Well, to save his life, when that truck took off, he was going so fast he could not get that finger loose. He knew it was too late to yell loud as he could. Finally, about the time he was giving out, my uncle slowed down just a little. Well, my brother got loose from that hook and finally told us he was scared his finger would be pulled from his hand. Now he had been told but failed to listen. With a lot of children around, all adults had to watch them, for things like this would happen.

As this year 1947 came to a close, we had gotten settled. I had Charles, Gilbert, Jeanette, and Janice in Sand Hill School again. They all liked this school and knew everyone. Vernon also started school that fall. Now I was a PTA member. I had been all along, but I really got with it now. I had Leona or Debbie McDaniel pick me up to give a hand at those projects that promoted a good fellowship between parents, teachers, and pupils. We quilted quilts, sold tickets, and put the money in the treasury. Some lucky one had a good quilt, and we enjoyed the making. We also had school jamborees, where we had cakewalks—which Webb liked to run—box suppers, fish pools, haunted houses, and a country store. At a box supper, a very neat box with a large capacity to hold something was filled with goodies, including a complete meal for two. Oh, these boxes were covered over to look beautiful with crepe paper. I once made one in the shape of an airplane, in the spirit of '76.

I also made a steamship and a coaster wagon. These were made in my courting days, but I helped make them now for others. Oh, it was fun. They were auctioned off to the highest bidder, who usually turned out to be the girl's boyfriend. The cakewalk was similar but a game of chance. All walked around a big circle of chairs while music played. When it stopped, all sat down, and the lucky number won a cake, sitting in a chair of the number drawn.

Also a project that got us all into it was the county fair, once a year in the fall. All schools entered a booth to show how productive the community was, also to carry out a theme or title. The Chamber of Commerce thought a good challenge as a work project. Then the PTA got to work as a prize was given to the best work represented and how it was displayed. Sand Hill won several times, and a lot of hard work went into these projects. This year I really worked with all the rest. This was the fall of 1947, end of the year. Melba was born at Brice's on April 17, 1946.

Webb lost no time getting his fishing gear together. We are again near Brice's Pond. Mostly all houses are now wired for electricity. This house of Mr. Crosby's was wired that year in the summer. I well remember using a kerosene lamp and stove that winter of 1947. This was the spring of '48.

I am raising baby chicks and already feeling sick to my tummy, and I know very well what is wrong with me. I would have my number-eight child before the year's end, but we tackled my first jobs first. We planted five acres of cabbage in February for a little early money. Webb and I cut and loaded all those cabbage. It made no difference if I were pregnant. We gathered the cabbage in May. Once or twice a week, we got between two rows, each with a tobacco sled in between our rows. We cut and filled the sled then drove the truck at the end of the rows and emptied the sled until we had a truckload. Then Webb would take them off to sell them while I made dinner. This was the big meal of the day on a farm. One never ate enough breakfast to keep from being hungry for the midday meal. Of course the evening meal was a welcome time of day also.

In the early spring, Webb took Gilbert, our second son, to help get the nets and lines and go fishing. He would make a good payday Saturday and Sunday mornings when all those fish-loving men would be waiting for the boat to come in. He also did stay out Friday and Saturday nights until midnight, fishing the nets and selling to anyone at the pond who did not catch any fish, or someone who wanted something to just eat on the spot for a fish fry. This was great for those who liked to rough it or a man who wanted to show his son what outdoor life is all about. Webb could always make a little extra money for groceries, school lunches, and whatever else we may need that we couldn't wait to sell a crop for. We were glad Webb at least could fish and we lived near a pond. Not all farmers had the know-how Webb had for getting out, fishing for a living and farming. He would do anything to bring in money to help keep his family going.

When we moved to this Guy Crosby's place, there were lots of rooms but no windows in the front room. Well, believe it or not, Leona and I made a couple! We had ne on each side of the fireplace. We just cut a couple of holes out where we wanted them. She had a couple of glass windows that she had stashed away, so when Webb and Mr. Crosby got home, there were two nice framed-out windows looking at them. One would not believe until they saw this, that beside all else, we were two pretty good carpenters. They even said so.

One night Webb went fishing, and I got very scared. My youngest was still little and had been crying a good bit too. Our house was near a big swamp that came from the Pilco Creek to the back of our house. When it got dark, I made a good fire then closed the windows and doors with latches and a chain at the door. I had gone to bed, when all at once, something made me wide awake. I had been asleep just a short while, when suddenly a bloodcurdling scream sounded right at my door. My first thought was, *don't panic!* I reached for my matches—my best policy being light the lamp—when I realized my hand was shaking so bad I almost knocked the lamp off the table. I just stopped, but I could speak and yelled "Get out, hey, you, get off my porch!" This animal had to be a big cat, for it sprang to jump so silently there was no noise made. It left the wooden floor with a rattling, cracking; board-slapping noise that sounded like my long porch was being torn from the house. Gee, was I ever petrified, I did not panic. I knew it was gone away to the woods, then I lit the kerosene lamp and let it burn until Webb came home from fishing that night, but for a few minutes, I felt my blood turn to water.

In all my married life, I was never this frightened as I don't scare too fast or for nothing. I guess having babies at home and looking after them myself taught me a lot. It is comparable to the Boy Scout rule: be prepared always.

Webb's sister Ethel and her husband, J. W. McCullar, came to see us late one afternoon. It was a cool, crisp day. Webb was plowing up the old dead cotton stalks, and we all were at work. We were picking them up by the armful, making huge piles for big bonfires as soon as they dried in a few days. J. W. had this Ford car. I don't know which model, but it had two separate seats in front, not a bench seat. Somehow, one was taken out, and J.

W. just replaced it with a straight chair, and Ethel was seated in it with the three little ones in back. We all enjoyed them coming down from Moultrie to visit us. My daughter Mavis and their oldest child Arlene were near the same age, and her little boys liked ours as we had them in all sizes.

At this time, the fishing was really going good in Brice's Pond, so Webb and J. W. gathered up the lines and bait and took off just after dark for J. W. to finally get to go fishing with Webb. They came home with a fine catch. We built a fire and had them dressed and cooking in no time. We fried the fish and made a Southern favorite, cheese grits and hush puppies made from cornmeal, which was a batter dropped with a spoon into the hot fat that the fish were cooked in. You knew a hush puppy was done when it floated to the top of the fat. We had a very delicious meal with good, fresh coleslaw.

That night our light was a kerosene lamp and the glass shade was missing. It had gotten broken while it was moved from room to room. We were used to it by now though. Ethel said, "Lorene, I don't see how you make it. I can't even see you, let alone see how to cook food." That night one of Ethel's little boys broke his bottle and that left one bottle for both boys all night. No, they were not twins, just close in age, and the older one had not been weaned before the other one came along. Did they ever give their mom a hard time!

The boys each took turns with that bottle all night. When one finished, the other one got it, so cute, but I had never made a bottle in my life. They were so close in age and truly close brothers. What one did, they were both blamed for it. They were about seven or eight years old, when one of them shot the little bright spot in the center of the television screen with a BB gun. Both of them had gotten BB guns for Christmas, so after shooting out the light in the television, both of their guns were destroyed. My son used to really love going fishing with them when they got older, and they caught many fish together.

We had a large kitchen, and my boys always had other boys with them who were from Moultrie and loved the country life. When we finally got electricity, we also got a radio, and the boys learned to dance right in my kitchen. Jitterbug, Charleston, and round dance, they loved it. Also standing by my stove while I cooked, they peeled potatoes, turned the chicken frying, or set the table and learned about the facts of life. I never heard my husband explaining anything about life, making babies, contracting a venereal disease, or how to prevent these things. Also the bitter mistake of having to marry a girl to find out the price was much more than the purchase, also boys like to choose their merchandise, not have it pushed on them. Well, my boys got around to discussing these things with me in the kitchen, so I guess Webb and the boys had their man talks without a big deal over it, and since it was man's talk, it was something Mama hadn't needed to hear.

The summer was almost gone and our crop nearly completed. Our horse took a sleeping sickness, which is caused by or from the bite of mosquitoes. We lived near two ponds as I have said and right near a thick swamp with all kinds of fish and birds as well as cats, raccoons, opossum, and squirrels. Yes, the horse died.

We really do not have any money this time. My baby is due the first of September, and now I have five children to dress for school, bless their little hearts. My children are not lazy. The first four would work hard, with all gathering peanuts and corn and cotton. They then would pick cotton at their Uncle Ellis and Aunt Leona's. The boys helped with hay making and peanut picking. We have not had a cash settlement with Guy Crosby, and my baby is now due. This was our first year at the Guy Crosby place, and I do help pick some of the cotton, the first to open. I don't feel as good as I did with my other children. I guess seven others took their toll.

I now have varicose veins bulging in the front of my legs. My doctor did not mention any support to take the load up above, off the lower part of my belly, where the baby is. I now know some support would have helped as the weight caused a blockage of the blood flow returning once it is in my legs. As most of you know, I am only five feet tall.

So I ended up giving out at the end of those long days. Now I lie down a couple of hours a day and the older children have to help with more chores. Especially cooking, washing, ironing, and cleaning. These things still have to go on now our family is beginning to be a load. Children's school clothes, new shoes, socks, workbooks, and school lunches. Gee! Looking back now, I wonder how Webb and I could bear to even sleep near each other anymore. I really think there was a good bit of stress in our marriage.

Now the boys also expected an allowance once a week and we suddenly found out Charles had started smoking cigarettes. He is picking up butts someone else threw away. So Webb said, "Charles, that is too bad, don't you ever pick up another, I'll buy you cigarettes. If they make you feel better or you think you must." Before this, you'll never believe, he kept something in his mouth, a small piece of rubber or even a piece of paper to chew on. He was a good boy, a hard worker, considerate of others, very patient, and not inclined to lie about things like some people do, even to get out of a situation. He was a dependable young man. Even though he was handicapped, he got the same treatment Gilbert did.

I had been over to Ma Furney's one Sunday, and she found out I had nothing made up for our little one to come. I was never too lazy to sew, and I had my mother's sewing machine. One day the next week, here she comes with a ton of stuff in her arms, all kinds of material and two dozen bird's-eye diapers. Now everyone used that kind of diaper. They were used and washed and dried on the line, every day by hand. The cloth she brought was a fine soft batiste white broadcloth and dimity checks. Did I ever get busy?

Melba Jean was the baby then, she was two years old in April. Now this was August of 1948, so she played a lot outside with Mavis and Vernon. Mavis was now five-and-a-half years old, and just crazy to start school. She won't be six until February, but she could count good, knew all the little nursery rhymes, so Mrs. Johennison took her into her first-grade class, and I really got busy with my sewing. I made every piece of cloth into little dresses and underclothes in time for my son's arrival.

Dennis Jerale Furney arrived on September 3, 1948. An election year I will never forget. I'll bet he was the youngest ever to go to the voting place with his mother. I did cast my vote on Tuesday, and Jerale was five days old. Durwood Crosby came and carried us down to the Tallokas precinct. Webb was helping hold the poles—he, my dad, and Ellis Copeland. I felt strong enough, but after all the work and babies, in a few weeks I would be giving out at my job. You feel so good after delivery you could shout, but it does take a few weeks to be back to your old self.

I remember so well the day I came home from the hospital. As one can expect, sisters, brothers, aunts, cousins all came to see the baby Jerale, number eight. I thought I was fixing to become like my mother if my health kept being good, as it usually was. I would have a complete dozen. You see, I am the oldest of twelve children. Six girls and six boys, so I am following close in her footsteps. Oh yes, I can hear you say, "Why so many children?" Well, times have changed. In those days almost anyone could have a baby, but only an expert on thinking then doing kept from having a good-sized family. This was an old Chinese Proverb: think, then do. Not do, then think.

My little niece quoted it right. Dorothy Crosby was a small little girl and was so excited to see all the children at Morven School seated at one huge table all eating away at lunchtime. She often said, "Mama, I wish we had enough children to fill up each side of this table, that would be nice." Now here she stood looking lovingly into the bassinet at my number eight, Jerale. She turned to me smiling beautifully. "Aunt Lorene, now you have enough children to have a big lunchroom table." And she was so right. Four on each side, seated on benches, one beside the other, with Webb and myself at each end, seated in chairs.

Oh yes, our children learned how to be nice at the table, are kind and sharing, polite to each other. No one ever missed a meal; all ate at the same time. Once I had a shortage of dinner plates as one now and then got broken. With girls learning to wash dishes, they get a little careless at times. We had an unexpected number of people with Uncle Rass Furney, Pa Furney's brother, who came by for breakfast. Two children ate out of a large platter together, having no trouble at all. Only a short time till I could get into town and purchase more dishes. I now have piles of dishes that I never use at all, and you guessed it! I still think of the days when there was not enough to go around.

This year my sister Leona could not wait another day for the electricity to come to their corner of the world. She went out and bought a nice electric washing machine and moved it over to our brother Wayne's house. He had electricity. I lived half a mile from Wayne and do not have power yet. He lived on a large main highway, and we were off the main road, and that would take time. My sister let us both use her washer, and are we ever delighted! For the first time I could wash all the laundry in two-and-a-half hours. I now had time for school affairs, parent-and-teacher's meeting, school programs, 4-H Club, and work with our children.

An old slogan comes to mind: "My work is done, I have time to play. I've a new Maytag washer; I'm queen for a day." This went over and over in my mind every time I went for a meeting at the school house for anything.

It was now 1949, and the school year was in full swing. One of Leona's daughters and two of my children, Jeanette and Gilbert, graduated from the seventh grade to junior high school. They would be moving schools, on to Barwick. Did we ever fix up the school stage for this occasion!

We used Leona's beautiful geraniums on the steps, and we improvised across the entire back of the stage. The green foliage was beautiful in each pot, on white paper-covered steps. If there were not at least two blooms on each plant, we promptly made a white paper flower, put it on a piece of wire, and stuck it in the pot. No one could look and tell this one from the real thing. Now the entire seventh grade stood in lines, in the front, and the flowers made the background. Then lower on the floor level, we used large heads of glossy magnolia leaves tacked to the foot of the stage. We really got the job well done, a beautiful job. All the flower-loving ladies wanted just a tiny cutting of those red or white geraniums.

We still talk of this day in our lives. Oh yes, times were hard, money was scarce, all we did have plenty of was time. Now we have it so different, a little money, plenty of clothes, and no time. Where has it gone? Days and nights are still twenty-four hours long. In thinking of clothes and money, as I've said before, we were taught at an early age: waste not, want not. As fast as guano fertilizer was emptied out of a sack (and plenty was used), not one was thrown away.

I gathered ours, Leona gathered theirs, and we washed them by getting all the guano fertilizer out. We hung them up to dry, folded them, and carried them back to the guano plant, where we received ten cents each for them. This money was carefully spent for a white shirt for Gilbert and materials and shoes for Jeanette. Each dress for the graduation was handmade by the mothers using one pattern design. One pattern, or maybe four, was passed around to all the mothers, so the lovely pastel eyelet embroidered dresses looked alike. There were all different colors but each made of the same kind of material. No one knew but my sister and me how hard we worked to accomplish this, with all our regular duties to home, husband, and children. Those were the days!

I now lived very near my sister. We had moved to my dad's new farm in a tenant house up on the hill. After finishing off Mom's house on the property adjoining Ellis and Leona's, my dad built us a new house on the opposite side of his house up on the hill. Mary Hart now lives there.

Jerale Furney, Melanie, Dennis, Delores, Lorene and Rodney Furney

Twentieth Move, 1949:
New Hart Place by Brice's Plantation

We now are living at my dad's tenant house near my mom's and my sister's. He had bought this property from Brice's plantation and built a new house for me (which now Mary Hart lives in). All land growing lush pine timber and wire grass. No house, not even a well there. My mother must have been a real pioneer as I never heard her complain once. If Daddy thought it a good idea, she backed him up 100 percent. Always like that. I always prayed that after I become a married woman that I might have such patience.

When I was a grown single girl, I myself would have liked to crash into some of his grand ideas. I thought we might have had more material things, but at least I learned men are pretty good planners and they do make some mistakes with so many things to be responsible for. Because Dad was the head authority in our home, I never even considered a decision being made without my dad making the plans. My mother usually agreed, and we sometimes did not like the idea too well, even if Dad brought us into the discussion, but he still made the final decision.

Mom's answer to our complaint was "Convince a man against his will, he will be of the same opinion still." She also quoted, "Beautiful hands are those that do work that is honest, brave, and true." Yes, we often complained that the work Dad set us to do was worse than men's work. Our hands would tell everybody we had to work hard.

We did enjoy going to the county fair the year we lived near Leona and Ellis. My children now were teenagers, as were Leona's and my youngest brother Louis. We would gather them up and go to the fair. They just needed a little looking after, not having to be right with them, just near so if things did not go right, we'd be right there. As usual, my brother Louis and my sister Wilma took in the fair too. She did fine, but Louis dropped his last quarter through the cracks in the floor of the merry-go-round. He promptly got off the horse he was riding, got on his hands and knees, and crawled under the thing, and it was still going. He got his money and finished his ride! When he told me he lost his money while riding, I said, "I'm sorry, but you should not hold money in your hand." He said, "Oh, don't worry I got off," and he told me how he recovered it. I nearly fainted, suppose some machinery had caught him. I felt responsible. This was just a little thing compared to others that took place in his and my older little boys' young days.

One Saturday night, as they were getting bathed and dressed to go to the nearby town of Berlin about three miles away, they were all chatter and giggles, nearly as bad as girls. As usual Louis was slower in getting ready to go. Now these boys were walking to town as moms had not started the "run me here and run me there" yet. Well, they had no underarm deodorant, and Louis knew Wilma kept a jar of Mum deodorant on her dresser. He put the jar in his pocket to use later when they got to Berlin. The three of them went into a bathroom where they used Mum under their sweaty arms. A good bit of it was left, so Louis asked, "What do we do with this?" Charles replied, "Throw it away." Louis replied it that would be wasting it, so he filled his hands and rubbed it on his face generously. By then Charles and Gilbert were bent double laughing at him. Those boys were something else.

They loved to dance to the jukebox at Teens Café and watch a few do the jitterbug or an older person do the Charleston. Rheba Miley could make them all laugh good at her antics. Believe me, she was a cut up. These same boys once told about a very bright light up in the sky shining down so bright, one could count the rocks under their feet that just shone and kept following them all the way up the Lang Dean Hill from the Pilco Creek. They were running for dear life. Now this was in 1950, before any talk of UFOs, and no war training or planes of that sort had started lighting up the sky.

These boys worked hard and loved a possum hunt or a good coon hunt. Gilbert loved hunting with a gun for birds and squirrel. He got his daddy's gun one morning early and killed his first squirrel while we lived at Brice's. Webb let him hunt for the first time when he was about ten years old. He and our neighbor close to his age, Arthur J. Croft, were great buddies. They stayed together every minute they could. They also did chores together. Yes, we really did enjoy living at my dad's. Those days, people were a lot more contented. If hard work, like clearing new ground, and having the bare necessities of life could be enjoyed, well, we did. Of course all life was not just about our teenagers. The younger ones kept us busy too. There were always cuts bruises and falls to tend to. While filling a barn of tobacco, my youngest, Jerale, decided to ride up to the road in the back of a truck, and he fell out, striking the hard clay and rocks of Mary's Hill. He was brought to me completely unconscious and stayed that way three or four hours. We kept wiping his face with cold water, and he finally came around. Such things are bad.

My sister Eula Mae and her family had a sad thing happen to them that year. She had a baby boy, born the year we left Guy Crosby's in the fall, just a year after my son Jerale was born in 1948. Her son, Horace Daniel Myers, was born the following July 25, 1949. He was a fine little boy. They called him Danny. He took pneumonia and was very sick. Eula Mae suspected other problems when he had really recovered. On taking him to a local doctor here in Moultrie, she found out he had a large growth between the eyes, in the center of the two optic nerves. She then went to Emery University, where it was confirmed as a malignant tumor of the optic nerves. He had cancer. He passed away in February of 1950. The loss of Eula Mae's seven-month-old baby was a very sad time for all of us.

We finished the farm year at my dad's, also a lot of hard work, land clearing and farming. I did enjoy living near my mom and dad's too. They were good to me and my family.

Yes, Webb and me still had our ups and downs, you bet. One thing I remember very well, when our crops' produce were sold, Webb forgot the Quitman Bank had to be paid first then we could spend what was left. Webb wanted to put the money in a used car. I had sense enough to know we desperately needed clothes for winter and starting school. We now had four boys and four girls to dress. Our oldest daughter Jeanette is now thirteen years old; Jan would be eleven in November. Well, my dad, I guess, was a little partial to me, being his daughter, and I worked just as hard as my husband did all year through. After the banknote was paid, for once, I got the money to buy school clothes.

I was actually almost afraid to spend a hundred dollars on clothes at one time. I could not believe I had so much money to go shopping with, but I did. I really fixed our children up good for school and winter. Webb was absolutely furious with my dad, and my dad did not care as Webb already was buying a little bottle of four roses, three or four times a week. There is a lot of hell in those little bottles. He took it out on all of us.

We were an upset family at this time. My oldest two boys had stopped school. One day in August, Charles came in from the field he had worked a week or so at the end of a peanut picker. The dust back there was enough to choke a person to death, and the heat from sunup to sundown so bad on your eyes, and poor Charles only had one to see with in the first place. Now he came rushing in, my brother Brant with him. He said, "Mama, I've got me a job. What do you think? I am going to work at the thread mill at Quitman. Uncle Brant says they need a man, and I am the one for the job." Well, he was so excited, I grabbed a sack, packed his clothes, and said for him to go while he can, and I hope him the very best. My sister Effie and Durwood, her husband, knew Charles was one hard worker and dependable, so he and my brother Brant boarded with them. Charles was tickled pink. There would be no more dusty field or hay baling.

Oh yes, Webb knew one had left the nest, and you know he was missed, but I never let Webb take the little money they did make. I also said, "Now you must support yourself, the choice is yours. Work hard, don't be foolish, keep your money, and act like a man should." It all worked out just wonderful.

Then we had a big decision: farm or no farm. Webb went to work at Jenkins's sawmill in Moultrie, Georgia, one dollar and twenty-five cents per hour. We would take a small farm with the best house we could get on it and tend the farmland and not have to pay rent. Just grow corn, peanuts, and tobacco. Tractors were now coming into use on all the farms. No one wanted to even plow mules again. They had to be looked after or cared for too, fed and watered, not counting the million miles one had to walk doing the plowing. We decided that me and the children would farm and Webb would work full time. Now our two older girls were in the seventh and ninth grades at school. Three children were in elementary school. We got this tiny little old house on the Mable Dill place. It looked like a big chicken house. Little side rooms for the boys, finished out making three bedrooms, a kitchen, and a living room. We moved there about the first of September that year and planned to grow a crop the coming year.

The Little Cotton Pickers: Velma, Gwen, Patsy, Jan, Vanada, and Mavis

Twenty-First Move, 1951:
The Mable Dill Place, behind Spence Field

We soon bought a car with Webb working full time, even if it is only a small paycheck. After he worked a while, Mr. Jenkins did really like his way of working and wanted to help us, or so it looked. The children were going to Culbertson School. I believe our oldest girl Jeanette, was going to junior high in Moultrie. Now her clothes had always been made by me on my sewing machine. She was proud to wear her little cotton print dresses, starched and ironed to a finish. They were worn twice before being washed as washing made them look old too soon. The color stayed pretty longer if they were not laundered after one day's wear. They were worn one day then changed and put on a hanger, and another one used then back to the first one again.

We soon found out Mrs. Dill had a brother living with her who was a bad drinker. He was really what soon was to be known as an alcoholic. He drank all the time, no work anytime. He would ease down to our house and beg at Webb—I mean *beg* at him—to just take him to get a pint of booze. He just had to have a drink. Now his sister did not want him to go to town to get boozed up.

So here we go again a few days after Christmas. We packed our belongings and furniture on one of Jenkins's trucks and moved to a brand-new little house in back of the Newsome's. Webb had already told me about this new house and little farm. Oh, it was so pretty, everything new, it just shone. It had a cute little kitchen, a back porch, and two bedrooms on one side, a kitchen, dining room, and living room on the other side. Nice large windows and pretty hardwood floors. Mr. Jenkins just wanted us to grow tobacco and cotton. We had a mule to plow with and a tractor if we needed it. The little place where the house and yard were laid out was a two-acre plum orchard. I mean as thick as a briar patch. We all fell in love with the place.

Twenty-Second Move, 1951: The Watt Jenkins Farm

The house was small, but we were the first to live there and we loved having a new home. The kitchen was so small, we used it to cook and eat in that winter, but come spring, we moved our dining table on the back porch. Webb had a man make our table big enough for twelve people to sit at comfortably, and our family of ten really filled it up. We had converted the dining room into another bedroom.

Charles was visiting us regularly on weekends. He now had bought himself a nice little red Ford Coupe, a one-seater, and now he thought he was hot stuff. We were within walking distance of Plummer's grocery store and only about five miles from Moultrie. The children caught the school bus to Culbertson School. Charles had worked a good while in Quitman, but he liked Moultrie and home best, so he came back and lived with us again. We always had other boys visit our house now. There was Guy and Billy Copeland, J. B. Hart, and my brother Louis. Charles went to work at the sawmill. In the early evening and summer nights, Buck Newsome and Gilbert surely did a lot of coon hunting and bird hunting. Gil really knew those woods near our house, and they spent many hours in the Pilco Creek swamp.

Mr. Watt Jenkins built us a new tobacco barn. We grew a fine tobacco crop, and our cotton was just beautiful. Yes, we had a small acreage of corn, the finest we ever grew. We also had a beautiful crop of tomatoes. Mr. Jenkins did not mind buying guano fertilizer and seed, and we knew how to grow things, believe me. I worked hard to keep every top and every sucker off that tobacco patch.

Now one day my son Gilbert was plowing the old mule in the cotton patch when a very strange thing happened. He was walking along paying close attention to his work, when all at once a really large animal came running up. Gilbert noticed the mule started trembling, something awful, at the same time the large dog-type animal did. He knew it was not a dog but large like a German shepherd but lighter in color. Well, this thing ran alongside him. The Pilco swamp was right at the end of the rows of cotton, and this animal let out a scream that scared Gilbert so bad he could not say a word, and of all things, the mule just fell broadside in his tracks. Gilbert thought he had died. The animal hit those woods and old dried pine tops and disappeared. This all happened within twenty minutes. He told us as soon as he got the mule up, everything was back to normal. Gilbert was fifteen years old.

Spence Field has been named as a training field for the Air Force as the good old USA has been busy building training fields to keep our military might up with or better than other countries so it is top-notch. I believe it was 1951 or 1952 that Spence Field actually became a base for training cadets for the Air Force.

We were chopping cotton when someone questioned "What in heaven's name can that noise be?" It was just deafening by now. All of us stopped our work and just looked. It was twelve or fifteen training planes with instructors ready for business, flying over our heads. We lived about one mile as the crow flies, over a few treetops and hedge rows from the base. These instructors and cadets made their way into our families. They were, as usual, from everywhere in our United States.

Now the air base was becoming the life of Moultrie, Georgia. I can't begin to tell you how many people were used to operate this new operation. There were common workers, cooks in the mess halls, waiters to carry food to tables, meat cutters, laundry workers, house cleaners, drivers for higher-ups, and special drivers for visiting generals. Boy, Spence Field was first class. The ground vibrated with marching, for all were involved. There were a couple of barracks of girl trainees called WAFS, not WACS. The little town of Moultrie became a city overnight. We had people move in from everywhere. There were jobs for everyone, but Webb stayed at the sawmill. One had to have an education to work at the base, not high school or college especially but good basic schooling and a desire to use it. Webb helped build the groundwork. Trucks hummed day and night, crews for day and night were on duty. When a shift ended, the lights never went out either. The streets of our little town were now abuzz with people.

My little sister Wilma had finished business school in Tampa, Florida, after graduating from good old Barwick High in Brooks County. She got her first job in business administration at Spence Field. All employees had to be checked out for security reasons, also anyone who worked on the base. This was why my sister worked toward a better education. She learned life needed her in higher places than being just a housewife and mother, cook and cleaner. So today, as then the job has no frills or flourishes, but the greater calling on this earth is never the same. There is no higher calling under the blue skies than a good wife and mother to see to her husband. She is to love and cherish, to have and to hold, to trust and obey for the rest of her life. To make a firm foundation with love and understanding, patience and nourishing, firmness and joy in bringing up a God-loving family, for her days will be many on this earth. There is no greater calling: my mother was this kind of material or person.

Now all five of the girls in the family had taken the step of marriage and had a family. Naturally the grass looked greener everywhere else, so when little sis was growing up; we wanted her to do great things. Especially finish school and get better training in a profession as far as she could go. To do so, she had to go away to school. Now this was where Mama came in. None of the girls had left the shelter of our home until they were married and had a husband to stand by her. By now, Mama had found we had it tough, and we found Mama very understanding about letting her baby girl go. Our sister Sarah lived in Tampa, so Wilma went to live with her and went to the business university in Tampa and did a fine job of learning, then came home.

We were all so happy for her, and more so when she got her first job here in our hometown. I went with Pearl Copeland, a good friend, to put in her application for a job in the mess hall at Spence Field. There sat Wilma at her desk with a big typewriter in front of her, asking the questions one has to do to fill out an application, looking Pearl in the eye, her fingers flying over the typewriter keys. To me it was breathtaking as I had never seen such work. Wilma was a lovely young lady, very calm, straight look in the eyes directly at you. Big blue-gray eyes, a peaches-and-cream complexion, blond hair, medium build with a slim waist. She really was an eye stopper. I think we have a picture taken at the Colquitt Hotel, where the nicest social young ladies were hosted to a dinner and dance to meet the new young flyers who had come to our little town.

Security was tight on the air base. A big swimming pool was built, also housing for regular maintenance, barracks for enlistees, houses for instructors and paved runways with a large landing field. Well, it took about five years to get it all set up. Many civilian jobs were available, that was why my sister was employed there. There was a large mess hall for cadets and then an officers' mess hall. Boy, Spence Field was the place then.

All the local girls thought they were very lucky or attractive to be able to date the flyers or instructors. Of course, a special party was arranged for boys to meet girls. The place was the Colquitt Hotel. The guys were sharp and the girls just lovely, dressed in beautiful long formal gowns. As each came down the curved staircase, all eyes were turned to the girl. A dozen of Moultrie beauties or well dressers were asked to come to the party, and Wilma, my sister, was to go. She looked lovely—tiny waist, bare shoulders, bouffant skirt with a huge crinoline of many layers of nylon net, and shoes completed the outfit. Yes, she met the young man who later became her husband. A commissioned officer who had just finished high school and two years of college at Clemson College in South Carolina. He then signed up in the Air Force as noncommissioned officer, a little higher than just a mechanic, for duty.

Now my children were still small, and Wilma stayed at my house some nights when she was expecting her young man to come pick her up. She would tell the children to have their faces clean and hair combed when she got home because Chuck was coming home with her in the afternoon. She later said, "Lorene, it was a sight to see those kids, all four, sitting on the doorsteps, their faces shining clean and hair combed perfect." They were so little but wanted to please her too, and see the boyfriend who flew the planes. These planes flew day and night except in bad weather.

We carried our little girls to get their hair permed for school. Everyone went to the beauty shop. Also dance halls were put into action, skating rinks and taxicabs. You can't believe this really happened. We even had prisoners of World War II, enclosed right here at Spence Field. They were the ones who rode out each day in big trucks under cover with guards to watch them as they cleared the land. My father used them to help clear his new farm, which we had previously lived on, of the pine trees. These prisoners were so glad to be allowed to work, just to get fresh air and not brood and think of loved ones at their home. A lot of the guys looked just like us here. If one of them had learned any English, they would tell you of their young families in Germany. It was the same there for our boys, but their concentration camps were barbarous, as you will find if you wish to explore.

My sister fell in love with her young Air Force man and, while still at Spence Field, married him the very week he was to transfer to Enid, Oklahoma. A separation my mom knew had to come sooner or later as the babies finally leave the nest, heartbreaking but so true. She only had a brief few minutes to stay after the wedding as "Just Married" was written all over their car, and they left, their clothes all packed for their next air base.

Now another winter was at hand. Mr. Watt had really improved this little farm. Little did we know our time was short there? Mr. Cecil Arwood had bought this farm before the cotton was picked, and he really took a liking to us also. We decided the house was just too small for us, so we were looking for somewhere the kids would be on the bus line going to school, and, oh, how I wanted a job working every day now. My youngest was getting to be a big boy.

For a woman used to having a little one in her arms all the time, I was at loose ends. I wanted to go to work and make a little money as too soon all my children would be in school. There was no one I could leave the two least ones with. No babysitters those days. When I worked, the children were right there with me. Oh yes, we worked every day in tobacco somewhere. I stood by my children and encouraged them to earn every cent they could. Honest work never hurt anyone. Those who could not work could care for the little ones at home while I worked with Gil, Jeanette, Jan, and Vernon. Mavis was my babysitter those years. Gilbert was too young to work at Jenkins's sawmill yet. The rest were in school. Until now we moved to a different house each year and lived only a short time at some of these. In all we have lived in twenty one different places by this year.

The excitement of that year was so pleasant to still think of. Jeanette got all of us interested in the Football games. A student got points for attending the weekly home games and she wanted everything that could make a good student better. She had never missed a day yet of school. Well things finally settled down at this place. The children had a good distance to walk to catch the school bus each day so we're looking for a short trip to the bus. Charles and Webb work every day at the sawmill in Moultrie now. Gilbert is almost a grown boy. He could put a nice straight fence, so one of Mr. Jenkins's brother's was already looking for someone to look after and work on his new farm.

There was no house, just barracks used by the Air Force trainees who were there before. These were the only buildings on the place. Sam Bo Jenkins had bought this airstrip at an auction, and he turned it into a cow-and-hog farm. It previously was used to land and take off planes. One unit was in use as a tool shelter for privately owned airplanes. There were a lot of runways and plenty of lights all over the place. There was no tobacco or other crops. So here we go again, from the back of Buck Newsome's place to Sunset Airstrip.

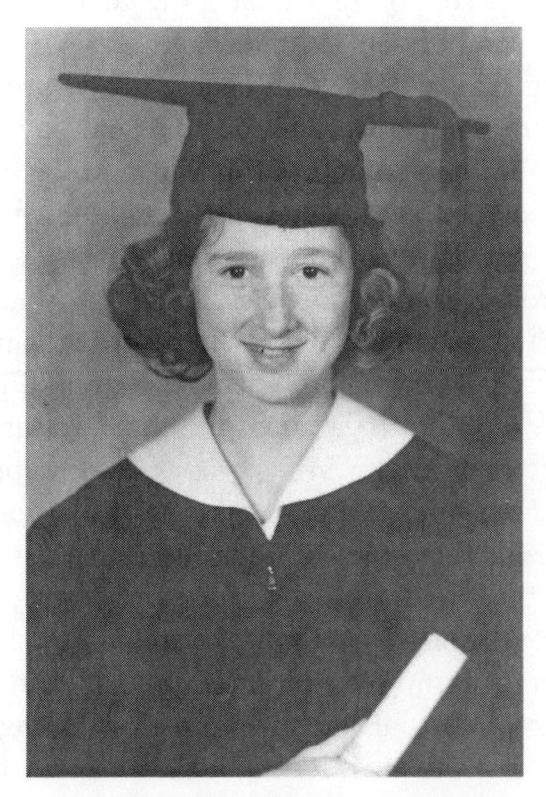

Jan graduates from Sunset Elementary

Twenty-Third Move, 1951 and 1952: Sunset Airstrip

Gil and I worked like a hand and glove from September until December at Sunset. We loved it and got paid for it every day. We measured off rooms, put up Sheetrock partitions, and cut out doors that Webb helped us hang. We made the bathroom around the already existing plumbing. We had a shower and bathtub, toilet and lavatory. I mean, we made it a good-looking job. We had made a large comfortable home for us to live in.

We worked eight hours every day and ate our lunch under an airplane wing. There must have been a dozen privately owned airplanes there. People were all out on Saturday and Sunday, like an air show, and sometimes we did have an air show. Bill Sheldon, an instructor at Spence Field, had his own plane and was a real daredevil in the air. I saw him and another pilot go up, unrolling a roll of colored toilet tissue just as long as it lasted, flying up straight as one could go then cutting it into as many pieces as could be done before hitting the ground! In the spring and summer, crop-dusting planes and their operators came in. Warmack and Schroder from Fort Valley and Ralph Philpott, a local, all used poison dust and sprayed pesticides for the tobacco and cotton fields they sprayed. Right away Webb went to work, helping load the planes with pesticides and destroying the bags. Destruction of the bags was a must because of the large number of animals on the farm. We really met some interesting people.

My children were all at an impressionable age. This was probably some of the most lasting memories they have of their childhood. Everyone in my family says how we liked living at Sunset. Most of the plane owners were single or had no family traveling with them because their jobs took them all over the United States. Because we had such a big family, they all merged right in with us, leaving their impressions with our family. Larry

Singer was a regular. His buddy, Lee Corvis, has communicated with Mavis through the years. He shared pictures he had taken of us all. He loved our family so much, he flew his beautiful girlfriend down from New York City to have dinner and meet us. Now you know the children were impressed. She worked for NBC Studios in New York City and sent a big box of butter cookies to the family when she got home. Which do you think made the biggest impression? You got it, the butter cookies.

My children all took their first rides in an airplane. My very smallest one cried every Sunday to go "wide" a plane. One day Mavis came in, wide eyes shining. "Mama, look up, Jerale is in that plane going over the house." Bill Sheldon, the stunt pilot, had sneaked him out while I was busy. Even my sixty-two-year-old mother took a first ride at Sunset. Jeanette learned what a real elevator ride was in a plane. Jan and Vernon were still small enough to fit into one seat, in Earl Garlick's two-seater Aircoupe. Something new every day was going on. While other children were happy to go to the store to put gas in the car, mine were going to Tallahassee to get fuel for airplanes. These pilots took care of my children as if they were their own. One couple who were married and lived in Moultrie would take Mavis for the weekend. They never wanted to bring her home.

Gilbert and I were very busy with all those sows and pigs, feeding, separating, pulling, or breaking off the tusks of the tiny newborns. If a sow was out of the farrow house when the pigs came in, Gil and I took a basket and went and got the pigs. The mama would follow us to the pigpen then we examined the pigs and shut them up there.

Webb enjoyed this too. After a hard day's work, the whole bunch of guys would go to the Maxwell House and drink a few cold ones and tell jokes and some dangerous truths. Like when a crop duster came in at sundown with several lengths of fence wire trailing. He just did make a landing. If a plane was late coming in, no one left. Everyone waited till the last plane came in.

One day Gil and I were putting up a fence by the runway, and I heard a small voice from way off say, "Hey, Mom, look here!" I listened and heard that voice again saying "Look at me," and there, a few hundred yards away, my least one and his sister were almost to the top rung of a ladder to the tower used for identifying the landing field at Sunset. It had been put out of order but was still standing, with my two young ones right at the top. My heart was in the bottom of my shoes as I carefully called, "I see you, now be very careful, and don't look down. You two come here. I want to show you something." I held my breath till their feet were on the ground—Jerale, three, and Melba, five, on such a place. I switched the two, you better believe, and told them to never cross the deep ditch again.

Polio was to hit Colquitt County, a very serious blow. Many had it, and some lost their lives because of it. Polio was rampant. All swimming pools and movies were closed. They even canceled the football season. A little girl lived at the little store where my children bought drinks. On Saturday, she was helping her very pregnant mother load a crate of drinks to take home. On Monday afternoon a large black wreath was on the door. We asked around and found out she had developed a pulmonary type of polio and could not get her breath. She even told her mom there was no need to take her to Augusta to a respirator as she would never make it, and she did not. She died in her daddy's arms about half the way there. The Vereen Memorial Hospital had no respirator, but almost immediately, donations to purchase one were collected. Many little children were left crippled for life, and some just never made it. The little girl was Vaden Murphy's daughter. That was a sad time for all families.

My children had one illness there, Hepatitis. It is caused by a virus, very contagious. Our children got it from Bill Furney's children when they came for a visit from Plant City. They went to a doctor for it, and Margie Furney told me how to get our children well. A no-fat diet and plenty of rest was all that could be done. I still can't believe it! Even the whites of their eyes turned a yellow or copper color. It was summer and no shade anywhere, and it was hot! Hot! We did have a nice pond to swim in though, and my children went swimming every day, believe it or not, sick or well. All did fine, lived on pans of JELL-O and Coke for two weeks. Then it was all over.

Now my oldest girl, Jeanette, is quite grown up, ready to start driving, driving to the store and everywhere. She nearly got caught one time. All the young ones got into the car to go to the store with her to get some Coke. They drove out to the highway. She circled our mailbox, and right back they all came. She stopped the car, and all fell out and ran into the bathroom. No one had time to talk, I soon saw why. The highway patrol was right there looking at me. I asked what the trouble was, and he said, "Where are all those kids I saw in the car out at the road just now?" None could be found, so I replied, "If you know who was driving, you should have stopped them. I have my washing to do." He said, "Tell her if she is going to drive to wear shoes and never let it happen again." She never drove on the highway again while we were there.

One thing we were cautioned to do was to burn all empty sacks that the pesticide was poured out of so no animals would get sick or die. Our milk cows were good milkers. We had lots of butter and good fresh milk for a family of ten people. We could make good use of it. These cows were expensive.

One Sunday morning we went to get the milking done, and one of the older and best milk cows was gone. The calf in another pen was bleating his poor head off. Well, we looked everywhere nearby. No gates open, the fence mashed down just a little. You see, on paved runways, it is impossible to track a cow. We were now looking in the fields of green corn just maturing everywhere then we saw tracks and checked them out. That cow must have walked all night, for some of us walked all day and there was no cow to be seen. We notified Sam Bo and Hazel, the owners. So right away he said, "She just got one of those poison sacks and ate it and is very sick, lying someplace, most likely near a water hole." Then we really looked for an unusual water hole we knew that was located just over into someone else's pasture. Sure enough, there she was, swelled up about three feet thick, just breathing.

We let Sam Bo know so he could call a veterinarian to come out. We were also sure she had gotten no poison. The veterinarian could not tell, but she died at sundown right by the water hole. We went back to the house and tended all the other cows and separated the calves as we always did. I sent the two girls to see for sure that all gates were closed and the animals were at rest and quiet. They came screaming back to the house and told us a long snake was just lying in the cow pen with his head in a cow stall. Gil had come in, so he grabbed a flashlight and rifle. A truer shot there never was. If Gil aimed at something and pulled the trigger, it was dead. So here he came with a moccasin four or five feet long. It was a monster cottonmouth. He was not to be outdone. We wanted to show the snake to Sam Bo and Hazel. Charles took the snake to town where Sam Bo just looked at it. He was sorry to lose a two-hundred-dollar cow.

He did not say much as he still was not convinced that the cow got snake bitten. We showed the snake to the vet, and he said to call Cope Rendering Co. They will get the cow and skin her, and the truth will be known. Sure enough, her whole front shoulder was dark green, even the flesh showed the poison of the snake venom, he said. So our conscience was cleared that the snake crawled up to the cow, and she must have lay down on it or disturbed it some way and had gotten bitten by it. Later we found many little snakes colored the same. The low flatland, fit only for pasture, was infested with little vipers.

Melba started school at Sunset Elementary that year. My children loved school there. Jeanette would finish ninth grade at Moultrie Junior High that year. The rest finished the year at Sunset—Jan, seventh grade; Vernon, fifth grade; Mavis, third grade; Melba finishing up first. I even liked Sunset school and helped there with the teachers, making costumes of crepe paper for the kids. When the circus came, Charles and Gil helped set up the tents and were rewarded with enough tickets for our whole family to go to the circus with real live animals. What a fun time.

I guess I could write a book about our living at the Sunset landing strip. All our children learned to meet and converse with people, be friendly, learned to drive a tractor and trailer, for feed was carried night and morning to cows and hogs. We even had to have the old bull follow the tractor when he was moved from one field to another. Every day that we were not working on our own little farm, we made extra money working someplace else for others. We all knew how to work in tobacco and we did. We were all self-supporting.

Well, Sam Bo sold his little place to the city of Moultrie. They wanted to make a municipal airport out of the place, and it was ideal. Even while we lived there that year, there was not even a telephone on the whole place. People flew in with private planes from everywhere to conduct business in the neighboring towns as well as Moultrie. I very well remember they were so surprised to find no transportation, except for the car we owned, and no telephone. My children really enjoyed every minute at Sunset, the planes and the people and being so close to town.

Our life has become so much easier as the children are now older, and we have developed friendships we will treasure all our lives. Just one thing, we were still trying to get ahead but still stay behind. Webb had been talking to Mr. Cecil Arwood again, and he has bought a farm in Brooks County, near Barwick and Pavo. So he took Webb down to look at a pretty good-sized farm and one hundred acres in wood pasture. A place very well known to us: the Joel Clark place. Pa Furney once lived on the place next door to it.

Twenty-Fourth Move, 1952 and 1953:
The Joel Clark Place

Webb could just see the quail flying and plenty of hunting for the boys at night. There were woods all around us. We even had to drive through the woods to get to the old house, and our children had a good long walk to even catch a school bus. No running water and lots of hard work. Mr. Arwood furnished us a nice little tractor. Some hogs and cows also came with the place. We also had a little plug mule all the children did enjoy riding. Oh, yes, we did grow what we ate, at least most of it. We sowed crimson clover in the pasture and picked green beans and chased Billy goats. When we finally caught up with things, we built a huge dam across a little stream and had a nice lake backed up for hopefully fishing one day. The stream was fed by a spring that came out of a cave with all sand in front. The children found arrowheads all over the pasture above it and around the spring. Of course they made spears and built tepees in the woods. This was a haven for kids.

Well, neither Webb nor me knew much about dam building. He took the tractor with a lift pan and filled the gulley with just plain dirt. The work was dangerous. Many people get killed trying to dig farm ponds or make dams. OK, Mr. Arwood thought it nice too. Well, the middle of May, the rains came about three or four days in a row, and we really had a tremendous large body of water up above the dam we had just made. As I just said, we did not make the dam right. We failed to dig our dirt to a clay foundation; also, clay should have been used to fill the gulley then topped with regular soil.

One day, a few days after the rains set in, everything else was so rain soaked no one could work. We were eating dinner (our midday meal) when a loud boom was heard and a deafening roar.

We all made a beeline for the door and yellow muddy water was to the doorsteps, just roaring away. I said, "We can't do a thing, there goes our two weeks' work we had put into it." We were just lucky our children were at the table and not in the woods picking berries, or not out with the two little dogs they played with. They were hunting dogs, and the boys didn't use them.

We did not do our job over. Too much work going on, we had six acres of tobacco to gather. All work to be done by hand, day and night, every day, all day long. We had to set the tobacco out by hand, bending over each little plant to secure the tiny root system in the ground. Poison it by hand; dusting with poison in a thin bag we shook gently over each budding plant. It was growing right along now. We broke out the tops so the leaves will spread and grow long. Then here comes a little shoot by every leaf called a sucker sprout. Each one must be picked off. One finger can do the trick if one gets with it in time. There are barns to heat, tobacco to color and cook, but we did make it a good high grade of tobacco.

We had five acres of green beans. These were to be picked by hand. Because of our help, we picked three days a week. I always said, "Webb, Jeanette has never missed a day of school. I'll pick her share." We also had peas of every kind growing, so we could carry them to the farmers' market when ready and get a good price for them to buy groceries with. I guess work was one thing there was plenty of. We just did not know how to make it provide money, and that is what we needed most of all. At least none of us could be called lazy.

Now this was a chapter in our lives that is quite personal. After we got the beans picked, the selling at the market Webb did. Now he seemed to love that job. Well, I am no fool really for some things that happened. I worked my behind off in the hot sun, and it was hot weather; also, one had to just keep encouraging the children to do a good job not to leave any beans or peas on the bushes.

I always felt let down when Webb loaded up and went into town sell them. I would not let him know I did not trust everything he did, but give an inch and they will take a mile. I am serious; he was there until three AM, getting home sometimes. I had let myself go to just nothing. My clothes were shabby, my shoes just plain sneakers, and in the field I usually work barefoot. Well, the only thing I still did a good job of was cooking. I cooked three meals a day, every day. Quick foods were unknown, although little beer parlors and barbecue places were springing up, girls work them. Also when crops were ready to be sold, there were loose women floating around the markets. If a man was looking for a good time, they were there, ready to share the money and show them a good time.

Well, after some late-night escapades, like at two or three AM, I began to catch on. The first time, the gas leaked out of the truck. The next time, he was on a lonely road and the battery failed and the lights went out on the truck. I was still listening to his tales of bad luck and the produce bringing practically nothing, but he could not make it home. You see, he had learned a new kind of people.

The old flyers from Sunset, some had found themselves live-in girlfriends. The two would share a travel trailer or camper. Oh, one could get by. You would not believe when I would go with Webb, he tried to make me believe anything but what it really was. I could not bring myself to think their cheap quality was equal to my standards in life. Yes, we would pack a nice basket of the prettiest red ripe tomatoes, fresh yellow squash, tender small pods of okra, and delicious sweet corn. No wonder they treated us to a sparkling cold drink and good conversation, for we certainly did not meet any country people like them out there in the woods where we lived.

Now Webb was getting quite bold when he went to carry the vegetables. He learned to love beer. The girls who ran the places did not care for anything but the money taken in, and pretty soon, beer and money for the jukebox was getting all our money, as well as Webb. He was seen all about town with girls who were just off work. He forgot he had a little family. Our oldest, Charles, was now eighteen, and Jerale, the youngest, was four years old. Of course he had seen enough of the good ole kind: trusting, not given to temper tantrums, and always depended on—Lorene. I could not hold these hussies a light. They used nice perfume, thin pastel silk dresses with spaghetti straps over their bare shoulders. Nice legs in pretty white sandals and curls on top of curls from the hairdresser.

No, I did not know about these things like this, but two of Webb's brothers worked in town and saw him getting around the Busy Bee, looking for watermelons at the farmers' market and playing the slot machine at AmVets, a drinking pub. I call it a staking-out spot for female trash! Do you ever believe the old saying "The one involved the closest is the last one to hear the gossip"? But you better believe I finally did hear.

Now one night he had not returned when the boys came home from work. He had carried a neighbor with him to the tobacco sales. He would bring him back when he returned home. Well, this old man was seventy-five years old, had no car and no way home. Webb had carried him to his dad's house in town, and after lunch there, they went to see the tobacco sell, and right there, Webb lost him. This old man finally decided he had better find a place to spend the night, so he went back to where he had eaten lunch at Webb's dad's house, and they took him in. When my boys came home and said, "Where's Dad?" I said, "Your guess is as good as mine." I had just finished taking a whole barn of tobacco off the sticks and piled it very neatly on a large tobacco sheet, or several sheets were more like it. A barn would hold seven hundred four-feet sticks of tobacco.

Of course the children did their fair share of work, and I did not have time to worry where Webb was. Right away I heard the boys leave. Webb worked at the sawmill when not working on the farm. Gil and I did most of the farming.

Well, here they went; they drove right up by the side of his truck. It was really Charles's truck, and he let his dad use it. OK, was he ever surprised: here sat his girlfriend in the truck? She had sent Webb back for her purse, which she had left inside, and she laid it on the dash just as the boys got there. Now they were seeing for themselves. Well, Webb was caught red-handed. You never heard such excuses. He was just giving her a ride home, she was sick, but when they drove up, everything looked real good. No one had any trouble getting her back into the door she had just eased out of, and the jukebox played on and the slot machines kept clicking. Slot machines were everywhere. They were legal then, and people were making money any way they could.

When the boys quit talking to their dad, Webb nearly burned that Dodge truck up getting home. That was why he forgot the old man who was a neighbor who rode to town with him. He never gave a thought as to what had become of him.

Well, was I ever ready to kill someone! He got ahead of the boys, and till yet, they wondered how he got home first. It was a good twenty-five miles to our house. The boys drove up right after Webb and confronted me on a small back porch about five feet off the ground. The steps were almost straight up, the full five feet. Well, an argument like we never had before or since was going on. I was crying mad (a woman and her tears). If I had possession of a gun, that man would have died way before his time. It ended with our oldest son packing his few clothes and leaving such a mess. He asked Gil if he wanted to go, and he said, "No, I'll stay here." The next thing I was so tempted to do was to shove Webb right out on his back in the yard, off that dinky porch. I guess it would have spattered him.

All the work I had done, and accomplished farming, was regretted in that moment of truth, plus my oldest son knew at that time from then on he could take care of himself. He moved in with his grandma and grandpa Furney. The next morning, the old man's son went and brought his dad home and found out why he spent the night away from his family, who was quite alarmed at his disappearance.

Well, if this had taken place in 1986, which is now, a divorce would have been in progress, but I am not a quitter then or now. We resolved our differences. We had seven fine children to divide, now that the oldest has gone from the nest. From that day on, I knew I had to make a change as there was no way to change Webb. I worked very hard to see where the mistakes really were and found a lot of improvements in me would help. The way I looked now, I would have been ashamed for my own relatives to have caught me in the field.

It was time for a change. First, a new hairdo then I bought some decent clothes, some nice-looking sandals, and some makeup. I no longer looked like a little country mouse. When Webb went to sell tobacco, I went with him. We came right back by Mr. Arwood's and brought the checks. We got our share and he got his share. I saw to that. Then it was cotton-picking time right away, and Webb had never found a cotton sack that would fit him. I made no plans to grow and pick any more cotton. Yes, we had grown lots of cotton, and our children worked very hard helping gather it. That helped us make a little more profit. I said, "Now if these children want to pick cotton, they can do it for so much per pound and use the money for school clothes," which they were very willing to do.

School was near at hand, and Leona and Ellis had acres and acres of cotton, so my girls went over there to make some money by picking the "country snow." Jan could pick maybe 150 pounds by working from sunup till sundown. Vara and Vivian were about the same. Jeanette could pick two hundred pounds in a day and quit before sundown. We still can't understand how she did it, for she was always right there with the other girls. Still, she got fifty pounds more of cotton. I guess she picked like fighting fire or whatever, she really did work fast. She tied tobacco like picking cotton the next year when we were farming.

Twenty-Fifth Move, 1952:
The Joel Clark Tenant House

One day, my youngest son Jerale, now soon to be five years old, and I were home alone. Webb was helping a neighbor lift a sick cow. Charles and Gilbert were at the sawmill at work as they both had gotten jobs there. Charles had come back home by now. I was preparing peas for dinner, and while shelling them, I had turned on the kerosene stove, which I used now and then when I had no wood to fire up the woodstove. I started a boiler with my meat in it for the meal, and I would put my peas in as soon as I finished shelling them. I went back to the porch swing, sat down in it to finish shelling my peas, when I heard this peculiar noise like a blowing wind, just a swooshing noise like I had never heard before. I went into the house through the dining room, and my whole kitchen was in flames!

I caught myself in time not to panic and grabbed a stack of dishes off the table, ran to the front yard, and put them down. I took another look at my beds, grabbed sheets and pillows just stripped them off. Near the door were the boys' and Webb's shotguns, so I took them out. I don't know how I did it, but I dragged my sewing machine to the door and lifted it out. My little one took one look and said, "Mama, are we fixing to move again?" The tears had my face covered. I don't think I was yelling as I knew no one would hear me, but I never knew how far away the smoke could be seen.

The roof of the house was handmade pine shingles. When they had started to leak, it was covered with a heavy roofing top. Now I was standing way off, just watching everything we had go up in smoke. Webb saw the smoke and nearly ran over the baby, who was alarmed to see Mama crying. By now Webb had joined me. We were both crying. My sister Eula Mae lived three miles away, and she saw the smoke, and she and Tony joined us. It is a terrible thing to see your home on fire, no matter how humble it is. Then you think you will never see or use again the valuable things, like thirty-five dollars, all the shoes, the dress clothes, the school clothes. Well, you just cry again. All of Jeanette's certificates of perfect attendance in nine years of school, a baby bed full of freshly washed clothes not yet folded, and on and on.

I went to Mama's and Leona's to tell the girls. We were as desolate as the day we married nineteen years before. Only now we had eight children to take care of. You can very well tell the country is still full of good, warmhearted people, who are your neighbors. We stayed at Bill Furney's that night in Autreyville. I did not sleep, I just had nightmares. My youngest two little girls were already at Bill's house. They loved Maureen and Annette and were staying a few days for vacation before school started. Bill was fixing to move back to Plant City, and they would not be able to play together for some time. The day after our house burned, Eula Mae and me went to the old dilapidated house at the end of the lane on the same farm and went to work.

We had used it for storing our tobacco when we were getting it ready for market. We made four beds up completely. We had benches and chairs for our kitchen, and someone brought us a good woodstove. The third night after the fire, we spent the night at home. What a relief! People shared towels, sheets, blankets, and kitchen utensils with pots. All of my pretty quilts got burned up, and all the early pictures of our family too. Our house was not much. Effie and Durwood brought us a nice old pie safe. It was nice to put our cooked food in.

Now this was the first week in September. The flying instructors who had been Webb's bird-hunting buddies sent word for us to go to Spence Field and stop at Bill Sheldon's. He had a surprise for us. When we stopped by, we talked a while then his wife brought out a cigar box and gave it to me. The box was full of money that was donated from all the flight line men. It was about two hundred dollars. We went that day and bought a couch and two living room chairs and a coffee table we needed so much.

The girls went to Moultrie and got new material for dresses and shoes for school. We fixed up the other three—Vernon, Mavis, and Melba Jean. They all started back to school at Barwick.

This house had no fireplace, so the weather grew crispy cool but not before all four of our youngest children came down with the whooping cough. They coughed and whooped, but it only lasted about four weeks after we found out they got it in school two weeks before. We knew it was whooping cough. They had all gotten well as soon as the season changed from summer to cool fall days. By then we had broken the corn, divided cows and hogs, and settled with Mr. Arwood. Me and little Jerale were home alone.

Twenty-Sixth Move, 1953:
Laura and Ralph Crosby's Autreyville Place

One day just before Thanksgiving, a bunch of kids skipped school at Barwick, and Jeanette did too. They were all there that morning but left right after lunch. She came home and told us she did not miss the whole day, just a couple of hours. The next morning, when Webb and the boys went to work, Jeanette started back to school at Moultrie High School. She had been there in the eighth and part of the ninth grade and was glad to be back in Moultrie. Vivian and the others at Barwick were given a huge amount of writing about never skipping school again, but Jeanette had gone her last day to Barwick. Vivian told her what happened, and Jeanette missed the punishment.

During Thanksgiving holidays, we left the Clark place and moved to Laura and Ralph's little farm at Autreyville. The house was so small and out of the way for all to go to work. You better believe it, Vernon and I had the corncrib (a small room in the barn) full of corn, ready to load on a truck at moving time. I sometimes think if Webb would have done all the work I had to do when we moved, we might have lived longer in the same place. Now I did this work because it took all Webb could make to feed and clothe our family. I had sense enough to know that.

You should have seen Ma Furney looking at me after our trouble about Webb's trips to town in the summer. I really did change my looks, and I liked the new look. I think Webb did too. I now have the two youngest with the next two older going to the movies at Gene Mills Theater. Webb and I go with the girls Jeanette and Jan to the Saturday night dance. The boys would be there also. If my husband wanted to dance, he did not need to look very far. All he needed was for some of the old bunch from Sunset to come near me to dance. I was right with him, and at eleven thirty, we would go get the little ones at the movies, pick up our teenage girls at the dance, and all go home happy. They learned to dance, meet people, make friends and learned to choose their company.

The reason we carried them home, it was twenty-five miles to our house and the girls were too young to let the boys bring them home. After eighteen years of babies and hard work, you'd think I would be a bag of woes and grunts, but the band plays on. God was good to me. Webb and I must have loved each other quite a lot to enjoy each other as we did. He stayed pretty good until the next summer, and then again he pulled some good ones. I also did some checking up, and we pretty well closed the book on a lot of things but not our personal lives.

We enjoyed living at the little new place. On weekends, Webb and some of the flying instructors would hunt quail and leave a few more little boys to play with ours. There was a nice pasture of Bermuda grass around the house and yard. Big yearling calves just walked and ate grass. The boys, ten to twelve years old, would rope one, a good-sized bull, a real tough one. They had a long rope, and sometimes three at a time would be hanging on to the rope, all laying on the ground, being flung all over the place. This was Vernon's thing. They would get up, brush off their clothes, and go at it again. The bull would make a dash, jerk the rope, and all would fall to the ground and in turn loosen the rope one at a time as it would be burning their hands so badly they could not hold on. Vernon thought he was a real bull wrestler, and so did the younger boys. Vernon was about twelve or almost thirteen then.

On my fortieth birthday, I won't forget what I did. I took Ralph Crosby's tractor and a long chain, went down into the woods, and pulled the chain tight around a big stump that had been pushed up out of the ground, hooked the other end to the tractor, and to the house I would go. After piling it onto the woodpile, I got an ax and busted the stump into small pieces and carried it to our fireplace. It made an excellent fire, which would furnish heat for the whole house. I felt good and enjoyed using the tractor as we were used to using a mule and sled and doing a lot of really hard lifting and pushing. Things were looking up for our big family. We still had to work hard but not the same as when we had no tractors or the modern conveniences we were now becoming used to. I only wore a size 16 boys' blue jeans. I am a lot bigger now.

It was time to celebrate a big occasion in the Furney family. Ma and Pa Furney will celebrate their fiftieth wedding anniversary. The party was at Laura and Ralph's home as it was the biggest and can accommodate more people in the country. All of Worth County relatives had been invited since that was the county home of both Lucy and Buster Furney.

The girls had given all the grandchildren jobs. The older boys were for parking cars, and the younger ones would escort the company into the house and hold umbrellas if it rains. The young granddaughters would help serve food and pass around the finger food. Thank goodness it wasn't hot. It was in February, and the entire community showed up as well as Leona and Ellis and my mother. The party was a big hit except for the boys, who all complained about being dressed up and wearing a tie all afternoon.

By this time Laura and Ralph were ready to move to town, Moultrie, Georgia. They were leaving their pretty country home and wanted us to move over there, nearer town. This was a real big house, and Ralph could sell his small place where we had just moved from. Now this was in February, and we could not believe this, but here we go again. All that big pile of corn to load again! I was about ready to run away because we were moving again after only four months. We had moved so often, the chickens sat with their legs crossed so we could tie them up pretty easy when we were ready to go again!

Twenty-Seventh Move, 1954:
Ralph and Laura's, near Moultrie

Now my little troubles had started to be big ones. These little children of ours had just grown out of sight. The boys were dating girls, and the girls were finding young men. They were taking a real liking to Charles, who was nineteen, and Gilbert, seventeen. Jeanette will be sixteen in October. The last of the eight will start school this fall. I—or we, I better say—will have six in school this year.

Webb's sister Melvin and her husband Doyle lived just right down the road from us. We liked the neighbors, some whom we had known for years, like the Alvis family. They had children who were my children's age, and they all played together and went to school together. Ralph had a big pond in the woods across the road from the house. All the children swam and really enjoyed playing in it all summer. We worked hard and played hard.

Yes, we had the usual crops of corn, cotton, and tobacco. Our children liked to work in tobacco. Jeanette could really tie it on the sticks. Jan liked to crop the tobacco and send it up to be tied. The croppers were usually boys, but Jan somehow got to crop so she could make more money. Vernon cropped also, and Mavis was getting right with it, learning to hand the tobacco to the tiers. I'd start the midday meal of meat and fresh vegetables, a big cake or chocolate pudding at six AM. By the time the first sled of tobacco came to the barn, I'd be there ready to tie. I made dinner for the whole crew, and we gathered tobacco on Saturday, filled a whole barn by one o'clock.

Jeanette helped our neighbor. She and her dear friend Shirley Flowers would sometimes tie off two barns full of tobacco in one day. Mr. Tom Gibbs thought those two girls were the very best. He used a very different method from us and grew a lot more tobacco too. About six or seven people all rode and worked on a newly developed thing called a tobacco harvester, with all the work going on in the field, all just riding along under a shelter. Boy, one that worked on one of those things had it made. Jeanette tied, Jan and Vernon cropped. This year Mr. Tom Gibb's daughter, Ona Faye, was getting married, and the girls were so excited. This would be the wedding of weddings in the community in June. With the girls riding the harvester all day, they got to hear all the details.

Now a new way of curing tobacco had started. Kerosene fuel had started being used in place of huge piles of cut or sawed wood. No more brick furnaces to fill to heat the barns to dry the tobacco. The kerosene was used in burners turned on as much as needed, and a heat indicator could be set and it would do the heating for hours at a time. One person could tend three or four barns at a time. Using wood to heat was wasting the timber on all the farms, which could raise the price of lumber and wood to heat our homes with. Before long, people had learned to heat their homes with heaters run by fuel, gas, or diesel oil, much more economical than burning up the wood. I got my first electric stove that year. I could not believe my eyes, just turn a button and the burners or oven got hot!

We really did enjoy our children even if we had a tough time. The older ones loved to go to the Little River and jump in the cool dark water, but they also loved to have their meals. So on Sunday, in order to see and be where the action was, every once in a while they would ask us to come along and bring a picnic lunch. Then their friends could eat dinner too. I'd bake a ham and a cake or fry some pear tarts, boil corn on the cob, make the usual potato salad. The girls would help till the last minute, when the boys would pack up the cars and throw in a few watermelons.

We would just have a day to remember. All this cost no money, just the effort to enjoy yourself and being with others. All my children did pretty well and my youngest Jerale turned five years old that summer, but he would scare the daylights out of other people who gathered there. He would just jump off a diving board into fifteen feet of water then swim facedown across the river, turning his head to get a breath of air and right back under again. He did this all summer. The next summer he swam like all the rest. Believe it or not, I was a sorry swimmer and scared to death of water. Webb was an excellent swimmer.

The best thing was that our children had not outgrown us, we realized this. They could ask their friends to eat lunch or come to our house where the good food was cooking three times a day. We brought our children up in what some people might say was the hard or tough way. Well, I never remember taking our family any place to eat away from home, unless it was to Webb's father's house or to my parents' home. We usually carried dinner to the Fourth of July barbecues at his dad's. I would carry a large box of food to my family's home if we were gathering for Thanksgiving or Christmas Day.

Most of the time, it was easier for them to come eat with us. That was where the crowd was. It wasn't easy to invite Webb and Lorene for dinner. That meant dinner for an additional ten people. I always planned balanced meals with an emphasis always on plenty of fresh vegetables, meat, and potatoes. When we got to the table there were no picky eaters. If so, while they were picking, the children thought the rest would eat all the food up. At least I got no complaints. They all shared chores. My first two girls, when old enough and big enough to help clean the table and dishes, took turns weekly. Each would take a week and ask Mavis or Melba to give a hand. That way they learned what it was all about. When Mavis and Melba was a little older, they did dishes alone also. Each had a week.

I can truthfully say one thing for my daughter Mavis: she never minded washing dishes. If she came in after the movies or anytime, if there were dishes in the sink, she promptly cleaned and put them away without saying one word. She still is the most unusual girl and has such a nice personality. I did not say she couldn't be mad or upset. She can be mean as a hornet if one tries to run over her, and she will let you have it. I was never too tired. I don't know where I got my strength. I guess I had a mother to set the example. Our family, before I got married, and a few years after, with my sisters and brothers, would go to the Little River on picnics and gather mayhaws (a little red berry that made delicious jelly). Some would fish, some swim, and those who were tired could sit in the shade. Those get-togethers were some more fun. My children still talk about how Grandma Hart wouldn't wear a swimsuit and Granddaddy Hart could float down the river like he was sitting up with his toes sticking straight out in front of him. We also had many outings at the spillway at Brice's dam, where all our families would gather almost once a year at least to swim, eat, and just enjoy each other's company.

After being married a short time, my sister Effie tried impressing her farmer husband, Durwood. She had so little to do keeping up the house. She expressed her ability by feeding the mule he was working then filling up the water trough. She just knew he would be all smiles. She got a surprise. Her husband took a look then came inside for dinner. So breathless, she waited. Finally, he said, "I am glad you fed and watered the mule for me. Now I want to know, do you think you can do this all the time, besides bringing up the children, keeping house and taking care of the garden, canning, and pickling?" Effie said, "Oh, I don't know about all that." Well, he told her not to take his job away from him, unless she felt pretty sure she could keep it up. "You will have enough work to do without doing mine." Was she ever surprised? That was the first and last time she tried doing his chores.

Over time, farming made great changes. My older boys had special chores to do when they were small, feeding up and watering all farm animals. Dependability was the name of the game. Most boys were told once what was expected. Feeding-up time was really important and also closing all barn doors and gates. If this was not done, just one trip to the woodshed where paddles were available and used on a fellow's backside taught them to think first, play later. It was tough, but good men were reared like this.

After the new tobacco planters came, the harvesters and the miracle of all miracles: a heating system that changed tobacco barns forever. The furnace system was replaced by a gadget called a thermostat hooked to a tank that heated pipes that circulated heat just wonderful. You never set up another night at the barn. Just set your heat, and the fuel flowed just right for any heat that was needed. One man could look after six barns, and some did. They worked here in Colquitt County and then went to Canada for six weeks after our season was over. They met new people and other ways to live and different cultures. Oh boy, that was living history. Some of the boys who went just kept going every summer then married a girl from Canada and came back here to live, and some liked the new land so well they stayed with their wife in Canada, but the tobacco harvesters made our day.

Well, we did quite well on the farm that year. Every one worked, even the youngest. Jerale was only five years old. I'd make him two biscuits with bacon and syrup, wrap them, and put them in the pocket of the tractor, and we would go to the field. I would turn over land, and he would play with the dog and make racetracks with his toy cars and a little tractor. I planted and put out fertilizer with the tractor. When they came in from Moultrie, where they worked, everyone worked at something until bedtime. Oh yes, we had no television at that time. Maybe that was why we lost no time having eight children. We were not lazy, so we kept busy at something even if the work was not too hard. We had good times and bad times, you can bet.

One day, when our twenty acres of cotton were snow white and me and the children were working our arses off, Webb slipped out. As usual to town he went. Well, this had been going on for some time. I was so tired of it. He had developed a kidney problem. I often wondered about that. He did take medicine from a kidney doctor. He was told not to lift anything heavy. So he was certain not to hurt himself and took off. Well, I'd had enough. I said to my cousin Junior Humphrey, "What do you say I take this bale of cotton to the gin this evening for Webb, in your truck?" We just needed a few more sheets packed and tied in huge round bundles then piled on top. So there I went to town. Really, I just wanted to check Webb out. Something told me he was into something. Well, no darn wonder he was not at home. When I saw his car, I pulled up and stopped.

Oh yes, I had dressed up good and put on my makeup before I left the house. I'd never been to a roadhouse before where cold beer, loud music, slot machines, and women—old and young and in between—were available. A sort of dark and ice-cold place compared to a cotton patch on a ninety-eight-degree summer day, sunup to sundown. When I came in, I knew a few people from the old airport days at Sunset Landing Strip where we lived and some of the well-dressed women who lived near the sawmill where Webb worked. There were also some of the women I rubbed elbows with while packing cucumbers a few times. I never drank. I spoke and got myself a cold beer. When I had downed that, I had picked up a little nerve. I still knew a fit of temper was not the thing to do.

I was sure they knew by then that Webb was outsmarted. So I just tried to act like I did this every day, but I bet I still looked like a plain ole cotton picker. Well, when the lump in my stomach settled, I went with Webb over to one of the slot machines. He was pretty good at winning and getting those lemons lined up. Well, he whispered to me he had been winning all along, and he knew the jackpot was coming up. He didn't want someone else to take over and win what he had put into it. He said, "You play it a few times, and maybe it will be ready to pay off."

Now thirty-five years later, I still remember every detail. Some gal walked over. She was also watching for the pay off. Believe me, there are some slick chicks around Moultrie, Georgia. She pushed herself right up beside Webb and asked him for a light for that everlasting cigarette. While they had their heads together (I always did wonder how they got the nerve to get so close to another woman's man), I noticed she had on tiny little sharp toe pumps with three-inch heels. I eased over right clumsily and stepped right on those crimped-up toes. It hurt so bad, she fell over backward and sat down on that dirty floor. I said, "I'm sorry I missed my shot" and pulled the handle on that slot machine one more time. That did it. All those lemons fell in one line. I heard a grinding sort of noise. After Webb gave her a hand, of course he rushed to the slot machine. He knew it was fixing to run over with change. It was quarters. He snatched off his cap and put it under a little thing that looked like something to get a drink of water from. Out of the lid came out about one hundred quarters, I'll bet. When they stopped coming out, Webb shook the thing good. I just knew he would break it. He said, "That's the way it's done." I said, "Isn't this about it for the day?" He said, "Heck, no," like he never had a child to send to school or a whole bale of cotton loaded and sitting parked right beside the road.

I said, "There's three or four more of these things, it's too bad you have a bale of cotton to take to the gin. My cousin Junior wants his truck back right away, he has to go someplace. Just taking this cotton to the gin won't hurt your back at all, isn't that nice." He glared at me, looked at the crowd in that little dimly lit smoke-filled room, and said, "You coming with me?" Right quick I decided he would not show out here, and I said, "Not on your life! You go on, and I'll take the car home as soon as you get back from the gin." Well, I thought to myself, come easy, go easy. I had more quarters than I had ever seen in my life at one time. Can you believe this? I pulled that handle on the machine until he got back. That was the quickest bale of cotton that ever went through a gin. I went home, but let me tell you, my arm needed to be put in a sling. It hurt so badly. I just let it hang lose all the next day.

I never went there again. Oh yes, Webb did a little better with his time from then on. However, he did not stop playing the slot machines until the law put a stop to all of them. No, we never got a divorce on that one. We still sent six children to school in September, from the first grade to the twelfth. Isn't that terrible? Or is it! Now believe it or not, I set my head to thinking. I was doing my job and trying to do his job too. Why not each just do his share and work for a payday every day? We moved so much, and we never owned a home. Farming helped us have a larger and better home as our family grew. Nice homes at that time were out of reach for us to rent.

We would tend or farm on a small acreage in order to have a nicer and larger home to live in. We could usually get a nice painted and screened family house in a deal, as long as we grew the corn and tobacco crops. The owners were happy and usually had grass pastures for cows. Webb and the boys could cut and bale hay or plant pasture grass on weekends, after their eight-hour days at work in the long summer days. Oh yes, with our family, anyone was glad to get us. I found working outside the farm was hard for me.

I didn't have any training or experience in any field outside the home and farm. After the years spent raising a large family and farming, I did not pick up job skills as fast as my sisters did. They always knew someone who had a friend or relative who could put in a good word for them. My sister Leona went right to work at the Georgia peanut plant with someone who knew how to get her on. I know the salary was not the greatest, but she could at least dress her girls in the new coat suits that were now in style. I thought Jeanette just had to have one. You see, we did not farm anymore, so no more borrowing money. It was work, get paid, and buy food and pay bills. Times were tough for us then. Instead of four, we had eight to care for. Webb was eventually picked up for drinking and driving and, for the only time in his life, was locked up, even though it was only for a few hours. He learned his lesson. We were leaving Ralph and Laura's nice home as they have decided to move back to the country.

Our Twenty Eighth Move, 1954: The Jack Lewis House

We had finally given up farming, and we planned to make a go of all getting jobs in Moultrie. We would make more money, and even though we may have to pay rent, it will put more money in our pockets.

Charles and Gilbert were still working at Jenkins's sawmill with their dad. I was busy herding children off to school and doing work in packing houses for an hourly wage. I worked nights for many weeks in spring and summer in the packing plants. First I packed tobacco plants until it was time to pack cabbage plants and then the tomato plants. I earned fifteen dollars for five nights' work. I worked until around eleven PM or sometimes twelve or one AM, depending on how many trucks were loaded out for places up north. Oh, it was hard work, but I did better on that than farm work.

The children still went back to do farm work when it was available. They earned enough money during the summer months to buy their school clothes and shoes. We now had to pay rent or live in dilapidated farmhouses.

We only lived in the Lewis house for two months. It was just too small for our large family. We planned to move to Sambo Jenkins's house.

Twenty-Ninth Move, 1954:
Sambo Jenkins's House in New Elm Community

We were now in Sambo Jenkins's house, and it was so much bigger and near the Okapilco School. Jerale was now six years old and had started at Culbertson School with the other children. They will attend the same school for the balance of the school year. The tobacco season was starting, and that was keeping us all busy. Jeanette was a junior in high school, and Jan had just started the ninth grade. Jeanette and Jan were still going to the skating rink and going to the dances with us and to the out-of-town dances with their brothers. Jeanette was dating local boys, and Jan was just going for the ride. Charles had met and fallen in love with a local girl. Her name was Shirley Whittington, and he was quite smitten with her and had proposed to her. They planned to marry in the fall. Of all things, he proposed to her at the Bethel Hill Church Cemetery. I think she was so scared she said yes so he would take her home.

It was now fall, and Webb and Durwood Crosby have had a nice quail hunt and killed a bunch. We all had a nice delicious bird supper. None of us like to live north of Moultrie in the New Elm Community, so we were looking for a house near town. We found one out near Greenfield Church on the Autreyville road. At this time, I know my family was the largest. It took a big house to hold all of us.

Thirtieth Move, 1954:
House near Greenfield Church on Autreyville Road

Well, we have moved into a bigger house before Christmas, and I am at my wit's end. So much is happening. My little problems are all becoming big ones at the same time.

Charles and Shirley have gotten married. She had a nice kitchen shower and received many nice gifts. They had a simple civil ceremony. Mattie Lou Ingram performed the ceremony with a few "I do and I will" then pronounced them man and wife. Charles had all his furniture and household goods ready, and they moved into a small house on the north side of town. The children all thought they should visit often. Jeanette has a special man in her life. Alfred J. Veglia, he is from Revere, a suburb of Boston, Massachusetts. She is now a senior in high school, and I know this is serious where she is concerned.

With all this going on, along with the everyday chores of housework and the never-ending lines of clothes that have to be laundered and ironed, I now am working at the peanut plant five days a week. I made it clear everyone did his share. While some washed the clothes, some others would hang them out to dry while I did the cooking. Now my third daughter, Mavis, was near as big as her mother. She was already as tall as me. I'll never forget one special time. She has always been this way and still is today. She thought if you were a decent human it made no difference where you came from or which side of town or who your family was. If she liked you, it was all right.

Right after we got settled here, she came home with two of the scrawniest little black-haired girls. They were the daughters of someone Webb had worked with. They were very skinny, with long unkempt hair, shy and afraid to talk to anyone, especially me. Mae had found out they had no mother. They lived with their father. Of course, as usual, Mae thought we would be just the right family environment for them. You should have seen Jeanette's and Jan's face when they thought she had brought home the worst trash she could find in the community. The girls raved and warned her if she associated with that kind, she would be thought of as the same. Now Mavis thought if you were human and had a sad life, it made no difference.

I'll tell you, some decisions are hard to make. Of course Melba, being two years younger and always looking up to Mae, didn't care if they had lice in their hair or not sure when they had a bath last. She was ready to be friends with them. They were just poor little girls, but she was told to find someone else to hunt violets with and make it quick. Jeanette was not happy to have Al visit her at this house anyway, and then to have Mae drag in two little girls with maybe lice in their hair. Well, it stopped right there. The only thing we like about this house is it has a pond on the side where Jerale can hunt bullfrogs and Jan can hide out and lay in the sun while she reads a book.

Now all the children think Charles made a good decision in marrying Shirley. We all had a good Christmas together. She fits right into our big family. Jeanette and Janice will stop at their little house when they come home from school if they are coming home with their dad. It is still very cold out, and Shirley always had a nice warm fire in her fireplace. This is the place to be while waiting for Webb to get off work, and they love being with Shirley. Everyone likes her a lot. Charles is real happy.

We are all unhappy living in this house, and me and Webb are hoping to find a house big enough for all of us in Moultrie. While on Christmas break at school, we find a place, and it is the upstairs of a big two-story house with two apartments downstairs. Charles and Shirley will move into one of the downstairs apartments.

Mr. and Mrs. Charles W. Furney

Thirty-First Move, 1955:
The Two-Story House on Old Adel Highway

Well, we are all excited to be moving into the big upstairs of this house. We will miss living in the country with the fishponds, farming, and the wide open spaces but are hoping to get into the city life, which we know nothing about. We will be paying rent from now on, and all our children will be walking to school all the way across town. We are on the Old Adel highway and across from Holman's lumber company. The Holman's was once a livestock place that only sold horses and mules and farm wagons, but tractors put a stop to that. Now they are a hardware and lumber company. We are right across from the sawmill where Webb and the boys work, and there are warehouses and a fertilizer company all the way toward the center of town.

Jeanette and Jan walked all the way to Moultrie High, and Vernon, Mavis, Melba, and Jerale walked to North Moultrie Elementary. Jerale had a very funny thing happen to him after he went to his new first-grade class. When he came home, he had his snack to eat, and I said, "How was school today?" He replied, "Oh, pretty good." I asked, "Why not really good?" "Oh heck, Mama, I almost got a whipping." I said, "You mean almost?" He said, "Yes, I would not let her whip me. She had a bad switch." It's hard to believe some teachers would go out in the country to get some tough switches over the weekend, trim up a gall berry sprout, and actually use it on the children. Usually the very sight of those switches made kids very careful to do as they were told. Jerale said, "I would not let her switch me." Well, I laughed. A little mite of a boy like he was, so small. I said, "What did you do to keep her off you?" He said, "It was like this, she hit at my legs, and I would scoot over to the far side of my desk and she could not reach me, then she ran over to the other side and tried to hit me, I would slide back over and she could not hit me. After a while she got tired, and then school was out, and I came home. Mama, I don't like that teacher one bit. I would not go back to school another day if I did not have to." Right away I thought of my dad and what he once told me.

When he was very small and going to school, there was one small room and one teacher for all grades, grade 1 through grade 9. And only about twenty-five or thirty children of the farm people, who lived very far apart. The children had to walk a long way to school. Of course this was during the 1890s. Lots of children went to school, but not all of them actually learned to write and read well enough to comprehend what they were reading. My dad's older brothers actually carried him to school on their backs. The first day of school, he was away from his mom for the first time and felt so alone. He began his plan not to go to school anymore. His mom asked why he didn't want to go back to school. My dad said, "Well, I don't need to go, I learned all things today," and from then on, he never liked school and put up every excuse possible to keep from going. He was one who did not write or read well enough to comprehend all he was reading. Years later, as a young man, he found out one had to have an education.

My dad became a lumberman in the early 1900s, when all of Colquitt County and the adjoining counties were rich with yellow pine timber. Dad bought himself a sawmill and learned to saw and figure lumber by the foot. He learned how many feet one tree would turn into board feet and also to cruise timber. That is to figure how many feet of lumber can be cut from a certain number of trees before they are ever cut down. Well, he mastered that, so when he got business letters, he had to take them to one of his brothers to assure himself he comprehended what was said and to return a letter confirming he wanted to do business with them. He was not to be outdone, so he taught himself to read well and to write and spell without difficulty. I think my mom must have helped him an awful lot. Later, when their children were growing up, he was one of the first to really push for nine months of school across the board. City schools had nine months of school, and the country schools did not. Formwork had to be done. That soon changed. Afterward, while a trustee on the school board, he pushed for hot lunches in every school, and in a short while, all schools had hot lunches. This created a big demand for farm produce. While giving children nourishing meals from farm surplus commodities and dairy products, it was also creating jobs for cooks and helpers for people who could work.

Now back to 1955. Charles and Shirley are living downstairs from us. The children are all doing well in school and not complaining about the long walk. The men all live close enough to come home for lunch, so there are no lunches to pack for them, just school lunches. Jeanette is no longer looking to work on farms. She has gotten a job at Mau's bakery. She works after school and on Saturdays. She and Jan enjoy stopping by there on their way to school and picking up three doughnuts for ten cents. They work in the cafeteria at school so they can have free lunches.

We are excited with the upcoming graduation of Jeanette. She is singing in the acapella choir and is in the beta club in school. For the choir, she needs a new black taffeta dress for the baccalaureate ceremony. She has ordered her class ring and yearbook. Now we are looking at prom dresses. Charles is so proud of her. He has offered to pay for the ring and yearbook. Jeanette is shopping for a prom dress and is not sure I will go along with a very modern dress. I have asked Mary Hart to go upstairs in Friedlander's to help her find the right dress and all the crinolines to go with it, as well as matching ballerina slippers. I almost choked when Mary told me the dress was seventy dollars, but I decided she would be the most beautiful girl there. When Al came to pick her up, he was so handsome in his black slacks and white sports coat. I won't forget him saying, "My mom should see me now." He was really dressed, and Jeanette was wearing her beautiful gown, and they were ready to go dancing at the country club.

Al and Jeanette before senior prom

Lorene, Jeanette, and Webb at graduation

The next big event was the baccalaureate ceremony at the place where the art center is now. Webb and I proudly went with her to hear the choir sing the day before graduation and see her proudly walk in her cap and gown the next day for her graduation ceremony. Little did I dream she would be my only one to graduate from Moultrie High? I could just see at least five more. We always went to all the football games with Webb, sitting way up in the bleachers with the Jenkins brothers and their little flasks. Jan's Spanish club sold black-and-gold chrysanthemum corsages at the game. We truly enjoyed our children's teen years and teaching all of them to dance.

Now Shirley is pregnant with her first child. We are all so excited. I am now working at the pickle plant in Adel, Georgia, packing cucumbers. It is a seasonal job and only lasts about six weeks, but I am happy to have a job. All the ladies I am working with who live near me ride in car pools to work. It is my last day of work for this season, and I have just walked to the car when up drives Webb. He had just left his job to come pick me up because he had sad news to tell me.

My mom had just had a fatal heart attack. I just couldn't believe it. She was so young and full of life. She was only sixty-two years old. I was just devastated. Nothing could be so unexpected, it was so sudden. On the way back home, I just had to keep saying, "Webb, slow down, or you will kill us before we get there." Facts must be faced, and although we all thought it just could not be true, it really was. Mom had a coronary thrombosis. A blood clot right to the aorta, completely blocking the blood flow through the heart. The rest for me was a time of not remembering faces. Yet all our friends were there to comfort and do anything that could be done for all of us eleven—no, ten children, and my dad. Wilma Ruth, the baby girl of our family, was in Germany with her husband, who was in the Air Force, and her two small children. When we contacted her, we learned there just was no way she could come home. She could not leave such little ones for a week with strangers. She herself was just getting settled into a foreign country. It was a very sad time to be so far apart without even a consoling word from all of us.

We are all getting settled in after the sad news of my mother, and our relatives from out of state have all gone back home. Jeanette and Al are now officially engaged. Al is spending a lot of time here in Moultrie with his new family-to-be. Jeanette has accepted a full-time job as a secretary at Taylor Manufacturing in Moultrie. She took all the business courses she could get in high school. With being able to write shorthand and type seventy words a minute, she would be an asset to this company. While Al is at our house, he is spoiling Melba Jean rotten. She is definitely his favorite. He is teaching us to make meals like his mom made at home. The children are not sure they will like salad and Italian food, but they have learned to eat anything Al cooks.

Charles and Shirley are all ready for the little one. Shirley is tired and has everything she can think of for a baby. It is August 24, 1955, and our first grandson, Charles Roger Furney, has decided to come into our life. We are trying to stay out of their business other than try to help do whatever we can. Shirley brings the baby home, and when Roger was about five days old or maybe it was a couple of weeks. He had been crying pretty bad, and Shirley and her mom had made some banana pudding that day, and as Roger kept crying, they gave him just a taste or so. Now Charles was not used to feeding tiny babies anything but mama's milk. I thought he would throw the whole family out. He ran up the stairs and told me like a crime had been committed. I said, "Oh, just a taste maybe won't hurt him," and it did not. We found out children do a lot better not so close to Mom and Dad.

Children will be children. Jan is now driving. Jan and Vernon and Mavis are hanging out with Dan Gay and his sisters. Jan, Vernon, and Dan are always trying to leave Mavis behind because they are afraid she will tell Dad if something is happening that she doesn't think is right. When they got older, it came out that once when they left Mavis behind, they went to Mable's Drive-In and bought a six-pack of beer just to see if they could, and they all drove over behind Spence Field to drink it. I don't know how many of them there were, but they said by the time they drank the beer it was already hot. None of them had ever tasted beer before, but they were always game for anything that sounded like fun. I think that was the only time they pulled a prank like that, but they were just out trying to have some fun. You better believe they would have some stripes on their butts if Webb would have found out. They were only sixteen and fifteen-year-olds. Later in life, Jan's friend, Annette Jacobs, sister Dorothy, married Dan Gay.

Thirty-Second Move, 1955: Down the Street Next to Doc McCoy

It is now the fall and we decided to move right down the hill from where we were, next to Doc and Juanita McCoy's house across from Buck Bisell. We are again in a house by ourselves, no more apartments. Jeanette is planning to get married in December, and I am working as an assistant to the chef at the Gold Leaf restaurant. I thought farm work was hard, but it looks like my boss wants to work me to death. Webb doesn't like me working so much, but the money is good and we need it. The weather is cool, and I walk to work each day. Webb picks me up at night.

The younger children are growing up so fast. Jan is going to the dances on Friday and Saturday nights with her older brothers and Jeanette and Al. Sometimes Al will bring a boy to our house to date Jan, and his friend Bob is crazy about Vivian Copeland. Vernon is learning how to dance, and Mavis and the younger two are enjoying the neighborhood kids. Ms. Kate across the street has a movie projector for her young son to watch movies. My children are so excited to be invited anytime they want to see a movie. Their favorite is Walt Disney with *Steamboat Willie*. What a classic.

Jeanette and Al are not planning a big church wedding. We cannot afford a big reception, and Al just wants to be married to Jeanette. He was baptized Catholic with godparents, attended CCD (Catholic Sunday School) classes, and received his First Communion as well as Confirmation. Until he left home, he was raised a very devout Catholic by his parents. He has told his parents he's getting married and is now getting all uptight as to what their reaction will be. They have let him know they will be coming down for his wedding with his older brother Pat.

Things are not as easy as one would think. You see, Al's parents migrated to America from Italy in the early part of the century. He has a very large family, and his oldest sister is very near my age. When they get excited, they will sometimes drop into their native language of Italian. We are very Southern with Southern accents. Will that be a problem? Also Jeanette is Southern Baptist. Al is determined to marry the love of his life in a simple ceremony without interference from anyone.

The big day has arrived, and Al's family is here. I am wondering what kind of family they think we are for not having the big Italian wedding and reception. After a tiring road trip from Massachusetts, his family is just happy to relax. At first the language barrier was a problem, but that dissolved quickly. They were such happy and fun-loving people we got past that in a hurry. Webb had more of a problem with the northern accent and fast pace of speech but managed as well as Pa Veglia did with the Southern expressions. Jan took Al's brother on a foot tour of Moultrie, and I became acquainted with Ma Veglia.

We all got dressed up and went to see Al and Jeanette get married then came back home for a good Southern meal. Vivian Copeland and Phil Cardin also got married around the same time. They also had a small wedding with family and close friends as well.

Al and Jeanette had already fixed up their little place in Albany with everything, including food, ready for them to go home to. They took Al's family back to Albany with them after the wedding. They would go on a trip for their honeymoon in February, when they would go to Massachusetts to meet the rest of Al's family. They lived near the Air Force base where Al was stationed in Albany, but they came home every weekend. We were so glad because we had gotten used to Al being part of our family, and we missed them when they weren't here.

My daughter Mavis is now about to have a birthday, and Jeanette and Al will be here for the weekend. When Jeanette got here, she said, "Mama, we just have to have a cake and a little party." Well, I went out and bought an angel food cake, put cardboard over the center hole, and decorated it with icing and made it look real nice with candles on top. I had also bought five pounds of hot dogs with marshmallows. I wondered if we might have a lot left over. I had told her she could invite her friends. As you might know, she invited all the kids on the block and half of her class from school. When night came, we went outside and roasted hot dogs and marshmallows. We had such a fun party, she still remembers it.

My Mavis has always been a person, a child, and an adult, who put all she had into every day she lives. Now nearing her midlife years, she still brings laughter and jokes to a crowd at reunions and just family get-togethers. The nieces and nephews all love "Aunt Mae." She is also a wonderful cook, both Italian and American dishes, and will give you her heart if she could. Most of all, she also gets things off her chest. Never puts off what she wants to say, good or bad. If it needs to be said, she wants to say it. In a nutshell, that's the way she is. In general, people just love Mae. I wish she were here right now to go for a walk with.

Charles is still working at the sawmill with Webb. Gil has gone down to Belle Glade to work with my brothers, who work for A. Duda. We have all left the farm, and life is so much better. I don't have to wish for ham or meat. We can afford to go buy one. Believe me, when we farmed, it was fresh meat when it was in season and smoked meat all at one time. Thank goodness people no longer have to worry about preserving meat. It was so unsanitary. The salt processing also was not good for your blood pressure. Thank goodness for progress and no more hot kitchens from woodstoves. The first three children are now out on their own. Jan is having a problem with an English teacher in school. She is now a junior at Moultrie High, a teenager, and she feels her teacher is being unfair with his grades because of the friends she is hanging out with. He has told her he is going to give her a failing grade in English, so she just drops out of school.

We are now moving to the southeast side of town, to the lower Meigs road to a nice-looking house with plenty of rooms for the children. Jeanette and Al still come home most every weekend, and there is plenty of room for us all.

Thirty-Third Move, 1956:
Murphy House on Lower Meigs Road

As usual we all worked every day when work was available. Vernon, Jan, and Mavis worked anytime they were not at school. There was nothing but farm work for me as I still had two small ones at home. I helped weed tobacco beds then pull the plants. Later I would drop the plants if the landowner did not have a tobacco planter. I don't complain. The little ones are in school all day, and the older ones help out around the house.

Jeanette and Al have planned a nice fishing trip for all of us to go to the Panacea Bridge down at the West Coast. Oh, we were looking forward to this trip so much. People we knew did relate how the fish did bite at the Panacea Bridge. My aunt Selma told me you could put two hooks on one line and catch two fish at a time. Now I sure didn't want to miss out on that. All the children loved to fish, and Jeanette could really fish and loved it, so she taught Al to fish. Since the house we lived in was a farmer's house, we had told him we would be able to help with farm work when he needed us. So on a Friday he wanted me to help pull plants from the tobacco bed. Jerale stayed home from school with a cold and a slight temperature. He played around the tobacco bed while I worked, and took a couple of naps in the car during the day. His fever got pretty high that night, and he got worse so I continued to give him aspirin. You should have seen him the next day. He had thousands of little bumps, even on his eyes. His eyes were so weak I had to put covers over the windows to keep the room dark. He really had a bad case of the measles. The rest of the family had already had the measles, but guess who had to stay home from the fishing trip with Melba and Jerale?

Oh, well, a couple of months later we all went to Panama City Beach and on over to Saint Joe, Florida, to visit Webb's brother

Iris and Mattie Lou. We certainly had a wonderful time visiting with Iris and Mattie Lou. The children had never been to see the ocean and beaches. Al had been stationed in Panama City, so he enjoyed going back but was a little leery of the ocean. He was raised in Revere Beach in Massachusetts and was a distance swimmer. While in Panama City he was swimming a distance off shore and was entangled in Portuguese man-of-war and almost lost his life before he got back to shore. He was a little cautious afterward. We all enjoyed being on Mexico Beach. It has been a favorite of ours since then.

While at Mexico Beach, Jeanette went out in the water with her new wristwatch, which Al had given her for her graduation, and she was upset. When we got home, Webb put it in the jewelry shop and they ordered new parts and it was as good as new. Talk about fair-haired children and sunburn. Well, Mavis looked cooked. She was so burned she missed two days of school the next week.

Mae was now at the primping age and was forever doing her hair in the morning and would keep fixing her hair until the school bus was there, making the driver wait for her. She had to have those crinolines just right for her dress. I said, "No more of this," but she continued her habit. I was also trying to teach her to value her time better. The next day the bus pulled off and left her still primping. Well, I just got me a switch and asked if she wanted me to use it. She began to cry, but I told her to get in the road. She was not missing school that day. I made her walk from our house all the way to Sunset School. I walked her to the railroad track then she went on by herself. You know what? She was not to wait for anymore.

The owner of the house, Mr. Murphy, had a really nice mother, and we talked often. She told me she had a sister who lived in Alabama whom she had not seen since the sister was married and moved away from the family. Alabama did not seem so far away to me. When their mother had passed away, the sister was not able to come home to the funeral, and now her sister was seventy-five years old. That was a long time for sisters to not see each other. Later I read of their reunion, and they were in their eighties.

The Murphys were good neighbors. By now Gil had moved back home, and fishing was in his blood. They always let us fish in their ponds. Gil would get up at first daylight, get in a boat, and fish for bass. He knew just where to look, and he did enjoy coaxing a nice one out with his reel and latest lure. He caught some nice ones too.

We only lived at the Murphy house a short while as we are always looking for a bigger and better house since we have never built one of our own. Al and Webb went into town one day, and when they got home, they brought a new television for us. We were so excited. This was our first television, and it was black and white. Of course we never dreamed TVs could be in color. Can you imagine the pleasure we had watching TV?

Thirty-Forth Move, 1956:
The Auger Place, off Meigs Road

Well, here we are in a beautiful home we were so pleased to get. The home has nice hardwood floors throughout, and we have a shower and bathtub in the bathroom, all laid out so well, with a fireplace in the big living room with a nice place for our wonderful new TV. We have a nice big green lawn around the house, so Vernon and Jan cut grass any time they are bored. The large back porch runs the length of the house, with bamboo at the end. Now the girls would have liked to live there always, with hardwood floors so shiny you could see yourself in them. This was the Auger's place.

Mr. Auger had built himself a very modern little home nearby. They had no children. He had a big farm and planted a big part of it in Bermuda grass for his fine herd of cows. Now this is why he wanted us on his farm: so we could help run a John Deere tractor and set out fields of Bermuda grass. We did help on Saturdays until the place was ready for us. We were soon ready to move in around Thanksgiving. It was the nicest place we had ever lived. Other than a nice home, we had a couple of fishponds we could fish in anytime we wanted. We caught a lot of fish, bream, and in one area was a lot of catfish.

You should have seen me on that tractor. I did a number-one job turning land. I think Mr. Auger was amazed at our family. We kept our home clean and looking well, and the grass was always cut and manicured looking. For once we had a country life we all enjoyed. We kept up the pastures, although the girls hated the dust from planting Bermuda grass, and we helped our neighbor Mr. Griffin pick tomatoes, squash, and cucumbers. He paid us good. Me, Vernon, Jan, and Mavis worked, and Melba and Jerale went along to learn.

Jan is back in school. She only had to take her English class over, and can you believe she got the same teacher. This time when she had a problem, she went to Mr. McDonald and he straightened that problem out. She continued where she left off as she had only missed a few months of school. Gil is back at the sawmill with Webb and Charles. He has grown into a young man of his own. At this time in our life, I have a hard time keeping the children in a church. We go as often as possible.

Jeanette and Al have been blessed in their marriage. They are neither Catholic nor Southern Baptist, and they have not taught their children either, and naturally, these children have not to this day committed themselves to any belief in this life, of which I do not approve. Jeanette was baptized in the Southern Baptist religion. The children attended Sunday school with their friends who are Baptists. I sometimes feel that what my children were taught did not sink in very deep, as all eight are not a very dedicated bunch of adults. None of them are true dedicated Baptists. Two are active and truly Catholic, although four of them married into Catholic families. These were Jeanette, Jan, Vernon, and Mavis. As Charles grew older and established in the community, his family always went to Hopewell Baptist Church, and his children have found their roots in that community. Gil did not establish a church for his family as they were moved from Florida in their early years back to Georgia. Gil's wife is from Florida. The children attended Baptist churches with their friends and cousins. Jan, Vernon, and Mavis all were married in the Catholic Church. They baptized their children in the church, and all their children were given godparents, whose responsibility is to be responsible for the children until they become adults, should something happen to their parents. Jan's and Vernon's families are devout Catholics. Mavis renewed her faith in the Baptist church as her children became older and continues her faith today. Melba was a believer of the Baptist faith but was not baptized as well as her son Sandy. Stacey, her daughter, was baptized into the Berlin Baptist church at eight years old. Jerale has not established a church for his family yet and has not been baptized. He did, however, put some study into the Mormon religion. Jerale now has two grown sons, and I do not know which church they prefer.

Many are the times I wonder where I have failed. Yes, I very well know the Scripture. "A tree is known by the fruit it bears. A good tree produces good fruit; a tree that produces no fruit is worth nothing and should be cut down." Well, this is very strange as I diligently cared for my family and took them to church every Sunday. This I did by myself as Webb did not really enjoy Sunday school or church. In his early life, his family was not dedicated to a particular church, but both his parents were baptized when they were older. My mom instilled God and his life into me and my brothers and sisters. We still stick by our faith. I think one reason my children did not follow my Southern Baptist faith is because we moved so often, which meant new people, new churches, and lots of times, we had no car to go in. Sometimes we were too tired from working. We needed to rest on Sundays.

I wanted my little girls to always look good when they went to church. Sometimes for a special gathering I have taken a good dress of mine and cut it at the seams because it was either too small or too big. I would turn it the wrong side out and cut another complete dress for one of my little girls. I still believe if one goes to church every Sunday, even if you have to wear the same dress, God will help you and provide for you to go to church.

I'll never forget what my mama said to me once when I was complaining. "Honey, when I was a young teenage girl, times were hard and I wore the same little rose-printed dress every Sunday and the same little shoes [mind you, they were not slippers, which were not durable enough, so money could not be spent on such]." The older adults could only afford two pairs of shoes. After she and my dad were married, he told her he knew she only had one little rose-print dress because she wore it every Sunday.

She and her sisters were very good singers in Pleasant Hill Church. She sang alto, like her Aunt Maggie, who raised her family after their parents' death in the early 1900s. They and two of their children died when typhoid fever was rampant in Colquitt County. Her grandparents took the family into their home, and Aunt Maggie helped raise them. When she sat on the front bench in Pleasant Hill, she was very happy with her voice blending into her six sisters' and Aunt Maggie's, who all sang together, she with her little rose-print dress. In that little church in the wild woods.

No wonder my dad spotted her and was soon asking if he might take her home from church. Dad, in his new shiny Buggy with his high-stepping horse. He was the envy of a dozen or so young men of the same community, all young farmers or businessmen of the day. He fell in love with the little girl in the rose-print dress who sang like a nightingale. He only could take her home from church. Very few girls were allowed to go riding with a young man. They would sit on the porch or in the wide hallways of the then-popular dogtrot-style house that was usually made of logs with a big room on either side of the big hall.

One of my mom's cousins was in his teens but had a very good head for business and was a hard worker. He told her brother one day he was going to own a fine horse and buggy if he had to eat garbage and go naked. He was very determined, and the seed was planted. He finally got the horse and buggy and married the most popular young schoolteacher of the day. He owned a large farm and one of the first cars that were made.

So much for religion. My children are all starting to develop into their own personalities. One day Gil went to work at the sawmill and was feeling young and sassy as boys will at that age. He was talking to my cousin and the others who worked with him when he said, "Heck, this is a good day to go fishing; I'll bet none of you have the nerve to just pick up and go."

Charles said, "I can't go, I might lose my job and I have a family to make a living for." Gil and all the others did not start the day. They just took off fishing. The ones that stayed waited till Everett (their boss) got there, and boy, was he mad. He did not have enough help to run the mill, so the rest got the day off too. I guess Gil hated that grind of eight to five, Monday through Friday.

Everett told them they were all fired and to stay off as long as they wanted to. Now Uncle Leonard was Frankie's (my cousin) dad, and he had been dead about six months. When this happened, Aunt Selma had to go to work for the first time in her life to provide income. She could not receive Social Security either, because she was not sixty-two years old. Well, the boys at work spoke a good word for little Frankie, and he got his job back. A few days later Everett let the rest come back, but he did not let them think he cared if they worked or not. They learned a good lesson in responsibility.

This same summer we set Bermuda grass on Saturdays. Mr. Auger tended the corn and cow feed after I turned the land. During the week, Me, Jan, Vernon, and Mavis worked in tobacco at a neighbor's, Mr. Russell Taylor. He had a nice tobacco harvester. He, his brother, and one other man were just enough to run the harvester with the four of us. Mavis and I tied the tobacco, and the rest cropped it. At noon the men would pull it in the barn. At noon when we got done, we did not get a hot cooked dinner. We all went to the nearest little country store and had cinnamon buns, milk, a moon pie, and RC Cola, sometimes sardines and crackers.

We made six dollars a day, five days a week. That was 120 dollars a week. We all had a blast working together, just joking around and laughing and happy. We all enjoyed fishing, working, shopping, and watching our new TV. Jeanette is still coming home on weekends and is pregnant but doesn't look it. We will have another baby to spoil in the fall. We did not seem to have any troubles getting along.

One day while we were having supper, Mr. Auger decided to come over for a visit. Of course it was like a madhouse with lots of food, lots of teenagers, and an in-law. He just came right into the house to tell Webb something but all the time taking a good look at our dining table made for twelve people, with two benches on each side. With all those peas, turnip greens, sliced tomatoes, and a picnic shoulder with plenty of baked corn bread on the side. I am sure his wife would have left home if she was to prepare meals for this kind of family. The difference was no vegetables up north or anyplace except down south cooked meat with vegetables. Georgia people call it soul food. The black cooks of slavery days handed down their good recipes that are used even up until now. The vegetables up north were cooked in one pot, the meat in a Dutch oven, or baked like we make a Virginia ham.

While living there at the Augers', we did enjoy going to a big pond cutting. I guess the last one I ever went to was at Mr. Watt Jenkins's pond. We took everything but the fish and prepared to cook what was caught. Webb and the three boys all fished then some dressed fish for dinner, and we cooked them in a big wash pot under a shelter nearby. Hush puppies, potato salad, coleslaw, and pickles. All you could eat with plenty of iced tea. Our family is really big now, and those grown kids can eat. They got lots more fish to take home for later.

We have finished the tobacco work. These days, acres and acres of cotton were planted and harvested in South Georgia. It all had to be picked by hand. We had not even heard of mechanical cotton pickers those days. So our fishing days were over. We had really enjoyed the summer, cooling off in the water and big fish fries to beat the band. We have to forget gathering tobacco. We must make more money some way. All the children must have something to do. We were taught ourselves that idle hands get into mischief more easily. We tried to keep something for our bunch of kids to do. You will notice only on the coldest days we were without work, in the winter.

That is when I would do my quilting and stitching up quilt tops for quilting. Blankets and bought covers were unthinkable up until then. Everyone's cover was homemade. The more energetic the ladies of the house, the more nice quilts were made. One never heard of selling these quilts. That was out of the question. Anyone too lazy to stitch up a cover for their beds was just unthinkable or considered too lazy for words. I always made one or two new quilts a year. I did have time while the kids were in school in the early fall and winter. One also made a few extra covers for the married children so they would have a good start. Nowadays, some young ladies getting married only hear about these things from the older generation. They know nothing of the care of old handmade pieced-up quilted quilts, and if you can find one you can get your hands on, it will cost plenty. Those things have gone the way of the horse and buggy.

The very elite housekeepers of today use blankets of every make, material, and color. The houses of today are also heated so well, in the coldest winter one can sleep comfortable under a sheet and spread.

I will have to back up a little here. When my mom passed away in 1955, within a short time afterward, my dad's big family home burned to the ground. There was nothing left but the ashes. My family was devastated. It wasn't just the loss of a home. It was my dad's home, and now we had to decide what to do with Daddy. My sister Sarah and Roy Copeland have just moved into their new home in Moultrie over behind the high school and have decided to let Daddy live there since they have plenty of room.

My brother Wayne has worked out a deal with Dad to buy the upper portion of Dad's farm, and is now living up on the hill where we used to live. He now owns the part of Dad's farm that reaches down to Uncle John Croft's pond.

Thirty-Fifth Move, 1956:
Mayor Wither's Place beside the Pilco Creek

The kids are back in the Moultrie schools. Thank goodness the high school is a consolidated county school, and as long as we are in Colquitt County, the older kids won't have to change schools, just how they walk to school. We are only here for a short while until we decide if we want to farm again.

Thirty-Sixth Move, 1956: Jim MacOdom's Place

Dad has offered to build a house for me where his old house was, down between Leona's and Wayne's. He is already working on it, and the foundation has been laid and they are getting ready to start laying the cement blocks. We will live here until the house is ready. When we moved from Auger's, Gil decided to move back to Belle Glade to work with my brothers. There is money to be made there.

OK, now we are into the fall of the year and cotton picking. I am helping my dad gather his white cotton. Dad lets me use his truck to haul people at my house, and also a bunch from Moultrie who had children who needed to work and uses cotton picking as a way to make money to buy school clothes before school gets started. Now these teenagers were really hard workers and made enough money, with their parents taking care of it for them, to buy all of their school clothes and supplies till at least midterm. That was a big help for the parents. If the parents would have let them use the money as they wished with no supervision, most of the kids would just never have had anything to show for it.

I always got up early and made grits, bacon or sausage, and scrambled eggs and a big pan of homemade biscuits. We never dreamed of any other kind. There was always homemade jelly and syrup to go with it. I also made dinner and put it in a box or bucket to eat at midday. The owner of the cotton field furnished drinks and water. Boy, when a person works in a field like that, it sure tastes good. In the late afternoon near sundown, the sheets we have piled high with cotton all day are tied up and weighed. You are then paid for as many pounds of cotton as you have picked. No more, no less.

Everyone wants their cotton weighed correctly, but after the weighing, someone looks at the weighing balances. There are usually two small ones that are used, and for some reason, there is an empty hole up in the center of these things they balance with. So if the fellow fills the hole up with lead that was melted and poured into it—it gets cold and is as smooth as the other material—you know it has been tampered with. If it is smoothed over, now that is cheating of the worse kind. A fellow will sometimes do these things, but believe me; if he is caught he has to buy new balances to get anyone into his fields to pick cotton anymore.

Every day we were in the fields as the sun rose. As it rose higher in the sky, the hotter it got. If it rained, we all went back to town. The cotton had to be dry before picking. We all looked to having nice dry weather for the cotton-picking days. In the late afternoon when we loaded up, we went home tired and all of us were hot. Now it is not to say some of the kids were bound to not work too hard. All that they could and would do was drag along, picking just enough cotton to sit on like a soft pillow then get into rich high cotton stalks and try not to go any farther down the rows.

They would just sit there and tell jokes and talk about what they would like to do. Maybe one of them will become a writer. Someone did always help pick their row out so they could all start back to the other end at one time. I noticed these particular ones were always to help. Also, they barely made enough money to pay for all the ice cream they could eat. Maybe one will become a politician. When we stopped at Edith Dea's grocery store going home, once a lady and her kids ate no ice cream because the quota for pounds picked was not what was expected of them. They were told they had to work more the next day or no ice cream. Boy, the next day they always did better.

I was not that strict with my kids. We did not try to make them provide everything for themselves, though I do think that is a good way to teach children. Money doesn't grow on trees. One has to work for it then can decide early in life why a parent wants them to get as much education as they possibly can.

Maybe one will become a writer

Vern "Red" Furney

DEMOCRATIC CANDIDATE PRECINCT COMMITTEEMAN
2nd Ward — 4th Precinct

Are you tired of having the feeling your vote doesn't count?
Are you tired of having no one listen to you about things that are wrong in your neighborhood?
Do you feel helpless and uninformed when you get into the voting booth?
I have all those feelings too!

That is why I am seeking your vote to help elect me Precinct Committeeman from our precinct. I have had to call my alderman repeatedly in order to talk with him. Your precinct committeeman should act in your behalf. He is the one who should be calling your alderman for you about neighborhood problems! There has never been any literature regarding a candidate or issue left at my house. As a result, most of us voters are not informed, and cannot make an intelligent decision when we vote.

My wife, two children and I have lived at our present home for five years. Until a year ago, I did not know who our precinct committeeman was! A precinct committeeman is elected to a position that is an unpaid honor, because he is civic-minded and interested in representing his neighbors and their needs in the precinct. He helps you to get your streets plowed and fixed. He helps to get a new street light installed. And he helps keep you informed on issues that will affect you and your taxes.

The last few years have spotlighted injustices in our government and the incompetence of the people we have elected to public office in the past. That is why it is so important this year that we elect people who are really dedicated to honest, open government and who are concerned with your best interests!!

I know that I can provide personal contact with you and your needs with the city. I will be most grateful for your vote.

THIS YEAR YOUR VOTE WILL COUNT, IF YOU VOTE FOR ME ON MARCH 16th.

Maybe one will become a politician

Thirty-Seventh Move, 1956 and 1957: The New Block House on Dad's Farm

Well, here we are finally into the block house my dad has had built. We are happy to get settled in now, and Dad is happy to be moved in with us. This year we have a lot happening. Jan is now a junior and is riding to Berlin with Leona's youngest, Vanada, where they ride with Jeanie Martin and Charlotte Chapman to Moultrie High on the school bus. Each day my brother Wayne drops them off in Berlin. While they are waiting, they will hang out at Miss Teen's Café, the same place my older kids used to hang out. Since Moultrie is a consolidated county school, Berlin is our designated spot to catch the bus to Moultrie. Wayne is farming Daddy's farm, and we are happy to get here, to be able to help out.

Jeanette and Al have invited me and my brother Wayne to go to Massachusetts with them before her baby is born. Webb won't hear of leaving the house to go any farther than to Florida. He cannot travel comfortably because of the bad leg and foot from his old coon-hunting days. He just doesn't like my being gone because I have never left him longer than to go to the hospital to have a baby. Well, I have decided that I don't have to stay home too. Webb is not happy with my decision, but I am ready to go somewhere I've never been and start seeing how other people live. This will be the first of many trips I have taken across these United States with my family. Wayne is excited to be invited into a real Italian home again. He was stationed in Italy in the service.

Our trip to Revere, Massachusetts, is everything I expected and more. Going through the cities was fun, and Boston was very exciting. We all had one good time seeing the Boston commons and all the historical parts of Boston. I had never seen a bowling alley, let alone go bowling, but Wayne and me even tried that. You could see the home of the Boston Red Sox from Al's brother

Frankie's house. My baby brother Louis was in the army and was stationed in Boston, so naturally we all got together for a visit. Everyone in Al's big family asked us to come over and eat dinner with them. They welcomed us like we were family. I can't remember when I have eaten so much. Jeanette kept getting sick to her stomach. She said the smell of garlic made her sick. Wayne just loves Al's family and said it reminded him of being in Italy. Al's mom and dad were very gracious hosts. They did everything they could to make us welcome. Now it is time to get back to reality and go home. We were sad to leave Al's family but glad to be back in good old Georgia after the long trip.

Now this is a very important time because my daughter Jeanette is having her first child at the same clinic I had my last baby. This is 1956, one year minus two months after she married. Boy, she was to say many times, "Why did I ever do it? Why did I not go to the base hospital in Albany, Georgia?" She had a bad enough time as it was, but if complications had come up, she would have been bad off for sure. Having it in that little hospital in Pavo, she would have had to be taken to a city hospital by car or ambulance. Thank God she made it after forty hours of labor with just enough contractions to worry her but not enough to give birth. She is not a quitter though. Her spirits were high when she went into the clinic. She knew she was lucky to have the little boy who looked just like his dad. Gerolamo J. Veglia (Jerry), born October 24, 1956, was a brunette if ever there was one. With black hair and big brown eyes, he was perfect, and Jeanette was none the worse after the long hours of childbirth.

Now that we have the cotton in, I am ready to get my sewing done. Jeanette and Al still come home for weekends. The children are all adjusted, and we are looking forward to a big Christmas with Gil at home and also with a baby in the house. Roger and Jerry keep everybody running. Mavis has met some little kids across the creek in the back of our house, and can you believe they have given her a real piano. She has always wanted to play the piano, and now she can try. Melba and Jerale are too little to do much work, so they mostly just play with Wayne and Mary's children, Larry and Gwen. Vernon is going to the sawmill now to help his dad out. He helps with farm work when he can, but he would rather work at the sawmill.

It is the beginning of a new year, and I don't quite know which way to turn first. My older children are out of the nest. Charles and Shirley are expecting another little bundle of joy, and we are all wanting a girl. We have two boys to spoil. Jerry, Jeanette's little boy, is growing like a weed. Al is going to reenlist in the Air Force and make a career of it. He will be stationed in Okinawa, and he wants to take Jeanette and the baby with him. Our house is too small for everyone, so Jeanette is planning to stay with my sister Sara and Roy until she leaves for Okinawa. They will close up their place in Albany, and all their belongings will be shipped over to Okinawa.

Charles and Shirley have added a really fine little boy to their family. Gilbert David Furney was born May 9, 1957. They are so happy even if it wasn't a girl. Charles is still working at the sawmill and so excited about his small family. They never have to look far for a babysitter. Jan is dating someone she really likes a lot; he is also a Yankee. Webb is not too happy with the girls taking such a liking to Italian boys, but Al has turned out to be fine son-in-law, and if Pat Acompora is as good, that will be OK.

Jan is just looking forward to being a senior in school this year. The children are working hard on the farm and spending all their money on school clothes. The girls have their friends working on the farm with them, and they have a lot of fun. They love when the Martin girls come out to help us. Our neighbor's children don't have to do farm work, and Jan and Vanada get so mad when their boyfriends come early and they are all hot and sweaty, and Jeannie comes prancing down the road all clean and cool looking. Vernon has grown into a young man and is working hard but has decided to not return to school this year because he has heard his brothers talk about a job in Florida on a dredge boat, and he wants to go there.

Well, my daughter is getting her paperwork in order to leave the good old US of A. Al is already in Okinawa and has gotten a house, in base housing for them, and it includes a live-in maid to help Jeanette out with Jerry. Jeanette is happy to go be with her husband, but as we are, she is sad to leave our family knowing full well it will be three years before we see each other again, and she is saying her good-byes and is on her way. My brother Wayne is taking her to the train station where she will travel to meet the ship in San Francisco, California, to sail for sixteen days to Okinawa, and is brave to be taking Jerry on such a trip by herself. She has sold her little black Plymouth car to her granddad, and all the kids here that have a driver's license are thinking of ways to borrow his car. She met other girls on the ship going to the same place. She has said Jerry was a good little traveler, and she, unlike the others, never got seasick. This would be one of many Air Force bases she would learn to call home, including Japan.

Well, Charles and Shirley have moved their small family down to West Palm Beach, Florida. Charles will be working on a dredge boat and has asked Gil to come help them out. My sister Eula Mae is working in a bank in West Palm Beach. They have moved Tony's mother in with them, and she helps with the home work and taking care of the girls. Her husband, Tony, is working with the county, and Webb is talking to Tony to see if he can help him get on with Palm Beach County. Webb has been working on the farm and with Ellis at Jim Walters Corp. for the last year or so. If he gets the job, this will be a real big move.

Jeanette and Jerry now live in Okinawa with Al

Thirty-Eighth Move, 1957:
West Palm Beach, Florida, High Ridge Road

Webb wants us to move on down to Florida, and he will work on the dredge with the boys. We are going to go down with the two youngest kids to try to find a place. Jan, Vernon, and Mavis will stay here in the house until we can settle in and come back to pick them up around November. They are old enough to know how to run the house and get themselves off to school. Jan does not want to move to Florida. She really likes Pat Acompora and wants to finish her senior year in high school.

Well, we are in West Palm Beach, and Webb is helping the boys dredge. Tony has gotten Webb a job with the county. He will start as soon as they check him out, and the pay will be the best we ever had. For the first time in our lives, we will have real good benefits, such as work toward a pension and the best health insurance that is available. We have found a house for all of us, including my brother Louis, to live in, over on High Ridge Road. There are big banyan trees and mango trees all over the large piece of property.

It is now November, and we are ready to pick up a few more of our things and our older children. Patrick A. Acompora Jr. has given Jan an engagement ring for her eighteenth birthday, and they will be getting married in December as it is too difficult for Jan to manage her finances by herself. We will make our trip a short one because we will be back for Christmas for her wedding. Mavis left her one-hundred head of 4-H club chickens in Georgia, of course, and I heard Pat cleaned chickens for Thanksgiving.

Well, coming back to Georgia this time feels really strange. All our family is now transplanted in Florida except Jan. She and Pat were married December 22, 1957, at Preacher Eason's home and had their little, or I should have said large apartment

Jan and Pat Acompora are now married, and it snowed in Valdosta

Jan Furney Acompora, family picture: Mariah, Caryn, Debbie, Jan, Shawna, Candice, Jennifer, back are Nick and Zack

in Valdosta all ready to live in. They love it because it is part of a big old Southern house on North Patterson Street. They even have a fireplace in it. Vanada Copeland was the maid of honor, and their best man's—Shorty Morgan—father had a heart attack, so Lawton Castleberry stood up for Pat. We were all invited back to their home after the wedding, but only Gil and Vanada went. Gil had bought some silverware for Jan's wedding present and dropped it off.

We are back from Georgia, and had a great time. I have all the family in one house again, including Gil. Vernon has also gotten a job with the county now, and I am working at the cafeteria at the school where the other three children go to school. I am so worried about the kids' education, but they worked it out themselves. Jan left Moultrie before graduation and later got her GED, so she could start taking college classes. Vernon later attended adult education classes and walked with his class to get his high school diploma as an adult. He was so proud because he became an active politician in the hometown where he raised his family, Rockford, Illinois. He eventually became a negotiator for the Auto Workers Union for Chrysler Corporation. When Jeanette settled in Florida, she was in banking. She retired as vice president of First Union Bank. She was responsible for the entire operations department in Orlando. All we can do is encourage the last three to do their best and get as much education as they can.

With Webb working with the county, with benefits, I can now look for a vocation that will carry me for some years. That became a professional cake decorator in the bakery at the farmers' market in West Palm Beach. I have always been creative, and this is my cup of tea. I am happy to be able to work an eight-hour day. The children can also work in the market at odd jobs while they are not in school.

As I have mentioned earlier, when my oldest, Charles, was born, he lost his eye because of a lack of knowledge about certain medical procedures at that time. As he grew up into elementary school age, he did not need glasses. He was nearsighted, and it became more evident as he grew older. I did all I could do except raise holy hell to get him help. I finally got him to a doctor who fitted him with proper glasses. Now I know he could not see half of what other kids saw. I saw him hitting objects with his fingers as he tried to feel for things. He could not do schoolwork and was failing grades, so at around the fifth grade, I let him leave school. When he was thirteen, he got pink eye and almost lost his vision in his only eye. Well, he did get through that with God's help and prayers. I know why his fingers always looked like a dog had chewed them.

He learned to feel the things he wanted to do. After getting proper glasses, he could see good and was a good driver. He became an excellent mechanic for small gas engines. When working with detailed parts, he still depended on his fingers. All his adult life he has managed to provide for his family very well, and not knowing how long his vision would last, he had paid for his home by the time he was thirty-eight years old. He worked a regular schedule at the sawmill then took on a second job as night watchman since he lived right across the street and would have time for some sleep between jobs.

He and Shirley had raised four little boys, and after the last one, they decided to give up on having a little girl. When Shirley went for her checkup after the last boy, she started discussing birth control with her doctor, and he announced it was too late. She was already pregnant. Would you believe, that was the girl? Their last child, Charlotte Diane Furney. Can you imagine how hard Charles must have worked those days with no education? They had five kids in six years. I am sure Shirley thought life was just one long struggle with diapers. Back then it was bird's-eye cloth diapers to wash every day. Pampers was just a dream.

Shirley's brothers have moved their families to West Palm Beach, Florida, and they are doing really well working on a dredge. Charles has two young boys and a wife to support, so he is ready to work with his brothers-in-law and has asked Gil to join them. They both like the dredge boat work and are making good money. This job has turned our life around. Now I'll explain something about dredging. Florida, as most people know, is low-lying ground. Very wet in rainy weather and has a sandy soil with lime rock base, so it lets the water run off fast. A small place in a building project was outlined and staked off to a depth the right height to allow for drainage then a road machine was set down. It was started up, and in a couple of days, a large hole existed where the wet sand, along with plenty of water, was pumped out. Huge pipes were used to get the sand pumped to where it was to be settled for a housing project to be built when finished.

Shirley's brother operated the machine, and it usually took five or six men to keep pipes in place and moving out. Soon we have a lake then a bigger lake as the sand is distributed through large pipes, and a village begins. As the hole gets bigger, so does the area of new houses. At this time a big place called Palm Springs, right on Congress Avenue in West Palm Beach had been developed. Three of my sons would be working for a period of six months for each development. While working on the boat one day, Charles went to get the Bendix started, a round little thing one had to get started before the starter kicked on. He stuck his finger into the hole to feel for it. The motor started up and just chewed the end of the poor boy's finger all around. He got twenty stitches to sew it up and two or three days in the hospital to fix it.

There go his fingers again. They looked so bad, I always told his sons and grandsons to get as much education as you can. Charles finished up a year later. The job in Florida on the dredge played out. His lack of education held him back again. The county could not hire him because when he would get his physical, they would turn him down because of his poor vision. He had to return to Georgia to continue work there. He did learn a lot while in Florida.

While looking to rent a house, once you found one, there were a lot of rules and extra rent to be paid. How many children, and do you have pets? We said just two then the owner would say, "Well, my septic tank is small and has not enough water to take care of four people." You know that will really make you mad? To consider children as pets: talk about abortion and talk about adopting. This older generation was not willing to share anything. No wonder they filled the nursing homes so quick when they were finally invented.

OK, so Charles has gotten together a nice little trailer and put his possessions in it. On Friday night, Webb and I are there to help, with one son David in our car with some of his things and Charles, Shirley, and their son Roger in the other, headed back to Moultrie, Georgia. It was a long tiresome twelve-hour trip. Everything on 441 North was under construction, things were going strong there. It always took us twelve hours to go to Georgia. The new Interstate Parkway and Highway 75 were in the dreaming stage. Poor Charles went home thinking, *How much longer will I be able to see how to work and make a living?* He went right back to the sawmill, and that is when he worked two jobs for some time. We went right back to West Palm.

Now his work is paying off. Wages are better, so he has bought a piece of property out on the lower Hopewell Church road. He built a nice home and had two more little boys and, finally, got the little girl Shirley was looking for. Who would know, thirty years later, he would be in the same place? His first house burned down to the ground. It was called an accident; an iron or the stove was left on accidentally. We lived in West Palm at the time but came home to help him if we could. By the time we got there, everyone was already at work helping him. In two or three days he had another place right close by to move into and plenty of furnishings to cook and keep house with, including clothes and groceries. Hopewell Community, then as now, was always helping in every way. His family also—aunts, uncles, and cousins—helped him get a new start. We went back to our home in West Palm, Webb to the county and me to Mama's Bakery, our new jobs and new experiences.

We are all writing to Jeanette and getting letters and pictures from her. They are doing just fine, and Jeanette has made friends; also, a good friend Frances Presley and her husband are from Moultrie. They live near the beach, of course, since they are on an island. She sends pictures of Little Jerry so we can see how big he is.

Webb and Lorene at Lucerne Avenue in 1959

Thirty-Ninth Move, 1958:
Lucerne Avenue, by WPB Canal

One of the guys Webb works with is leaving his home and has offered to let us rent from him. This is a big place with plenty of room for all of us and my brother Louis, who has lived with us since Mama passed away. I'm so happy to have a nice house near my job. We girls try to keep up the inside, and we want the boys to take care of the outside. I never knew grass could grow so fast. We have a canal between our yard and the street. It's always full of water, and the grass just grows faster than we can cut it.

Webb now has both Gil and Vernon working with him at the county. He is responsible for the maintenance, for keeping an area looking manicured. That includes Lake Osborne. This is a good job for a former farmer who likes plants and takes pride in how things grow. At this time in West Palm Beach, if you want to plant a tree, you just give the county a call and they will come right out and plant it for free. With all the beautiful palms and other such trees you see along the road, it's hard to believe other counties don't do the same thing. Because of his bad legs and feet, this job suits him to a tee. He just rides on a tractor most of the time. The boys do whatever else that needs to be done, like repairing a fence or planting a tree.

I am staying with the bakery business; I have to get up very early, but that means I get off early. I am baking very little now in the kitchen. I mostly just stand in the front area of the bakery and decorate the cakes. I am amazed to see how people will just stand and watch me. If they want a special cake, I can decorate it while they stand and watch me. My boss Kathy said her business has really picked up. We have become pretty good friends, and that has lasted us all these years. I have never had to look for a job since I found what suited me best. The money is good, and I can schedule vacations and have enough money to go wherever I want.

Mavis is too young to be working, but she has a job for when she is not in school. She and her girlfriend Irene Hendershot are both big girls. They work hard to earn a little extra money. You see, the children like to go to the wrestling matches, and even the women wrestle. We all like to go, and Mavis, Melba, and Irene wouldn't miss a match unless they absolutely had to. While I am working now, I can depend on Mavis to watch out for the two younger ones. No one dares mess with them. They do not want Mae mad at them. They all love to go with Webb and me when we go to Wellman's dance hall. We take all their friends, and it is just like it was in Georgia, with me, Webb, Gil, and Louis teaching all the children to dance and going over to the beach at the Lake Worth casino or Lake Osborne for cookouts. Webb and I go swimming almost every night.

Now things are looking good back in Georgia, with everyone taking care of their own little problems. Charles is just getting a new little one. Tommy Ray Furney came into this world on June 25, 1958. He is another little cotton top with pretty blond hair and those big blue eyes that he got from his mom and his dad. I know Shirley has the most patience in the world with her little ones, and Charles never comes home without a big welcome and dinner on the table. Roger is the responsible child.

Jan and Pat are doing good and enjoying their married life. Jan loves living in Valdosta and walks the twelve blocks to town, just for the exercise. Pat had an insurance policy that his mom gave him, for when it matured on his twenty-first birthday, he could cash it in. They could finally buy a car in March, and right after that, they took off to New York for two weeks so Jan could meet his folks. They had a very small Italian family.

Pat's only brother was born when he was fourteen years old, so he grew up as an only child, you might say. He lived out on the north shore of Long Island, which is just a commuter town for people who live there instead of in New York City. They ride the train to the city to work each day. Pat's godmother is a seamstress and makes the sample dresses for a dress designer, and she commutes each day. Other than that, it is just rolling farms, mostly potato farms. His family is a butcher-shop family. Most of the men have private butcher shops in different areas of town. Pat's dad's butcher shop is out by Walt Whitman's birthplace, on Walt Whitman Road.

Webb's brother Coley is down here looking for a job. The poor man just doesn't have many job skills even though he was in the army. He finally just gives up on jobs down here and has reenlisted in the army and is now going to live in Oregon, I believe. My brother is a meter reader for the water company, and that keeps him busy enough to keep him out of trouble, I thought. But I did just find out he and the boys decided to make a jug of homemade Corn Buck and let it ferment on the roof so no one would see it. I guess they are always up to something, and with Jan and Pat coming for Thanksgiving, I'm just fit to be tied.

I am all excited Pat and Jan are here for the Thanksgiving holiday, and we have a real good one. They both look good, and Jan has just found out she is going to give us our next grandchild in March of 1959. Maybe this time I will get to make a little dress. She was out picking up the grass for Gil when he cut it beside the canal and just scooped it up by the armful. A little brown snake fell out of the grass and scared her so bad she just screamed. Gil told her to get inside, a scare like that would mark the baby. She laughed at his superstition and went inside, but when my first granddaughter, Deborah Acompora, was born on January 27, 1959, she did have a birthmark on her belly button. She wasn't premature because of that, but she was early by a couple of months and reached five pounds in ten days, and they got to bring their beautiful little daughter home. Debbie was baptized in the Catholic Church as was her mom, Jan.

We didn't have to wait too long before we saw Debbie. We had some very sad news. Webb's mother had a stroke in the first of March and passed away. We had to go home to the funeral, and the whole family was devastated. She truly was the matriarch of that family. Jan didn't have time to get someone to watch her baby on such short notice, but when she got to Ma Furney's house, there was Aunt Leona Head, taking care of Ona Fay's baby, Carla Kay. Aunt Leona was the black lady that had taken care of Jan when she was small, and she was just so excited to take care of Jan's baby too. Jan was sure glad to see her.

I no longer make quilts except for my grandchildren. Of course we don't need them in Florida, but I did finally get to make some little baby clothes in a preemie size. You see, they didn't make preemie sizes back in 1959, so I was happy to make Debbie her first clothes. The kids are wasting no time now with the grandkids. Charles's little boy Roy Earnest Furney was born on September 4, 1959. What a fine healthy boy. We now have five grandsons and just one little girl. Shirley has said that is it, she has no intention of having another boy, four is enough. When she lines up four little boys for a bath at night, with the oldest barely five years old, she has her hands full. Charles is now working for Destiny, building mobile homes. That's OK. Webb and I have decided what we will take to Georgia this year for Christmas: a great big swing set we can strap on the roof of the car that we have already bought and we pray we get it there in one piece.

My sister's daughter Vanada Copeland has also married her high school sweetheart, Harry Lanzillotti, of Richmond, Virginia. They were the first to have a wedding in the new Pleasant Hill Church on November 26, 1959.

Webb's friend is returning to Florida, and we will be moving over the holidays. We have enjoyed this nice home beside the canal so much. We will go move into Kinzy Apartments right down the road.

Jerale, far right at Kinzy Apartments

Roger, Shirley, Tommy, David, and Charles Furney in Florida

Part 2

Lorene Continues

Hereafter Lorene will be referred to in the second person. This portion was written by Jan Furney Acompora.

Lorene at Twin Lakes with Charles, Mae, Jeanette, Vern, Jan, Jerale, and Gil

Fortieth Move, 1960: Kinzy Apartments

Yes, Lorene's hard work and good ethics along with her deep faith in God to help her and her family survive are paying off. As she watched Jeanette become a world traveler leaving for Okinawa with her young son Jerry, who was only seven or eight months old, she reminded Jeanette to make sure her cash was pinned by a big safety pin in her bra. There was no doubt in her mind that she could safely travel alone, and she prayed to pass these ethics along to her last four children who were at such an impressionable age. Hard work and good ethics was the passport to the world. If one worked hard and saved his money, there were no limits to what one could do, but you must always share what you have with others. What good is something you think is wonderful if you can't share it with others? There will always be the poor among us and those who can't take care of themselves. Of course, Mae is the one who is always looking for these people, with her big heart.

Lorene and Webb have moved their family into an apartment complex. They are not too happy about this situation as their family has never adjusted to apartment living very well. Their big family has shrunk. Three of their children have left the nest, so to speak. Charles, Jeanette, and Jan are all married and have started their own families. The four young ones miss living in a house where they could just walk out the door and fish in the canal if they wanted to. However, the apartment complex is on a big lake, and that isn't hard to get adjusted to as there are many families with children in the complex. Jerale has already made friends with a bunch of little boys around eight to ten years old. Melba, Mavis, and Jerale have new friends at school.

With the apartment complex being even closer to the market, Lorene and Webb commute to work together, where she is at work very early and Webb is on his job by daybreak. She loves her job in the bakery and has at last gotten out of farm work. She is such an accomplished cake decorator she no longer feels she is only suited for being a laborer the rest of her life. The people she meets on a daily basis have heightened her curiosity about the world around her, and the other merchants in the market love being with her. Her happy disposition spreads out to all around her, and she is so well read she can communicate with people from all walks of life.

They still go to Wellman's dance on Saturday night and continue to take the neighborhood children with them, where there is an alcohol-free environment and the teenagers can have fun, and they all love to dance. Melba is now starting to become a lovely young lady. The young ones are at the Lake Worth Casino beach so much; Melba has almost become a blonde. Her natural strawberry-blond hair is even lighter, and the hairdresser just won't believe she doesn't bleach her hair. Mae is starting to notice boys as she and Melba hang out at the Sugar Shack where they go after school. They are both in Lake Worth Junior High. Jerale still loves the woods, and he and his little friends are forever exploring through them along the canals. While on one of the explorations, Jerale decided to see if he could outrun an alligator. After a short run, he decided to climb up a tree. He definitely couldn't outrun the gator. Vernon has met a young lady named Ethel and is getting quite serious with her. She is from Indiana, and her family lives near us.

Jeanette and her family are doing well in Okinawa. They live on the base in housing that is called Quonset huts. They are built to withstand very bad monsoons. Jeanette has experienced one and said she was a little worried, but they just lit up their light sticks, and when the fierce winds let down and the sliding glass door stopped bowing, everything was fine. Her *mamasan* (the maid) is very good with Jerry. When he isn't feeling well or he gets a cold, the *mamasan* uses local remedies on him, and Jeanette is amazed at how well they work. She is very happy, and she and

Al have so many new friends, and she has friends from Georgia there. Because they are all so far away from their families, they are like a big family there.

Lorene is happy that Charles is moving forward with his four boys. His hard work and belief that he can do well, even with a disability, is paying off. Like his mother, he is never a quitter. His new home, which he built after the first one burned, is in the same location, on three acres of property where the boys can run and play outside with plenty of room in their new home for his large family. When any of our family goes to visit Georgia, they end up at Charles's house. Shirley keeps a tight rein on the boys and is really happy she will soon have one in school. Roger will be the first one to start school at Culbertson.

Jan and Pat are still in Valdosta, Georgia, and are planning to move to Palm Beach in April. Pat is leaving the Air Force and will use his aircraft and engines skills to work at Pratt & Whitney in West Palm. Lorene is all excited about this move, and her only granddaughter will finally be near her grandma Furney and granddad. She was happy that last summer Jan and Debbie spent a couple of months on Long Island with Pat's family. Jan loved Long Island and was happy to be able to get around with a good road map. Lorene's family was always so transient Jan was surprised to find out that Pat's family had never traveled much and never took advantage of living near the water. They didn't go fishing or to the beach. Of course, she took Debbie and Pat's little brother Joe to the beach often. When she was ready to go into Brooklyn, New York, to visit Debbie's godfather, she was surprised when Pat's mother commented, "You aren't taking the baby, are you?" The women in their family never ventured outside their hometown and especially without their husbands. Well, they found out Jan did travel and, yes, with the baby. Lorene was happy Jan was traveling but couldn't wait for them to travel south with Debbie.

Forty-First Move, 1960: Florida Drive, near Lake

Lorene is getting settled into her home on Florida Drive. This is a very nice little subdivision with nice lawns, and the hedges between the houses are all beautiful with very thick hibiscus plants. There is a big lake a couple of blocks in back of the house, which the neighborhood children enjoy swimming in. The children gather there almost every day to swim, and the girls enjoy working on their tans.

In the meantime, Jeanette has returned from Okinawa with Al, who has been stationed in Rapid City, South Dakota. Lorene was so happy when they came for a visit before they went to their new home. Jerry is now quite a big little boy, almost four years old. After some discussions with Jeanette, Gil has decided to move to South Dakota and see how he likes the Midwest. He has found a job he likes and an apartment. Jeanette is delighted to have some of her family with her. Shortly afterward Mae has decided to go join Jeanette and Gil in South Dakota and moves in with Jeanette and Al in their home. At first she just babysits Jerry, but she quickly adjusts and finds a job also.

Lorene is having quite a few changes in her life. She only has Vernon, Melba, and Jerale left at home. They can enjoy their children at home and enjoy visiting the ones who live out of state. Lorene enjoys going to the lake and Lantana Beach to swim after work. She likes to be in the water in the late afternoon when the sun isn't quite so hot.

It is finally April, and Pat and Jan have moved to West Palm with little Debbie, and Pat is working at Pratt and Whitney. They have gotten an apartment nearby and are starting to look at houses, but Webb has encouraged them to revisit the developments after hurricane season is over. Pat carpools out to Pratt and Whitney with Darrell Presley, who is from Moultrie and has taken a position there and moved down with his wife, Linda McCoy Presley, who is from Berlin.

Debbie has made their life complete for the moment. Lorene stops by and picks Debbie up before she even picks Webb up from work each day, and they take Debbie to play in the shallow water at Lake Osborn after dinner. On the way to the lake, there is a big roadside sign advertising a dairy with a huge picture of a cow on it. The minute Debbie sees it, she jumps up and down saying, "Cow, cow," and they stop the car and let her run to the sign with her little arms reaching up for the cow. You better believe Webb will have his men (he is now a supervisor in his department) keep that grass cut short in front of the sign so his only granddaughter can run to it each time she sees it.

It has been a great summer, but hurricane season is here, and Hurricane Carol has her eye on Florida. She finally makes it to shore in September. Jan, Pat, and Vernon tried swimming, but the surf beat them up pretty good. Lorene and Webb are bringing Debbie to Jan's house to sit out the hurricane. Jan has insisted it will be safer there since her house had a higher elevation. Well, so much for her idea of higher elevation. After the storm passed, she had water up to her front porch for three weeks and Lorene had maybe a little puddle in her yard when she got home.

Her happy moments with Jan's baby were about to slow down as in October, Pat had to take a leave of absence from Pratt and Whitney. His dad needed him in New York. He would have to help his family out with the butcher shop. Little did they know that would turn into twelve years? Her and Webb's heart are broken when they took their baby granddaughter away. They had bought every cute little sun suit and pair of sneakers she had worn, and now they felt empty. Vernon has also decided to move to South Dakota with his siblings. Their family was decreasing, and their neighbor was a grouch who complained about everything. They were ready to leave their home near the lake.

Forty-Second Move, 1960: Bermuda Road, Stucco House near County Barn

They only have Melba and Jerale living home now, and Lorene has advanced in the bakery and now has a follow-up business where they are very busy, but she still has time to do all the specialty cakes. Webb now has a lot of time on his hands if he finishes work before her, and he now drops her off at work and picks her up in the afternoon. When she has to finish up a cake before she leaves, he is unhappy, and he has become jealous of her devotion to her job, but she is happy that she can have a job that she really loves and that is rewarding to her, as well as she is providing income for her family.

She is happy living near her sister and her brothers in Belle Glade. On their days off, she and Webb can really enjoy their time to travel around south Florida as well as their trips to Lantana and Riviera beaches. The children at home still enjoy going to Wellman's to dance on Saturday nights and also taking their friends to the beach for cookouts on Sundays.

They are getting ready for their trip to Georgia for the holidays. They will go to Charles and Shirley's with Melba and Jerale. There is very little room in the car. It is packed with toys for those four little boys as well as Melba's and Jerale's gifts. The children in Georgia can't wait for their grandparents to get there. They know Grandmother and Granddad always bring a lot of stuff for them.

This year there is a big announcement. Shirley has had a tubal ligation, but surprise! Shirley became pregnant before the surgery. She is expecting a little one in April. Everyone is excited, except Shirley. She is not ready to go through this again. With their smaller family, Lorene is moving again after the holidays. She and Webb are back home, and her brother J. E. from Belle Glade is coming to help her and Webb move into the Tradewind

Apartments over by West Palm Beach Airport. She no longer has that big bunch of boys to help out. Jerale is still just a preteen. Melba is in her teens and is planning to join Mae in South Dakota. She will live in Jeanette's home with Mae.

Forty-Third Move, 1961: Tradewind Apartments, near West Palm Beach Airport

Well, her family has certainly been busy. Charles's wife, Shirley, is expecting a baby in April, and now Jeanette and Jan are both pregnant, expecting babies in the late summer. Melba is now living with Jeanette in South Dakota, and Jeanette is having Jerale move there. He is old enough to be a bag boy at the Base Exchange and make quite a bit of money in tips while he is not in school. He will attend school in Rapid City.

It is now springtime, and Lorene has just learned she actually has another granddaughter. Charles and Shirley are in seventh heaven. Charlotte Diane Furney arrived on April 8, 1961. Shirley finally has her little girl, and she knows that definitely is her last baby. She can now go out and buy all the little dresses she wants.

Most of Lorene's family is in South Dakota, and now that Vernon is living with Gil, they are having a ton of fun. When everyone is home for the weekends, they all head for the hills, the hills of South Dakota. Gil and Jeanette always know where all the best fishing spots are, and Al goes along with the rest. The boys hunt a lot, and even Jerale knows how to hunt rabbits and tells Jerry about how to shoot a—rabbit. This bunch of little Southern kids is getting quite an education.

Mavis and Melba have bought a car together to get back and forth to work. They just forgot you were supposed to check the oil periodically. Now they all have to learn how to drive in snow. Little did they imagine they would ever see so much snow that was so deep, it was to the top of the windows to their homes. They assure Lorene that they are all just fine, and Jerale is doing really good in school with some special tutoring. At that time, no one knew Jerale was dyslexic, or that it was hereditary, and he wasn't the only Hart child who had it.

Well, she has some time for herself now and actually has time to read anytime she wants to. She and Webb are still going to Lantana Beach in the evenings. Once the surf was a little rough, but Webb convinced her she would be fine as long as she stayed by the lifeguard rope that went out in the water. That day they both learned what a riptide was. As they were trying to get back to shore, the undertow kept dragging them both back out. They finally made it in but became very aware a person had to pay attention when there was a riptide warning.

Jan is away from her family, and Lorene knows she is having a few problems with her pregnancy now that she is five months along. Lorene can't just jump up and run to New York even though she wants to. Jan's doctor is giving her hormone shots every week and everything seems fine, but Nicholas Charles Acompora, II, was born June 25, 1961, looking just like his mom with strawberry-blond hair to match his sister's auburn red hair. He was born a month early, but everything went well and he is just fine. A month after Nick's birth he was baptized in the Catholic Church the same as his sister was. His godparents took him with his dad to be christened, and of course, there was the big party after.

Lorene barely had time for a breather before she got the call: Jeanette had just had her another little granddaughter. Diane Veglia was born on August 29, 1961. Diane was another beautiful little brunette who looked very Italian like her dad. Perfect in every way.

Well, just as Vivian and Jeanette had done when they had their boys, Vivian had just had a little girl. Penny Laura Cardin was born a few days before Jeanette's baby, on August 25, 1961. It seems like the Hart family was on a roll. Leona's daughter Velma, who was a week older than Jan, had her son James Garrett Nelson Jr. on October 13, 1961. Then Neal Hart and Verdie had their little girl Rhonda Gail Hart on August 18, 1961. These were all the great-grand children of Jerry and Eva Hart. Their grandchild was also born in 1961 to Brannon and Bunny Hart. Brannon Jerome "Jerry" Hart was born January 5, 1961. It must have been a cold winter in 1960.

It is now the fall of the year, and Lorene and Webb are deciding what to take to Georgia for Christmas when they go. They can't wait to see the grandchildren and especially the baby Charlotte. She must be spoiled rotten by now. The boys are all old enough to really have a good time playing with trucks and cap pistols or maybe a little fishing rod for Roger.

She and Webb are very happy with their lives and feel they have made some big headways into their future. They have some good benefits, and Webb is proud to be investing into their future, but they miss their family who has now moved to different states.

Melba decides she will return home. Lorene is missing the quiet life, and she and Webb have decided to move back to her dad's house in Georgia. Mavis, Gil, Vernon, and Jerale are still enjoying South Dakota.

Our Forty-fourth Move, 1962: Back to My Dad's Place in Georgia

Lorene is back in her dad's block house that he had originally built for her. They are all excited about being back among family in Georgia. She and Webb are getting older and not as anxious to do farm work anymore. They spend some time doing farm work but have just gotten themselves involved in a business of Lorene's brother-in-law Ellis Copeland. He has built a beer joint just outside of Berlin and decided Webb would be just the one to work it. Webb knows the bar business, but Lorene knows Webb and has decided she will go along to help, not that she doesn't trust him.

Her big family is very busy as they are all growing up and meeting the big world with open arms. Melba is now dating a local boy, Sandy Deas, and they are really serious about each other. The group from South Dakota are still working hard and having fun. Jeanette's husband, Al, has plans for transferring to New Hampshire this year, and Jeanette will move with him. Charles's family is going at full speed. The oldest is now in school. Roger is such a smart little boy and loves his brothers and sister. He is such a reliable child and is a big help with the older children. He will be in second grade, and his little brother David will be going to school with him this year. Shirley won't know what to do with only three children at home.

Jan and Pat have found a piece of property they like and have started construction on a new home for their family. She said it is a Cape Cod style with upstairs and a basement. Pat's grandfather died in the beginning of the year, and they will live in his home until the construction on their home is finished. Mavis has moved to Jan's home in New York to see if she would like living in the northeast. She is only nineteen years old and has already gotten a job and is dating and has met some nice friends. Gil has returned to West Palm Beach and has also started building a new home off Kirk Road. He is not far from the area where she and Webb have lived and worked since they first moved to Florida. Lorene is thinking of the advantages she enjoyed living in Florida as opposed to running a beer joint in Georgia with no benefits and no health insurance in case one of them should become ill. Gil is pressuring Lorene to move back and live with him in his new home when it is finished.

Jan and Pat build a home in New York

Forty-Fifth Move 1963, Hypoluxo Road, West Palm Beach

Well, this is the beginning of 1963, and a very busy time. Lorene was laid back and not too busy while they were tending the beer joint, but now her life is back to work every day. She has gotten her job back in the bakery and is so glad to once again be the top cake decorator. Her boss, Kathy, was only too happy to see her smiling face and know her old customers would be back to have the cake lady handle their special orders.

She and Webb have moved into a small little house over on Hypoluxo Road where they will live until Gil gets his house finished. The new house is over by her sister Eula Mae's. She will be so happy to be back in that area with her sister, and Lorene has a deep affection for Eula Mae's mother-in-law, Ma Taylor. Ma Taylor is a great cook, and all the kids look forward to eating anything she cooks.

Well, she has bought all new furniture again and is really happy. Jerale is now getting ready to return to West Palm Beach when the school term is out. He will be traveling from South Dakota to Florida by bus, and it will take a few days for the trip. She is a little concerned but knows he only has bus changes a couple of times. The biggest was to change from Greyhound to Trailways about halfway home. Her youngest, Jerale, is back home with them. He has become quite a handsome young man. He is just fifteen years old now but looks all grown up. Webb got his seniority back and is working every day with the county in his old position. It is comforting to know they will now have health insurance, and Webb can again put something into a pension for when they retire.

Melba married her young man, Sandy Deas, and remained in Georgia when Lorene left. She is in love and happy. Sandy's family is prominent, and his dad owns a little grocery store in Berlin.

Sandy is a talented musician and plays guitar in a country music band. He wears his hair like Elvis Presley's, and Melba is crazy about it. She does not have to work and will be a stay-at-home wife to just take care of the home. She is quite sure his family will make sure they are OK.

In the meantime, Mae is also in love and is marrying her new love, Michael Vanacore Jr. Yes, Lorene is getting another Italian son in law. They have a big wedding, and the reception is at the Vernon Valley Inn, in Huntington, New York, where Jan and Pat also live. Jan and Pat moved into their new home in October last year, and the girls are really close. Jan is a stay-at-home mom, and JR, Mae's new husband, doesn't want her to work, just be a stay-at-home wife also.

JR's mom took Mae out shopping before they were married and told her to pick out whatever she wanted for their apartment and not to worry about cost. They shopped until Mae had every piece of furniture, all the linens, everything for the kitchen and bath she could find. When she walked into her new apartment, everything in it was new, and her husband was madly in love with her. She was happy. She had made all new friends, her sister lived nearby, and she loved Jan's kids, and the kids were crazy about their Aunt Mae and uncle JR.

Italian families are a lot of fun and want to party over anything. Mae's new Italian family was really warm and friendly. Her father-in-law had about three acres of property where JR's family lived, and the back of the property was all garden where he grew all kinds of vegetables and fruit for the family. He owned a wholesale greenery business, which sells greenery products to florist shops. This was in New York City, in Harlem. JR and his brother Dominick worked in the family business and commuted to the city each day. Pat and JR have a lot of the same friends, and both their families migrated to Long Island from Italy around the same time, so both families are well established in the Huntington community.

With the weddings and such all going on, Jeanette is preparing to move to New Hampshire. Al is being transferred there from South Dakota. Everyone up north is happy. Jeanette will be closer to Jan and Mavis. They can visit by car in only two or three hours.

Mr. Sandy D. Deas Jr. marries Melba Furney

Mavis Furney marries Michael Vanacore Jr.

Forty-Sixth Move, 1963 and 1964: Pine Drive, Gil's New Home

Lorene is all moved into Gil's new home, and everyone is so happy. She now has an all-new kitchen with the latest appliances, the bedrooms are all nice, and the house is big enough for them all. Jerale is the only child still living home other than Gil.

Vernon has met a young lady from Denver, Colorado, and is going to stay out in the Midwest. They plan to marry in the near future, and Vern will be converting to Catholicism. Cynthia Cunningham is Catholic, and her older sister is a nun in the Catholic Church. Lorene is happy to hear of Vern and Cyndi's wedding plans and is looking forward to meeting Cyndi. She will now only have her two sons that are single. Gil, so far shows, no intentions of getting married in the near future, and Jerale is still having too much fun. Once when he was telling Jan about swinging from a long vine into the Palm Beach canal to go swimming, she asked him if he was nuts because of the alligators. He replied, "Do you really think I'm stupid? I let my friends swing in first."

The year of 1964 is another banner year for additions to the Furney family. Melba started it out first. Sandy Divadus Deas Jr. was born on January 23, 1964. Melba was such a small little woman to have such a big baby. He was such a healthy-looking baby, and the grandparents on both sides of the family were ecstatic. Her baby girl is starting her own family. Mavis and Jan are each expecting babies in August of 1964.

Vernon has now married the young lady he met in Denver. Lorene so wanted to go and be present at her son and Cyndi's wedding but just could see no way at that time. Vernon and Cynthia Cunningham were married on March 31, 1964, in Rapid City, South Dakota. Just a small wedding, which later was followed up by a Catholic Church wedding. She planned to visit them when they were settled into their own home and did fly into Chicago for that visit with them in their home in Rockford, Illinois, where they would raise their family.

In 1964 it was also the year of the World's Fair in New York. Jeanette and Al are now living in New Hampshire, which is fairly close to Al's family. Even though they live in New Hampshire, they have bought a home in Amesbury, Massachusetts, for rental property until they retire. They brought Al's family down to New York for the World's Fair. Jan couldn't go because of her pregnancy, but she could enjoy having guests like Al's family. Everyone went to the World's Fair, and when the whole thing was over, Pat's dad, bought a picnic table from the Belgium pavilion, which Pat and Jan used for years. Al's family had a big lunch of Italian food on one of the days they were on Long Island. Jan had met some of his family but not Al's sisters and their husbands. They all had a good time.

Jan is anxious to have her children come visit Lorene, and she can't seem to get away because she is again having a difficult pregnancy. At five months pregnant again, the doctor has put her on bed rest this time. She is not allowed out of bed for two months. Thank God she lives near Mae, and Mae goes over to care for Jan's family each day while Pat is at work. When he comes home, she then goes home. JR is so fond of Jan's children, and each Friday he brings little Debbie a small bouquet of sweetheart roses. She thinks she is so special. Finally the two months are up, and Jan is so happy to be able to bring her young family to visit Lorene for two weeks.

She can't wait. Jan, Pat, and children are all checked into the nearby motel and are so happy to be in Florida. She is anxious to renew her friendship with little Debbie, and this is the first time she has seen Nicky. Nicky at first clings to his sister but then warms up to her and the family. After she takes them on a fishing trip and teaches Nicky how to catch little fish, the kids are ready to go anywhere with them. They go to the lake and the beach to go swimming. After this visit she always sees Jan's family every year on or around Nicky's birthday, depending when school is out. Nicky always wants his grandma Furney to make his birthday cake for June 25, and she does.

Pat and Jan are barely gone, it seems, when Pat is telephoning to say Jan is about to deliver baby number 3. Stephanie Acompora is born on August 4, 1964. With all the excitement, Mae goes into the hospital the day after Jan. Her doctor says the baby is too small and stops the contractions. That night Lorene gets another phone call. Jan's baby has a congenital heart disease and passed away around midnight on August 7, 1964. It was a sad time, with Pat and Jan not knowing what to do next. On the day Jan was going home from the hospital, the doctor had successfully stopped Mae's contractions, and Mae will be going home from the hospital with Jan. This is such a shock to Lorene. Nobody expected this. Her heart is broken, but there is no way she can go to New York, so she just thanks the good Lord that Mae and Jan have each other, along with their families.

They had a private burial, and Stephanie was buried in the National Cemetery, near where the other Acomporas are buried, which is located in Melville, Long Island. This is part of the Huntington Township. She was baptized a Catholic before she died. Mae and JR were listed as the godparents, although they didn't really have a christening.

Mae returned to the hospital two days later and delivered a healthy big baby boy. Michael Vanacore III was born on August 9, 1964. Mae and baby Michael are doing fine. Lorene was so happy to get the good news her new grandson was a big healthy baby, and Mae was doing good as a brand-new mom. Michael was taken to be baptized in the Catholic Church. JR's sister Betty is Michael's godmother, and a nephew was the godfather. There was a big party after the christening, and all the *Comadas* (old Italians) came to leave money under the pillow of the new baby Vanacore. This was an Old Italian tradition.

After the busy summer, Lorene is ready for a trip to Georgia to clear up her brain. This year she will be going to Georgia for Christmas. She can at least hold Little Sandy, and spoil him. They always have Christmas at Charles's home. She knows Charles's family can't wait to see her and Webb.

Forty-Seventh Move, 1965: Back to Kinzy Apartments

Lorene lived with Gil in his new house for about two years and again discovered it is not too wise to live too near your children. They decided to move back into an apartment since they only had Jerale home now, and rather than put the pressure of living with parents on Gil, they would move to their own place.

So many things are happening this year; Lorene can barely keep up with work and family. Jerale is the only child at home now. She is keeping up with the bakery work, and she and her family are well known and loved in the family at the farmers' market. The market is like a strip mall with many different businesses that have been there for years, as has the bakery. When Kathy leaves for vacation, Lorene is in charge of the bakery. She tends it most of the time anyhow. The bakers look to her to find out what she needs baked for the next day. She makes sure the display is full of anyone's baked fantasies. She and her children have been there so many years now; they know all the other stores and its owners. Her favorite is the hoagie shop. Many times after her retirement, she would say, "What I wouldn't give for a good hoagie." Even when visiting other cities, she would order a hoagie but claimed they just didn't match up with her friend's.

She and Webb still have a good life and no longer have the troubles they had raising a large family. The finances are much better. Webb is more attentive to her now that she is out working on her on and not stuck on a farm with a new baby every two years. He no longer goes off to bars alone. He is more worried that she will go alone if he does, so he makes sure she is with him. When the children come for visits with their families, there is always a big picnic lunch packed by her, and off they go to Jupiter or John Prince Park. The families from West Palm and Belle Glade try to get together at least once a year for a big cookout. This year

Lorene's entire family, with all the grandchildren, hosted a big cookout over at Lake Worth Casino. Charles's children hadn't been to the beach since Charlotte was born. She was amazed and said to Shirley, "Mama, look at the size of that pond, you can't even see the other side." All had a good laugh with that.

Forty-Eighth Move, 1965: Mrs. Tiner's House

Lorene needs a home for when all those children come to visit now. They are all settled into Mrs. Tiner's house. Webb is really into auctions, and she makes sure to accompany him, to remind him he cannot buy everything he comes across that he fancies. Otherwise he will continue to buy things he likes even if they don't need it. Webb tends to get attached to things he likes and then never wants to resell them. She is good at putting a limit on how many treasures he brings home.

She and the boys love to fish. I don't think she has bought a fish since she moved to Florida. The men in her family really love fresh fish and know how to catch them. They always fish for snapper and snook, which are the family's favorites.

Sad times fell upon the family this year. Lorene's younger brother J. E., who lived in Belle Glade, had a pancreas attack and died suddenly. The family had to be rounded up as this was July, and many were on vacation. The highway patrol tracked down Wayne in Virginia, where he was on vacation with his family. This was a devastating loss since it was the first death of a sibling in the family. As years passed, several family members had bouts with pancreatitis, but not all were fatal or a result of being a heavy drinker. Decades later, one of her grandsons also died of pancreatitis.

There is big excitement in the family. Lorene has been invited to visit Jeanette's family in New Hampshire. She will be flying out in the fall. This will be her first trip by air, and Webb isn't happy. She has always traveled by car, and he wasn't able to travel for a long distance. Now he doesn't want to fly even though he will be there in a few hours. She is unhappy he doesn't want to fly, so she has decided to take her trips and will fly solo. She has learned if she wants to travel, all she has to do is say yes to her children.

It is time to leave for New Hampshire, and she is a little nervous. She remembered her friends' advice: "Just order a nice martini while you are on your flight." Lorene has never been one to have cocktails, but as soon as she boarded the flight, she ordered a double martini, relaxed, and she had a wonderful flight.

This was now October, in the fall of the year, and she had read and seen so many pictures of New England in the fall. It exceeded her expectations. As her plane was coming in to Logan Airport in Boston, the entire ground was ablaze with the trees colored with orange, brown, and green. As Jeanette and family picked up Lorene and returned to the north for New Hampshire, she was just in awe. She asked Jeanette "Are all the roads here as beautiful as this?" as they were driving through the country with red and orange maple trees and green spruce trees, and the winding streams with white birch trees covered at the top with golden leaves. Jeanette couldn't wait to show her around, and she was so happy to be with her grandkids Jerry and Diane and renew her acquaintance with Al's family.

They went to Amesbury to see a house that Al and Jeanette had just purchased as an investment. Then it was time for her to go up to Maine and have a New England lobster, which had big claws that had to be cracked to eat (Florida lobsters don't have claws, you just eat the lobster tail). She was treated to homemade ice cream from Ben and Jerry's ice cream stand. (This was before they went commercial.) Now it is on up to Vermont, and that is where the fall colors are so spectacular, and also to purchase some maple syrup, which definitely didn't taste like Georgia's cane syrup but was very tasty.

On the way back, they took her to see Green Mountains. She had never seen a mountain let alone one in the fall of the year in Vermont. The little villages like Woodstock and the other little villages nestled in the foothills with their little country churches and stores were true beauty. Very much like the little towns down south where everybody knew their neighbors. When they came to the Green Mountain National Forest, Lorene just loved it with all the color. Some of Al's family has summer homes in Vermont.

Unfortunately she will have to leave Jeanette and Al and her wonderful grandchildren to return home to Florida, but not before she makes a quick trip to Long Island. Jeanette and family take her to the airport and see her off in a small propeller-driven plane heading to Long Island. They are all sad but make plans for a trip to Florida soon.

Mae and JR, along with little Michael, pick her up at the airport, and she is surprised to see that Long Island is all wooded with little villages here and there among the farms. She is happy to see Mae and JR and so excited to see her grandson Michael for the first time. Mae will take her all around Huntington and Huntington Station, which is on Long Island's north shore.

The beaches here are different since Huntington is a harbor town located on Long Island Sound. She gets to visit the Vanderbilt museum and Centerport beach. Michael is such a wonderful baby. You can tell his mom, Mae, stays at home and enjoys him. After a couple of days with them, Mae then takes her to Jan's home, which is in the country. She and Michael stay with Jan while the kids take her on a tour of the woods.

They are so anxious to spend some time with Grandma Furney. The children take her up the hill into the woods they love to play in. There is a five-acre zoning on the hill, and the houses are all far apart. There is just one road through the woods to each house. They are happy to show her where they make their sled run in the winter when it snows and the oak tree Debbie ran into before she was old enough to have better control of her sled. Of course every wood's has a pond, and this one is where the neighbor boy catches bullfrogs and sells them to the little kids for fifty cents each. Nicky was sad his had all hopped away after he brought them home. They show Lorene where their dad, Pat, banks the snow in a circle in the winter and keeps putting water into the circle, freezing it, until they have an ice-skating rink in their own backyard. After coming out of the woods with her arms full of branches of fall foliage, she is sad to have to leave her family in Huntington. The next day Mae and JR are picking her up to go to Kennedy Airport for her return flight to Florida. They all bid Grandma Furney good-bye until they get to Florida next summer for Nicky's birthday.

Her Florida family was so happy to see their favorite cook back home. They all missed her but couldn't wait to hear her stories of her visit to see the Yankees in the family. Jerale is now growing up fast and dating. Gil has his eye on someone special, and she is surprised as he has been able to remain single until now.

She wasn't the only one to lose a brother this year. Webb's brother Bill committed suicide on New Year's Eve after attending a party. Bill moved to Plant City when Lorene and Webb were newlyweds.

Forty-Ninth Move, 1966: High Ridge Road

Well, things are moving right along for Lorene. She is so thankful for her life with a good job for herself and Webb, with benefits and promise of a retirement pension sometime in the future. Her home in her heart will always be in Georgia, but they just can't produce enough income and satisfy her yearning for knowing more about the world she lives in. Her children are all living up and down the East Coast and the Midwest.

Their house on High Ridge Road has a big field of mangos behind them. There is plenty of room for the dog to run and to keep Jerale's sense of adventure going. All of the kids can come and visit with plenty for everybody to do.

The northern families were down in June just as soon as school was out up north, Mae and Jan's families included. Everyone stayed at the Sage and Sand Motel in Boynton Beach. All the kids stayed in the rooms there, and she and Webb came over during the day to visit while all the kids whoop it up in the swimming pool. Her family has grown too large for everyone to stay in one home. Webb's brother Coy used to take his family here on vacation, and now her family will find it just the place to be when visiting their parents.

Al has gone to Korea for a temporary tour of duty for eighteen months, and Jeanette will not be accompanying him. She, with Jerry and Diane, will be staying near Lorene in an apartment down by the Intracoastal Waterway. The children will really miss their dad but are happy to be in warm Florida, where summer lasts all year. Diane has played on the steps of the pool until she has actually learned to swim by herself. Jerry has started a saltwater aquarium inside the apartment and fills it with baby fish from the water by the front door. Jeanette has taken a part-time job, and Diane will be the queen at Lorene and Webb's. As far as her grandparents are concerned, while her mom is at work, she can do no wrong.

Without failure, every weekend Lorene gets the food ready, and Webb is ready for a cookout at John Prince Park. All the children and friends they like will be there. They can kayak, fish, swim, or just sit in the shade and enjoy the outdoors, but they all get together on weekends.

Webb, Lorene, and Jan at Sage and Sand Motel

Gil is finally ready to make the big step. In April he married Betty Herrell, whom he has known and danced with for quite some time. They had a beautiful wedding, with Jerale as his best man and Jerry as ring bearer, and Diane was the flower girl. Everyone had a great time, and Gil and Betty finally got away from the family and friends who were still lingering around. Lorene, of course, made their wedding cake. She sees all the children all the time, but only Jerale is left at home now.

Mavis and Jan have made their trips home this year for a vacation, but Mae is now spending a lot of time at home. She has just had a beautiful little girl who is a spitting image of her dad, JR. Michelina Vanacore, born August 2, 1966, named after JR's mom, is so beautiful, with very Italian features and is the best baby ever. Michael is only two, and Mae has her hands full. He is smart, and just before Michelina was born, she heard a crash and was so surprised to see Michael in a heap of blankets on the floor with his crib. He had unscrewed the screws that held his crib up. Once when Mae and JR were sleeping, he decided to go next door, in the snow, to have breakfast with his friend. When questioned how he got the chain lock off the door, he promptly picked up the broom and showed them how to slide the chain lock over. He was only two years old. Well, his sister is very smart too. When she was in her playpen, she looked up and said, "What's that?" as she pointed to the leaves in a tree. Most kids say Mama or Dada, but she started out with sentences. Aunt Jan is so tickled that she and Uncle Pat are Michelina's Godparents. She had a beautiful christening and is just the best baby ever. Grandma Lorene is just dying to get her hands on her but will have to wait a few months until Mae will be ready to visit Florida.

Jerale has settled down a little, and his girlfriend, Delores, is Jeanette's babysitter when Jeanette is working. Jerale is working with his dad at the county still and has become pretty responsible. He goes fishing with Webb's friend Bill. Jerale is a certified diver and is always looking for a good place to dive, and Bill can always dive with Jerale. He just never gets enough of fishing and diving.

It is now time to go to Charles's home for Christmas. Jeanette and her family will also be going. They will all meet up with Melba's family and Jeanette and Charles will help Santa put together five bicycles this Christmas Eve and, they finish in time to even get in a little sleep before the kids all wake up.

Lorene is pleased to announce she now has another new daughter-in-law. It is September 1967, and Jerale has married

Delores Ball, the attractive young lady who is babysitting Jeanette's children now that Jeanette is back in Florida. They are very young and very much in love. Their wedding was a simple ceremony with close friends and family. Jerale and Delores have moved into their own apartment, and since the family has known her for some time, everyone is wishing them the best of luck.

Now all the children are out and on their own. Lorene now has something new to think about. She and Webb are back to living their own life without the bustle of a big family. Mae's baby is now almost two years old, and she has brought her family to Florida. Her husband is a hard worker and has no problem with finding a job immediately. Mae is back where she grew up, and with family and old friends. Lorene is so happy to have Mae in her everyday life again. She is such a fun person. Mae has now found a huge house on Military Trail, and there is plenty of room for all of them to live in together. They will all move into the new home, and the children will have an opportunity to bond with their grandparents.

Mr. D. Jerale and Delores Furney are married

Mr. Gilbert and Betty Furney get married

Fiftieth Move, 1967 and 1968:
Military Trail with Mae and JR and Children

Now that Lorene has moved in with Mae, she is starting to rethink her sanity. She didn't ever want to be a burden to her children. She is now under someone else's roof, and all the decisions are made by someone else. Is this the independence she was thinking? It has been a long time since she and Webb have heard the regular patter of little feet and having someone else doing the disciplining. She is definitely not happy having someone else controlling her life. She decides to speak with Webb. "Are you really happy with someone else running your life?" His answer was quick: "I have always been the head of our family, and we are still a family, it's time to do something." It didn't take long to explain the situation, and Mae agreed with her mom. After only being there for two months or so, it is time to start packing.

Fifty-First Move, 1967 and 1968: Back to Tradewinds Apartments

She and Webb are so relieved to be alone again. They are so happy to not be bothered by anything but going to work and enjoying their family, which is in a growth spurt again. They are back into their habit of going swimming in the evenings, going to the auction, and enjoying their grandchildren, as they can now spoil them and take them home to their parents. They love having Jerry, Diane, Michael, and Michelina to spoil by taking them to the market and buying things their parents won't buy them, and then going for an ice cream cone.

It has been eighteen months since Al went to Korea, and Jeanette has to meet him in Japan. Again Lorene has to swallow her hurt, having Jeanette go overseas again and taking those darling grandchildren with her. Al will not be coming back to the States this time. He has shipped out to Japan, and Jeanette has had everything shipped to Japan as she did before when Al was transferred. She and the rest of the family have good cookouts at the park on Sundays and watch the children swim and play. It is with heavy hearts as they all bid Al and Jeanette's family good-bye and watch them fly out for Japan. Thank God she doesn't have to go by ship this time. They have now arrived safely and can now communicate by telephone.

Since Jeanette and Al are now settled down, they have managed to be able to call the States at a better discount than they had in Okinawa. It is so good to be able to talk to them even if it is five hours' difference. The children are so excited to be in Japan and are experiencing things they never dreamed of. Jerry is in the Boy Scouts and gets to tell his grandma Furney about the areas around Tokyo he is seeing on field trips, and Diane is dancing Japanese dances and sings little Japanese songs to her.

Hopefully the time will go faster these three years. Jeanette has bought her mom a tape machine, and they exchange tapes more than letters so Lorene can hear the children's voices.

Things are also happening at home as well in Georgia. She exclaims, "Webb, we have to go to Georgia soon. Melba has just had a little girl." Yes, Stacey Adonice Deas was born on October 31, 1967. Everyone is so excited, and she was given Mae's middle name also. She is a beautiful little blonde and has the bluest eyes. They made a quick trip to Georgia to visit her daughter Melba's family and reassure herself everything was fine. Lorene has had a very busy year. Jan and her family were there in the summer, and Jan took a young lady named Judy back to Long Island to help her out with the children now that she is working part time. Judy's mother was not getting along with the daughter, and Lorene took her in. Her mom gave Jan permission to take her out of state. Judy was only fifteen years old. Jan and Pat raised her with their own children until she was an adult.

Now that Mae is in town, they are all getting some good homemade Italian dishes. She cooks good, anyhow you like it, but no one ever has had meatballs and spaghetti like Mae cooks. Jan swears it's all in the sauce. She told Lorene to taste the sauce, and if you don't like the sauce, don't bother eating anything else.

Now she has had her holiday season with all the children down in West Palm. They had a beautiful spring in Georgia when she was there to visit the kids. She always loved the azaleas blooming along with the dogwood and redbud trees. It is hard to express the joy of seeing the southeast side of Moultrie at that time of year, and then on to Thomasville, which is the City of Roses. It has almost every home as a showcase of roses.

Now Lorene's family are all working hard to make up time so they can take those treasured holidays and vacations. Gil has announced they will be having a little one this year. Everyone either goes to the park for cookouts or Mae will surprise all of them with a big spaghetti dinner. She no longer tries to make a picnic big enough for everyone. She announces they should have a cookout, and everyone brings something, with the boys doing the grill work and the women watching all those babies.

Jan's and Charles's families have been for a visit this year. They all love going to the market where Lorene works and meeting her friends in the different stores. Charles's little boys love the Western wear store with the boots and hats. Jan's family likes the glass blower's store. They went home with glass paperweights, with *Nicky* and *Debbie* written on them. Of course, when Grandma says let's go swim, they are all ready.

Now the big day has arrived. Gil, the last one to get married, now has a new little girl. Carrie Lynn Furney has arrived on October 28, 1968. A beautiful little girl with her mother's big blue eyes. Betty and daughter are fine; we're not so sure about the anxious father. Now Gil is getting bored with his life of just working and fishing. He has managed to save enough to invest in property. He bought a forty-acre spread of part woodland and part fields near Moultrie, Georgia.

He can just imagine going squirrel hunting in those woods. He works very hard and gets a little pond established in the back field where his family of brothers, sisters, and their children will have many fish fries and a big bonfire the day after Thanksgiving for many years to come. He has a large section of property fenced in where he raises calves for market. The property came with a huge old barn, and by the time Carrie was two years old, she was proud to show Grandma Furney her new pony, whose name was Princess. By the time she was three or four years old, she would take Grandma Furney's hand and they would walk over to the fence and she would call Princess. As soon as she climbed up on the fence, the pony would come along beside her so she could grab her mane, jump up on her, and off they would go at a gallop. No bridle and no saddle. They were like one, with the wind blowing their hair.

Things are moving along quite nicely in the Furney family. Lorene tries to share their time evenly among the children as they have so many grandchildren now. It is pretty well established that Christmas is almost always at Charles and Shirley's home. Everyone agrees where they should have Easter because by now they have a big egg hunt after dinner with lots of egg hunters.

The baby of her family, Jerale, is now starting his own family. His first child, Dennis Gerald Furney, born June 24, 1969, came into the world with the blond hair and the big blue eyes. Delores and baby were doing fine and came home from the hospital as scheduled but were called to bring the baby back to the hospital after three days. There had been an outbreak of meningitis in the nursery in the hospital. Dennis tested positive, and they had to leave their new baby in for another few days with all those new baby gifts at home just waiting to be opened. Finally, baby Dennis was allowed to return home, and by then, Vernon had his big announcement.

Christopher Vernon Furney was born on July 30, 1969. What a big healthy boy he is. There was excitement all around. Cyndi and Vernon couldn't have been happier. Christopher had a big party after his godparents took him to be baptized in the Catholic Church. Lorene's family just continues to grow, and they are all happy and she is so pleased they are all buying property and building new homes. Vernon and Cyndi have just moved into their new home in Rockford, Illinois. As we all know, she and Webb has yet to buy their own home, but she passes on her dad's wisdom of how important it is to own property. By the time her last grandchild was born, each of her children owned their own home, and so did Lorene.

Time is just flying by, and it is time for Jeanette's husband, Al, to return to the United States. He will be stationed at McCoy Air Force Base in Orlando, Florida. It is 1970 this year, and Al will be retiring soon. They will buy a home this time instead of renting.

Orlando will be their permanent home. Lorene is excited to know the little birds are all flying back to Florida again.

Vernon will be the only one to remain in the Midwest. He and Cyndi have just had a new baby. Nichole Catherine Furney was born on February 11, 1971. She came into a family of love with both families so excited to have a new granddaughter. Her brother Christopher is excited, and Cyndi and this beautiful little redheaded baby with the big blue eyes are just fine. Her godparents also walked down with her to be baptized in the Catholic Church.

Charles, of course, would never move his family from the Hopewell community in Moultrie, Georgia. Gil is now established also in Moultrie, Georgia. Melba's family is still in Berlin, Georgia, and will remain there. Jan's husband, Pat, has asked for a transfer from his management in a nationwide company and wants to move his business to Orlando, Florida. They buy a house in Winter Park, Florida, which is a suburb of Orlando, and are just waiting to close on it. Mavis and Jerale will remain in West Palm with Lorene and Webb.

It is now the spring of 1971, with so much happening. The Hart family is having their family reunion this year in Orlando, out at the old gun club. She is so happy to get to see all her brothers and sisters with their families. All the families from out of town have set up tents and have a big camp out, with access to the commercial-sized kitchen and the big clubhouse. There are about 150 people here. It is Friday night, and the food is all in the refrigerators, including Vernon's birthday cake, because it is May and his birthday.

Well, the rains also come to Central Florida in May. After about two hours of a heavy downpour of rain, Jan has decided her entire family should go to her house. The furniture was delivered from New York that morning, and the four bedrooms all have beds set up and the linens set up in each room. Everybody else can grab sheets and pillows and sleep in the living room and den. Well, the rain continued to just pour all night. The young ones set up music in the kitchen, and everyone danced in the kitchen, living room, and den until the wee hours of the morning. What a party.

She was so glad she and Webb were in the Master bedroom with their own bath and no one to bother them. After everyone got coffee and breakfast, they all went down to the club, and it was so flooded. The tents had about six to twelve inches of water (depending where they were) in them. She knew the kids were all noisy, but at least they were all dry. After a few hours of drying out, everybody had a great time at the Hart reunion, which has continued all these years the last weekend of May and is now held in Valdosta, Georgia, at the Girl Scout camp.

Well, Lorene is back home getting ready for another trip. It is summer in Illinois, and she will be flying into O'Hare Airport to visit Vernon's family with the new baby. She has her usual double martini, which she only has when she is flying and before she knows it, she is on the ground.

Vernon meets her and brings her to Rockford, which is a little suburb to the west of Chicago. Vernon's little family is just wonderful in his new home. He has been taking classes in stained glass and has made the little stained glass window at the bottom of the stairs. Little Chris is a very active toddler, and he keeps his parents on their toes. Nichole is still an infant and is just happy to be held by her grandma Furney. They live near the river that runs through the center of the town of Rockford, and she enjoys walking along the banks and seeing all the wild geese that come in from Canada, and for the first time ever, she sees a chipmunk running around. Vernon and Cyndi take her somewhere new every day.

She has been on all the tours of Chicago. The boat tour and the bus tours, then a trip on an elevator to see Chicago from the top of the Sears Tower. She now learns they are going camping for a few days in Janesville, Wisconsin. It is only a couple of hours away and is so beautiful. She sees fauna and flowers she has never seen before, and the quiet woods are so relaxing. While there, she is taken on a boat tour of the Wisconsin dells. While riding in the boat in the dells, she looked up at solid stone cliffs and was amazed that the Indians lived in the caves on these cliffs. While they were there, the descendants of these Indians invited them to an Indian powwow. She saw the dances they performed and the native dress of their times. (These powwows were discontinued just before Jeanette and Jan were taken there by Vern in 2007.) This was all performed up in the woods above the steep cliffs of the dells. It was a little steep climb but well worth it. She has seen some great natural sights and is back to the reality of leaving her northwest family, and heading back to the airport and going home to Florida.

She is back home and back at work but not over all the excitement. She just loves to remember the great trip to the northwest. Now it is time for her to get back on the ground. The family is all planning to meet at Jan's home for Christmas this year, and she and Webb will be there. The girls have started cooking already. When Jeanette, Jan, Mavis, and Melba put their cooking hats on, you better believe there is some good food coming out of those ovens. Christmas Eve is traditional Italian, with pasta, fish, shrimp, and any kind of seafood.

When they have eaten all they can, and are ready for coffee, then the gift opening starts. The children can only open one personal gift because Santa is coming. Everyone is so excited because Lorene is getting a special present she wants very badly. The boys go into the garage and bring out her three-wheel bike. She is just overcome with joy. She goes out to the sidewalk where she and the kids ride all over the neighborhood.

Christmas Day is traditional American with the turkey and dressing and all the side dishes. She is out riding her bike with all the kids for the day. She just can't wait to get back to West Palm, where she can ride her bike to work on the sidewalk each day. Now that Jeanette and Jan are in Orlando, everybody takes a turn for Christmas. Next year Jeanette will host Christmas dinner. Little did Lorene know that the next year she and Webb would finally be in their own home where she would never have to move again?

Lorene is thanking God for all the wonderful gifts he has given her and her large family. Only God knows what is in her heart. At the end of last year, she felt as if she just couldn't continue moving forward. On November 3, 1970, her dad, Jerry E. Hart, passed away. After several years of Alzheimer's, his body gave up, and she dearly missed that creative mind of her dad's.

Fifty-Second Move, 1972:
Our Own Home by the Pecan Tree in Georgia

Well, she is so excited; she is showing off her biking skills, and depending on the weather, she rides her bike everywhere. The children are all settling down in their homes, and the boys are all at work again. The little ones are all back in school. Jan hasn't decided to go to work yet even though her children are in school. She, Charles, and Jeanette are cooking up a plan.

They have learned Webb will have to retire soon, and Lorene wants to move back to Georgia and leave her job also. Webb has had to go on disability because of his legs, and he will be able to collect his pension early as well as his disability benefits. They are concerned about where they will live, and the children don't want them to ever have to move again once they retire.

Jeanette has talked to Uncle Wayne's wife, Mary, about them having a home by the big pecan tree up the road from the block house her dad built for her. Uncle Wayne lost his life in a tragedy in 1970, and Aunt Mary will make the decision. She has agreed in writing that Lorene and Webb can live on that property until the last one passes away, and the property will revert back to her. Thank you, Aunt Mary; the children can get busy getting a permanent home that will be theirs.

Lorene doesn't know she will soon live in her old Pleasant Hill community again. The children go up to Georgia and spend every weekend working on getting the home ready and all the landscaping done. Charles's wife, Shirley, watches the children, cooks, and washes the children's clothes and sneakers that get muddy. Charles takes care of the local contractors, and the rest just pick up cotton stalks, clear the land, and help out where it is needed. When everything is ready and the last shrub is in, she and Webb come to look for houses. As she stood there with tears in her eyes, she couldn't believe the new home under the pecan tree is really theirs. Everything in it is new. She knows she is really home.

Now she is ready to just kick back and plant all the pretty flowers she wants to and is already picking on Webb to get the floor for the carport poured with concrete. She is back in church with the rest of her family, and she and Leona can see each other every day if they like and can go to church together on Sunday.

It has been a long journey. Lorene and Webb are married for forty years now and are celebrating their anniversary with Pa Furney on his eighty-seventh birthday. The whole immediate and extended family and friends are there for the celebration. Everyone is taking pictures with the happy couple. What a happy day for her. She is so happy she was not a "quitter." She is very happy with that big bunch of children and grandkids.

Lorene and Webb celebrate their fortieth wedding anniversary

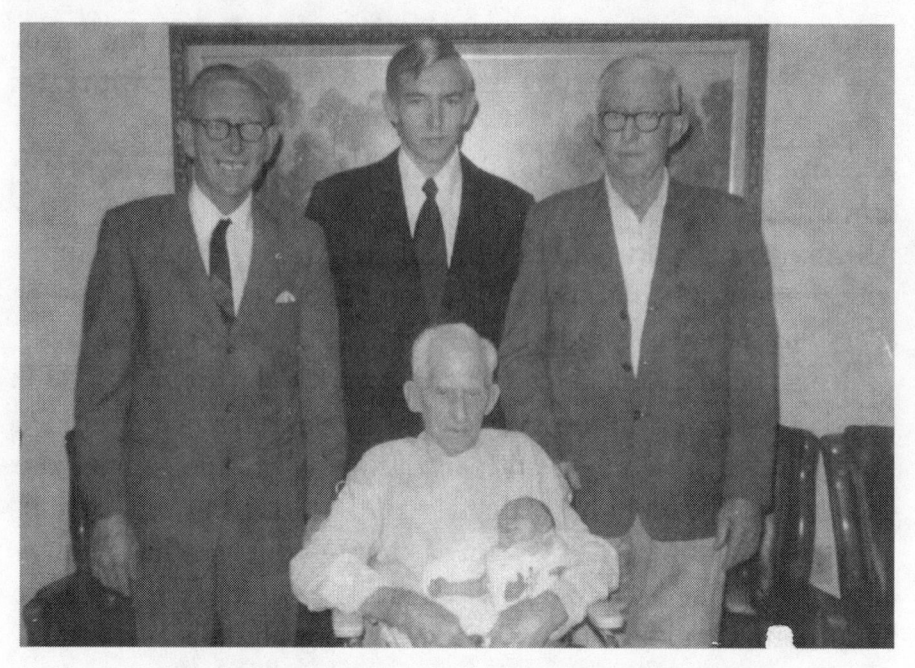

Five generations of Furneys: Charles, Roger, Webb and
Pa Furney holding baby Allen

Jan has had to make a move to Jacksonville to be with her husband. His company has lost a manager in the Jacksonville office, and Pat will take over there for three years before they can return to Winter Park. Not everyone is happy, but they will adjust. Jan is closer to Lorene now, and it is only an hour-and-a-half drive to her home. Nicky is now a preteen and has spent the summer at Grandma's working on the farm.

He loves it and doesn't want to return but has to be home before school starts. She loves having him there. Even she and Webb will help on the farm if it is necessary. She loves when Jan calls and says she is coming to be with them overnight if Pat is out of town for business. She just reminds Nicky not to get too excited about farming. He will not inherit his daddy's farm. He told Grandma he didn't even know where his bedroom was when he got home.

Now Jerale has called to let them know they have just had a new little boy. Rodney Furney was born on December 5, 1973. He is another blond with big blue eyes. Delores has a fever and has not been able to keep Rodney in her room at the hospital. They have found out she has gotten a staph infection from the delivery room, but the baby is fine. Of course Lorene doesn't slow down and is rushing Webb to get back to West Palm to see if she can help out. At three days old, Rodney was ready to be released from the hospital, and she was there to bring him home with his dad, Jerale. She was fifty-nine years old but figured she had some good times left in her, so she helped with the new baby. Delores would be in isolation at the hospital for thirty days.

Things were going along just fine, and Dennis the older brother had just turned five and was determined to play the big brother role. She walked into the baby's room, and Dennis was holding his baby brother on the floor. She almost had a heart attack and asked how he got him, and Dennis promptly responded, "I crawled into the crib and picked him up and put him on the floor so we could play."

After that, the baby was kept in the playpen with a netting that zipped up. Needless to say, the baby was only in his crib when someone was in his nursery. Of course, after bonding with Rodney those first few days, she became very attached to him. She enjoyed getting to play mom with the boys for just a short time but was relieved when Delores could finally be home with her babies.

Now it is time to get back home for retirement and see if they can stay in their new home for a while. Now the children always come to visit, and a new motel has opened in Moultrie so they can all come at once. Shoney's is new and nice, with a restaurant that serves great breakfasts and dinners if they don't want to cook out.

It is the springtime, and she loves planting all the flowers and getting the lawn started. She loves to just ride down the streets when she goes into Moultrie. One street is more beautiful than the other with all the snow-white dogwoods against those fresh green lawns and just piles of colorful azalea bushes scattered all around the houses with little redbud trees all over the place. She thanks God for the beauty in her life. She has just gotten an invitation to visit Vernon in Illinois, and by gosh, she has decided she will go, but she does not want to fly any more.

She has confirmed with Vernon that she would like to take a train trip and get to see the country while she is traveling. Webb has dropped her off in Thomasville, and she is on the way to Illinois with Amtrak.

She has gotten all settled in on the train and has found the club car where she can get a cold drink, and by then, it was time to go to the dining car. She sat looking out the window and enjoyed the scenery while she enjoyed an elegant dinner. This is the life. She should have thought of it sooner. After dinner she read a magazine and dozed off to sleep with the hum of the tracks lulling her as if it were a lullaby. Even though the train made a couple of stops during the night, you just slept through them. They were smooth quick stops.

Now the sunlight is filtering in, and she goes to freshen up for this bright beautiful day. She is completely happy to have her nice hot coffee and breakfast ready when she gets to the dining car. As she is watching the scenes go by, she notices the weather is cloudy and it begins to storm. She's not sure how close to Chicago they are and isn't concerned until the train suddenly slows down and stops in the middle of nowhere. Everyone is getting nervous, and the conductor announces there has been bad weather ahead, and with all the flooding that took place, trees have littered all over the track and they will be stalled until they can clear the tracks. Other than being anxious to get to her destination, she is now getting nervous. *Maybe this wasn't such a good idea.* The short wait lasted two days. Finally they are moving again, and she is so glad to see Vernon's face at the station.

The little ones are all excited to get to show Grandma their swimming skills (they both started swimming at six months) and their personal treasures. Nichole is all into her girl toys, and Christopher is all about anything that has to do with Star Wars. He has a walk-in closet full of Star Wars action figures. Vernon and Cyndi have trips planned to include the children, and they enjoy the museums and the butterfly exhibit as well as two weeks of fun things to do with children, now that Chris is five years old and Nichole is a feisty three-year-old.

The time goes too fast, and Lorene feels sad to leave her children as she probably won't be back for a couple of years. She finds comfort that she will see them more often now when they come to Georgia. Cyndi has found out about Shoney's Motel and can stay in a nice place, so she hopefully won't have to go to the ER as often because Chris has a lot of allergies. It is now back to Amtrak and, hopefully, an uneventful trip back to Georgia. She has changed her mind about flying now that she has experienced how easily a land trip can be delayed. She will just have time to get rested up and get organized again before they will be going down to Orlando in the last of May.

Jeanette's son Jerry is graduating in May from Boone High School and everyone will be there. Lorene and Webb are so proud their grandson is walking down in his cap and gown to graduate. She is reminiscing about getting to see his mother Jeanette also take that big step into adulthood. This is just the beginning of graduations and weddings. These grandchildren have grown up fast. Along with traveling all over to visit the out-of-town children, she still has Charles, Gil, and Melba to visit and it seems the little ones are always needing a costume for a school play.

Grandma is just the creative one to know how to make a "Pocahontas dress." Of course everyone knows she is a cake decorator, and she is making a birthday cake or wedding cake at least once or twice a month. Finally the cold weather will be here, so she can start making quilts again for her grandchildren. They do treasure them. Her fingers are starting to get arthritic, but she can still sew a fine seam.

Melba's children, Stacey and Little Sandy, are getting big. Little Sandy is now ten and stays with his mom a lot when she has to run the store for his Grandpa Deas. He has seen the older boys buy chewing tobacco, and they keep it in their pants pocket, so he gets some and puts it in his pocket. She reminds him not to decide to use tobacco because it will make him very sick. He carries it around for a long time, but the day finally came when he called and told his mom he was very sick. When Melba got to him, he was almost green in the face. When she called Lorene to say he was sick, she just smiled and asked, "Have you forgotten the chewing tobacco he has carried around so long?" They both had a good laugh and knew he didn't need to be reminded not to use it again.

Charles now has some grown children, and the oldest son, Roger, has gotten married and has given Lorene her first great-grandson. Allen Roger Furney was born on February 9, 1975, a big fine boy and was born on Mae's birthday. Now this is the fifth generation of Furneys to be born in their family. Everyone wants a picture of the five—Pa Furney, Webb, Charles, Roger, and the baby Allen. They finally published the picture in the *Moultrie Observer*, and now everybody can have a picture. Now for some more good news. Lorene was overjoyed when Gil called to announce he had a new son. Gil is now thirty-eight years old and pushing the biological clock. What a big beautiful red-haired little boy. Laran David Furney was born on August 4, 1975. Now Gil has his seven-year-old daughter, Carrie, and his new son has made his and Betty's life complete.

It is now the fall of the year, and the grandchildren are back in school, and Lorene knows they will soon start looking for costumes for the Thanksgiving plays at school. It is November 10, Jan's birthday, and she gets a call to rush to the hospital. Her baby girl Melba is in an ambulance and headed that way. She and Webb hurry out and head for Moultrie Hospital.

Webb's sister Laura was a nurse in the emergency room that day and came out to let them know the situation looked bad. She is stunned and cannot believe what she is hearing. Melba was at her home last night, and she was fine. By then Charles is there with Melba. He comes out to confirm what Laura has said. It looks as if her twenty-nine-year-old daughter has had a stroke. That just is not possible. Charles runs back to be with Melba. They are transporting her to the hospital in Albany. He rode in the ambulance with her. After two failed attempts to get her to Albany, they have reached the hospital and the neurologist has run the test. Melba has had a massive cerebral hemorrhage. As Lorene sits there praying for her youngest daughter, she knows she has to be strong for the rest of the family. She cannot expect her husband, Webb, to be the strong one this time. He is in a state of shock already. Just before midnight on November 10, 1975, the doctor pronounced Melba dead.

Fortunately they lived in a small town, and the policeman, Leland Dampier, was courteous enough to start looking for the rest of the children's cars as they came through Berlin and directed them all to Charles's house. There was no need to go to Albany.

As can be expected, the entire family was in a state of shock, and tried to direct their attention to the young children who had spent numerous hours and overnight visits with their young aunt who was always there for them when they needed to talk. Lorene maintained her composure as well as she could, and she and the family managed to withstand the outpouring of grief and comforting of the many family members and friends that one could expect with a huge family and a small town where everybody knew each other.

After the funeral, she just had the words "no parent should have to bury their child" going through her mind over and over. Now she knew where those words came from. As children are known to be resilient, Melba's are, but they sadly need the mothering because Stacey is only five and Sandy, eleven years old. Thank you, God, for her strong faith.

Lorene has just experienced the worst nightmare of her life and is determined to move forward and help Webb get through this. Most of the children have packed up their grief and gone back to their respective homes. None of them wanted to leave Lorene and Webb alone. They just wanted to be near them. Now it's back to work and school for all of the family.

It seemed to be a dark and dreary winter, but spring has sprung and the violets are blooming. The dogwood has filled the woods with white patches, and the redbud trees are in full bloom. The birds are all chirping and busy getting their nests ready for eggs. Lorene is now getting ready to start coloring Easter eggs and round her family up for the sunrise service on Easter morning at Pleasant Hill Church. Of course she will try to bring Melba's children with her, and they will drop off fresh flowers in the cemetery to decorate their mom's grave for Easter. The beginning of 1976 is already so much brighter.

The farmers are going strong and trying to get the most they can from every acre. It is time to start harvesting the tobacco, and everyone who can is trying to help, even Lorene. Jan and Leona's daughter Vanada are both here, Jan for the weekend, and Vanada is on vacation. They both climbed up on the tobacco harvester to try to help out. Jan just wanted to know why they wanted her to tie tobacco now, but when she was a little girl they never would let her. She and Vanada are looking at Lorene's sister Sarah's new house under construction and realized the road going to it had no name, so they promptly got a board and made a road sign while on their lunch break. There is now a street sign, "Sarah Lane," that goes down to her home. All the young cousins that are out of school are on the farm working. She and Leona are enjoying the children being home and making farm work fun again. They all work hard all day and then head for the river to go swimming after a long day's work.

It is time for the old turkey to be on the run. Thanksgiving is here, and just about everyone is coming home for Thanksgiving this year. Lorene has her kitchen overrun by cooks. Her son-in-law Pat is taking care of the turkey and will make sure he slices it properly before dinner. She is trying to get the corn bread dressing ready with Mae's help, and the rest are all making a contribution, it will all come out great. There is never a shortage of food or cooks. She is now starting to experience some problems with her legs. All those years of hard work standing all day are starting to show.

She is heading to Charles's home for Christmas again this year, and there is excitement in the air. Everyone can come home at one time now and stay at Shoney's. Charles always has so many things for the children to do and manages to get a big bonfire, and a hayride going, as well as football games (we now have enough for two teams) and fireworks. The games and the fireworks are held in the front road by the big oak tree. It's just a lot of fun. They all love to gather at Charles's. Everyone brings a dish, so no one person has to do more than their share. She again feels a great surge of pride for the large family she has produced. She and Webb have had a blessed marriage, and he is so glad she has been home this year with only being away for short intervals.

She is all ready for the coming New Year and her new experiences that this New Year will entail. Her first little granddaughter, Debbie, will be graduating this year, and she is so proud of her. The Acompora family is all excited, and Lorene is on her way to Jacksonville to experience the big event. She is so proud to see another one walk in her cap and gown and become another young woman to go off to make her way into the big open world.

She is now seeing the awakening of the women of the world, taking on bigger responsibilities outside the home. Debbie graduated from Terry Parker High, class of 1977. The after-graduation party is a great time to meet the young people's friends as they all head off to full-time jobs and college. Debbie is heading off to Orlando where she will graduate from the University of Central Florida and lead the other girls in the family into a world that was not open to Lorene. What a wonderful time.

Lorene is also excited to know she will be taking another trip to Illinois. Vernon has found out the museum in Chicago is receiving the King Tut exhibition, which is on loan from Egypt, and will only be in a few cities in the United States. When she was invited to visit, of course she said yes. She feels guilty at leaving Webb alone again but knows her grandsons keep him good company while she goes away. Most of the time, Charles's son David will even stay with Granddad until she returns home, or the other boys will come and go so that Granddad has company.

This time, when she flies, she will have Cyndi meet her with a wheelchair. Her old knees are giving her a problem, but they have worked it out so she will not have to walk long distances. She has had a lot of fun with her family in Vernon's home, and the big day has arrived. They will be staying overnight in the convent with Cyndi's sister Christa, who is a nun. This is a home for the nuns of the Chicago parish. They are treated so well, and they are accepted as any family would be into the home of a relative. The line around the museum is at least a mile-and-a-half long, and she sighs a big sigh of relief when she found she was not expected to be in that line. Christa has a pass to get into the museum anytime and has the tickets all ready. When they arrive, they are taken to the front of the line and she is just in awe from the time her foot hit the inside.

This is the young Pharaoh she had read about as a young girl. King Tutankhamen's tomb was found in 1922, and the stories of the curse on anyone who entered, and all of the artifacts, suddenly became very real.

She was so impressed with all the artifacts and all the stories. One that most fascinated her was the little golden statue of the child king with his little slippers. It is fascinating to imagine a frail young man becoming a king when he was around ten years old and learning about the wise men who helped him rule his kingdom. It was said he was only a teen when he first went into war. His rule saw many changes, one of which was to disclaim his father's belief that there was only one god. The young Pharaoh reinstated the belief of many gods and ruled his kingdom with a firm hand until he died suddenly around the age of twenty. The mystery of his death was never solved. She took a very long time to view all the artifacts and digest the information and the one chance in a lifetime to experience this great opportunity. Vernon stayed very close to her to make sure no one rushed her. She was so glad she said yes to the invitation. She sure would not be able to travel to New York or Philadelphia in such comfort.

She is back in Vern's home in Rockford, and they are all ready for a rest. However, after they are rested up, she has promised Cyndi she would ride up to Minnesota with her to the Mayo Clinic. While in the clinic, she happened to meet a Dr. Waterman, who was a nephrologist. Her younger sister Wilma's last name is Waterman, and she asked if he knew her husband who lived in the area. He laughed and said, "Yes, John is my brother." Dr. Waterman took her into his office after they realized John was her brother-in-law, and they chatted for a while. He then took her on a personal tour of the Mayo clinic. Can you believe she got to see firsthand how, along with the nurturing staff to comfort people, they were extending people's lives with the technology they had in every department? Dr. Waterman was head of the transplant team. (Little did she realize that one day her son-in-law would receive a heart transplant from a team at the University of Florida who were dedicated to giving him a more comfortable life and extend it for more than a decade?) She was very proud of the book he gave her about the Mayo Clinic, and the young professional who gave it to her. She couldn't wait to tell her little sister Wilma that she had met her brother-in-law.

These two weeks have been so exciting and more than Lorene would ever have expected to happen to her in her humble life. She is saying good-bye to her little Illinois family and is happy just thinking about being back in Georgia again with Webb. It is so great to go away and experience so much, but as usual, it will be good to be back home in Georgia again.

After such exciting things happening this year, she will have a hard time getting her head wrapped around the rural life in Georgia. She is so happy to be back singing God's praises in Pleasant Hill Church. She thanks the boys for taking care of Webb and keeping him busy while she was gone. School has started, and all the little ones are back in school, and the big ones too. Debbie is now living in Orlando and going to the University of Central Florida. Her granddaughter Charlotte and Leonard have just given her another great-grandchild. Robbie Jay Blaxton was born on October 3, 1977. What a healthy baby, and he is also a blond with those big blue eyes.

With the beginning of the New Year in 1978, she is just happy to be able to get some sewing in. Her quilting frames are up and her fingers are flying over all the delicate little stitches. She is so glad the little ones are all busy in school during the week, and she doesn't have to put things away until the weekend. Her daughter Jan and her husband have sold their home in Jacksonville and will be moving back to Winter Park in the summer. Pat has already moved back, and he and Debbie will stay in Orlando and take turns visiting Jacksonville every other week, with Jan and Nick checking out the construction on the new home when it is their turn to go to Orlando. Nick is in his junior year of high school, and his parents don't want to move him at midyear. Jan and Nick are having a blast living home alone and come visit as often as they can before the ride gets longer. Debbie and Pat just want the house to get finished.

Charles and his family have had an occasion to visit Jan as Shirley's brother, who lives in Orange Park, is very sick. She and Webb also get in another visit before they have to go all the way to Orlando to visit them. Of course the time flies by, and she and Webb are on the road headed south. They stop by in Orlando and stay at Jeanette's while they visit the families there, and then they are off again to visit Jerale and his young family for Christmas. It is nice not to have to drive straight through like they used to. Now they can break up the trip with a stopover in Orlando. The families in West Palm are so glad to see them. They are staying with Jerale's young family, but they all get together with Mae's family and her children to make it complete. Michael and Michelina are older, but Dennis and Rodney can still get a lot of attention with their young antics.

They are so happy to get together with family and old friends, go to the beach with the children, and put in a lot of time fishing, but all things must end, and she is on their way back to Georgia to get going after the beginning of the new year.

The farming and planting are getting started all around them, but she and Webb are not too anxious to get too involved. She has completely given up riding her three-wheel bike, and her legs are so bad she has started to use a walker. This is too much, so she has gone to see Dr. Adcock and scheduled the first surgery for a knee replacement. The girls are all working now, and Gil insists he is going to be her nurse when she comes home.

He will show her he can do anything the girls can do. The first surgery is over, and it went without a hitch. She was in the hospital and had pain medication the first three days, and by the time she was released from the hospital, she had no pain and was ready for the therapy part. Gil is the best ever. He cleans and exercises her leg every day and keeps her house as clean as a pin. He pays extra attention to keeping her bathroom sanitary, making sure she won't get an infection from anything. She knows from here on it is all about keeping that leg moving, and she and Gil do a great job of that. She will miss out on the family activities, but she is gung-ho to get ready for the other leg to be done.

She has two grandchildren graduating this spring. Jeanette's daughter Diane is graduating with special honors for being involved with FBLA, where she was a national officer. Future Business Leaders of America has gotten her a part-time job with Southeast Bank during her high school years and is only getting her more attention now that she will be a full-time employee after her graduation. She is now a graduate from Boone High School, class of 1979, and off to a great future. Her grandma Furney can't be there, but she is mighty proud of the young woman and the young professional she has become.

Jan's son Nick has also graduated this same month from Winter Park High School, class of 1979. Their ceremony was outside in the football stadium at eight in the morning. She was sorry she had to miss seeing Nick in his cap and gown but heard how unbearably hot it was. Nick spent his senior year working in the swimming pool business with his friend's dad. After the hot summer, he will be glad to get inside out of the heat, in the classrooms of the University of Central Florida with his sister.

WINTER PARK HIGH SCHOOL
Commencement Ceremony
June 8, 1979

Nick Acompora, class of 1979

UNIVERSITY OF CENTRAL FLORIDA
5:00 PM Summer Commencement
August 6, 1994

Debbie graduates, receives degree from UCF

They will all be coming home for Thanksgiving this year, and she will be glad to see them all again after her full year at home. She has limited her travel and concentrated on getting her leg back in shape. She was happy. Jan and Pat had stayed at her house for Thanksgiving this year, and the rest just came over for dinner. Jan's youngest son, Nicky (he likes to be called Nick now), has decided to withdraw from college. He has been an entrepreneur since he was ten years old and started his own lawn service. He now just wants to work outside and has a number of different jobs he would like to do. If he runs out of work, he can always go back to swimming pool work. They are just letting him choose for himself right now.

The New Year is here again, and we have a few new high school graduates coming up. They appear every couple of years. The New Year has started, and we have all had the biggest surprise of all. We will be having a new grandson in August. Can you believe it, Jan is pregnant. They always wanted four children, and now that the last two are in college, she gets pregnant. They were so excited but didn't tell anyone until after she had an amniocentesis confirming the baby was perfectly healthy and a boy. Now that they have built their retirement home, which is the smallest house ever, they are ready to start filling it up again. She couldn't believe it.

Jeanette's son Jerry is working as a manager for a His store, which is a man's clothing store in Clearwater. Her daughter Diane is just moving right along in the bank as well as Jeanette at First Union. Her husband, Al, is working in accounting with the expressway toll agency since his retirement from the Air Force. Charles's five are all grown up and working in different areas in Georgia. He now has Roger, David, Tommy, Roy, and Charlotte who have left the nest and starting families of their own. Shirley can just love those grandbabies and send them home with their parents.

Mavis's two are still in school, and Michael will graduate this year from West Palm Beach at John I. Leonard High, class of 1982. He has been awarded a football scholarship to Valdosta State here in Georgia. His mom's friend has rented out a catering place for a big after-graduation party, where all the family who can make it and all their friends will eat and party into the night. Melba's oldest, Sandy, is also graduating here in Moultrie. Thank goodness Gil and Jerale still has two each to go before they are all out of school.

Michael Vanacore III, class of 1982, and Michelina Vanacore
on her graduation day a few years later

She knows Gil is happy on his little spread raising his kids in the country. Jerale is putting his time in at the county and is working on a good retirement as well as his wife Delores, showing up at Costco every day and also establishing her own share of retirement. Vernon also has two to go, but he is so busy with his job and his involvement with politics, he leaves the domestic work up to Cyndi. He has always been very busy in politics on a local level and now has expanded to the national level. He is a negotiator for Chrysler and represents his company's union when it is time for elections. Lorene couldn't believe it when he sent her pictures from Ethel Kennedy's home, where he had met with Ted

Kennedy and Walter Mondale. He has always enjoyed shooting the bull with intelligent people, and she used to worry about his education. She is proud of the young man he has become even though she worries about his biting off more than he can chew. At a young age, he started investing in real estate with apartment complexes and now has narrowed it down to a couple of houses and a couple of apartment complexes, which Cyndi helps, manage.

She and Webb are on their way south to visit the children there. They missed their trip down south last year and are looking forward to the beaches they love, and the West Palm crew has a fishing trip planned for Sebastian Inlet. Everybody gets strung up and down the pier, Webb starts pulling in the drum as fast as he can get another hook back in the water. The drums are running. He and Lorene are excited, and he yells for Jan to fish it in. She lived in New York too long, and he starts laughing when he realizes she doesn't remember what to do, and he has to yell for Lorene. What fun. They all fished until they were tired and then went to breakfast before they go to get some sleep before hitting the Lake Worth pier the next night. As they were fishing at the Lake Worth pier, Pat remembers how Lorene's younger brother, Uncle Paul, taught him how to catch a snook right there.

The birth announcements are on the way. Brian Anthony Acompora was born on August 2, 1980. A fine healthy boy, looking just like his dad. No red hair this time. He is baptized, and his sister Debbie and his brother Nick are his godparents. What more could a child want than to be born into a family with four doting adults. She is happy with having a new child this late in life, knowing he will be the last. Everyone is coming over to see the new baby, and when he is about a month old, his sister has an announcement. Debbie is pregnant.

Vern with Ted Kennedy

There will only be seven months between the babies. Debbie is now twenty-two years old, and so is the baby's father. Since he is still in college, they have decided not to get married. Pat and Jan have supported her decision and will stick through this with her.

Pat is involved in their new neighborhood and is president of the homeowners' association. On September 19, he is scheduled to speak out at the university with the state utilities commission. He isn't feeling well and walks up and out the stairs from the engineering building and drives home. As he comes in, Jan knows he is in trouble and calls 911. Later that night, her neighbor from the old neighborhood, who is a cardiologist, confirms Pat has had a massive heart attack.

Lorene's entire family is upset and ready to go to Jan. Jan has a six-week-old baby and a sick husband on her hands. She was the calm hand that kept them all home when there was nothing they could do but babysit, and there were plenty of babysitters in Jan's house. She and Webb took turns visiting when Pat finally made it home. Jeanette was always there for Jan's family and took all family calls while Jan's friend Linda Miller took all business calls to cut down on incoming calls. Her family has continued this practice to this day: "If someone in the family has a crisis, there is a go-to person, and then the chain of calls begins."

Pat did get out of the hospital in October and was never allowed to work after that. After the first of the following year Jan went to work for the Equitable of New York and took over Pat's clientele as well as adding her own clients. Brian grew up with a mom who went to the office every day, and his dad quickly became "Mr. Mom" through the following years.

After all the action in Florida, Lorene has kept a cool head and is right there when her grandson Tommy proudly walks into the waiting room to announce the arrival of his first son, Jason Van, who was born on November 7, 1980. We have another cotton top with a head of blond hair and the big blue eyes. Lori Ann and baby are just doing fine. Before you know it, two weeks have passed and her grandson Roy is with his wife, Becky, at the hospital for the delivery of their first son. Bryan Paul was born on November 30, 1980. What excitement in the Furney family, another big healthy baby boy. Becky and Bryan are doing just fine. That's three new ones this year.

She is excited about how things are going down south. Jan goes to work each day with Debbie and Nick also working, and Pat stays home with the baby until he goes for bypass surgery in August. Then the baby will go into day care. Now the babies are coming again. First her granddaughter Charlotte and Leonard have a beautiful little girl, Cynthia Ann, born on January 23, 1981. Can you believe she is going to be a redhead? What a beautiful little baby. Before she even gets a breather in between, she gets another announcement. Her granddaughter Debbie has given birth to Shawna Marie Acompora, born on March 25, 1981. She is a real brunette with the dark eyes to match and is absolutely beautiful. Her grandma Jan says so.

She is wondering who the joke is on. Jan has to go to Atlanta for a week or two for training. Debbie and Pat are being left home with Brian, who is already to starting to walk, and the baby Shawna. She knows Jan will have a good time in Atlanta, but she does feel kind of sorry for Pat and Debbie. That's a lot of diapers to change, but they are all doing well.

Things are going along really at a fast pace, and it is time for her to get her yard in order. She has a pretty good St. Augustine lawn in front and has planted some iris lilies around the perimeter of the sandbox she has for the kids to play in. Now Webb heads in the other direction when he sees her coming with that big smile on her face. He knows she wants another hole dug. She has even planted jonquils along the top of the ditch where the vegetable garden is. He knows she will holler at him if he runs over even one when he plows the garden. Well, at least she has her flowers to keep her happy until the vegetables come in and then all she does is either can or freeze everything in it. She just wants to get everything ready. She is having her other knee replaced.

Gil has come over again and helped her through the last surgery, but this knee isn't as comfortable as the last one, but she finally gets the kinks out and is ready to go again. They are enjoying the quiet of the country as they sit under the large pecan tree out front with a big glass of iced tea. The group of kids in Georgia is all growing up fast. It seems there is always a new group to go into the sandbox. When one group outgrows it, another baby or two moves in. Of course they will be ready to roll as soon as it gets cool out.

The boys let Webb know when the fish are biting down south, and he will be ready to go again. They can stop and visit Jeanette and Jan's families on the way to West Palm Beach. When they get to Mae and Jerale's, the fun begins as they both enjoy fishing with their children and the grandchildren. All of the children in the family have great memories of Grandma Furney fishing with a cane pole. They all can remember her pulling in a big one. If she can't land it, she just puts the pole over her shoulder and drags it onto shore. Sometimes they refer to her as the "little grandma" because she is so short.

Her grandson Nick Acompora (Jan's son) has joined the army and will be ready to serve his country as his father was when he joined the Air Force. Nick has completed his basic training in Oklahoma and has now been deployed to Germany. He already misses the family but is in New Ulm, Germany, and loves to snow ski. He says it is the best place ever. The cost to stay in one of the rooms overnight is only $5. However, he does not know the area well enough and ended up on the wrong side of a slope landing in the wrong area. Fortunately a nice person brought him back into Germany.

This spring the big Easter egg hunt will be at Lorene's son Gil and Betty's. The whole family is here, and there are more toddlers than you can believe. The newest baby this year is her grandson Roy and Becky's. Jennifer Lynn was born January 23, 1982. We have another beautiful little blonde. Her older brother Bryan is one of the toddlers who will get to go to hunt eggs before the very anxious older kids. Jan has her son Brian's hand and Jeanette has Shawna in tow. Now the over-four group gets in, and it is time to get serious. Grandma Furney is helping anyone who needs her, but nobody will let Granddad watch the hiding of the eggs. Sometimes he picks a favorite. An exhausted group of kids and the excited bunch of parents are now ready for the big buffet Betty has set up inside. In the rush for food, someone forgot to say the blessing of the food. Laran is upset and crying; everyone is ashamed to think a child had to remind them to say Grace. It was a huge success and so much fun to be with a big family at this blessed event.

Now the spring festivities are over, and everyone is into the harvesting. She has a garden that reaches all the way down to the old block house, probably about two acres. There is more than she can preserve by herself, so everyone is coming over to pick the vegetables, and every kid who comes through Morven or Barney wants to stop and pick peaches. She also reminds them the next time they come the blueberries will be ripe.

Nicholas C. Acompora II joins the U.S Army

She and Webb will be spending the rest of the year in Georgia with only short trips out of town this year, now that the kids come to visit Georgia often and they all have big families of their own. They pretty much spend their Christmas holidays with the nearest group of relatives. Charles and Gil's families gather at Charles's house with Grandma Furney and Granddad, and as often as they can, this will include Melba's children. Jeanette and Jan's bunch rotate holidays at their respective homes, as do Mae's and Jerale's. It is not practical for Vernon to try to get south and, by chance, get caught in a snowstorm.

Now Lorene is in for a big surprise. Vernon will be coming in very soon. So will the whole bunch. The children can't keep it from her any longer. She and Webb will be married for fifty years on January 14, 1983. The children have planned a big celebration for them with a big dinner and dance at the old officers' club out at Spence Field. That is the only place big enough for three hundred people. That is the best estimate they could come up with. The invitations have been sent out, and the RSVPs are back. The dinner menu has been planned, with the reception line at five and dinner at six PM, and the band will be there at seven. The Frank Gay band will be there to play country and Western music, and if someone can't make it for dinner, they can join them for the dance.

She is so happy she doesn't know what to do, and the children won't let them do anything. The children all come into Moultrie a week before the party on Saturday night. They will do all the cooking. They have rented the commercial-size kitchen at the old Berlin School. The first things first: decorate the clubhouse. Anyone who could make a bow or hang a streamer had a job. They have decorated every inch of it to perfection and ordered all the flowers from Napier's. They have made sure the kitchen stoves are in working order to keep the food warm when it is transported to the club. You wouldn't recognize the place, and they even have two white rockers in front of that big fireplace, which is big enough for a man to stand in. Because it is January, they will have a fire lit in it.

Lorene and Webb's golden wedding anniversary

Lorene and Webb with their children
at their fiftieth wedding anniversary party

Somewhere they have managed to rent gold linen tablecloths and napkins. The steam tables will be set up the day of the buffet. Can you believe this? Each morning and evening they evaluate their waitresses that wait on them at Shoney's. They decide which ones they like best, and that is where the waitresses came from to help with the party.

Now that is done, it is time to cook. But first we have just one little incident! Lorene's little grandson Brian, who is only two and a half, has slipped with his new cowboy boots, so they run him down to the hospital to get a couple of stitches in that booboo he has on his head. There, that was fast. Back to the kitchen and get that cooking going. Anyone who missed out on that deal missed the boat. Her sister Effie said it was more fun cooking with everybody than it was at the party. Anyone who could wash a scallion or a radish was qualified. The relish trays were set up and stored in the refrigerators with the condiments. The turkey and roast beef were cooked, along with the rice and all the vegetables. The hot trays were set up and filled as the meat was being sliced by the boys in the club kitchen. The waitresses had all the tables set up with flowers and condiments on each. The food was put out on three buffet tables, and it was time to open the doors.

Finally everybody has made it through the reception line, and she and Webb are happy to just sit down at the head table and marvel at the great immediate and extended family they have plus their old and new friends. When they have all eaten such a wonderful dinner, it is time to cut that beautiful tiered cake she made for herself. The band starts up, and she and Webb are the featured dancers. She didn't have a big wedding fifty years ago, and this is more than she could ever have dreamed of, and now all her children are joining them. They all danced and never sat down the rest of the evening. She wonders who those rocking chairs were for. At midnight they asked the band to play for another hour, and they all just kept dancing. Finally the children took them home, and they fell into bed exhausted. The next day

Webb's sister Laura called to let her know she was up all night with pains in her legs, but she never remembers having so much fun.

The party is over, and the kids have all gone home. Now they can enjoy some quiet time in their nice warm home. Webb has not been quite as active lately, and she worries about him. They are getting to the age where they have started to pay closer attention to each other. She has had him in for a checkup, and he is healthy, just slowing down. While in town, she schedules a doctor's visit for herself. She appears to have a problem breathing. By the time she gets back to the doctor, she has acute bronchitis. She is taking medicine, but it gets worse and she cannot sleep lying down. Her son Charles comes and takes her to the emergency room, where she gets more medicine. After a couple of days, she is continually getting worse, and her sister Leona comes over to check on her. One look tells her the girls need to know, so she calls Jeanette. Within a few hours Jeanette and Jan are there.

They arrange for a couple of her grandsons to stay with Webb, and she is heading back to the Winter Park hospital in Florida. Within a couple of hours in the hospital, she is ready to go eat dinner. She has been overmedicated. The hospital doctor in Moultrie did not get the name of the medicine she was on and gave her the same medicine with a different name. After a couple of hours of Gatorade and a stern lecture on telling one doctor what another doctor had given her, she was released and went out for dinner with the girls. The children know that it is time to pay closer attention. She nor Webb have been sick and are not on a lot of medications. Thank God they are both in good health to enjoy the rest of the summer going fishing, visiting the grandchildren, and sitting under their favorite pecan tree with a big iced tea. They now have another great grandson from Tommy and Lori Ann. Justin Ray was born on August 4, 1984.

Lorene has noticed that Webb sometimes is not too focused when he is outside walking around. Just the other day, he fell into the ditch out by the garden and she had to have her grandson Roy come over and pick him up. At first she was afraid he had been drinking a little of his "four roses," but he denied it. He had given up his drinking habit a couple of years ago. Now he seems disoriented, and she calls the doctor for an appointment, and he won't even feed himself. She has an appointment for tomorrow morning.

During the night, she heard a loud thump in his bedroom and ran to find him sprawled on the floor. The ambulance got to the hospital, and her son Charles was right behind it. The doctor comes out and tells them Webb has had a massive stroke. Of course her daughter Mae was the first one to get home to them, with the rest of the family close behind. The doctor shows them the gray area in the x-ray and shares with them that he already has paralysis on his left side and cannot speak. In 1984 there was not as much emphasis as there is today on physical therapy. Webb was discharged to a nursing home, and she was determined not to leave him for long.

Before the month is out, Webb has developed pneumonia and is sent to the hospital. She doesn't want him in another nursing home and has planned to move next door to Charles's home, where she can have a few more hands helping out. This sounds good, but before long, even with a lot of equipment, she will find she tires easily. Mae has a VNA license and has taken care of a lot of elderly people, so she feels she can give her mother some much-needed help. Within no time, she has moved into a home in Moultrie and has a bedroom for Mom and a bedroom with a hospital bed all set up for Dad.

Things are looking a lot brighter. The children stay at Shoney's when they come home and can visit at Mae's house. It appears Webb doesn't recognize a lot of the family and cannot communicate at all. Jan is there for a visit and has the toddlers Brian and Shawna with her. All of a sudden they realize they have disappeared and start a frantic search, only to find both of them in the bed with Webb. When they walk into the room, there is one on either side of him at the head of the bed, and they are talking to their grandfather, each with an arm around his neck and rubbing his head. He may not have recognized them, but he sure had a big smile on his face, lying there between two loving children. Of course she just broke out laughing, and they were not scolded too badly.

She now has less responsibility and plans most of her day just learning how to use the lift and being able to care for Webb herself. She enjoys getting out shopping and maybe going to church with Charles's family at Hopewell. Eventually, when she feels comfortable with her new lifestyle, she tells Mae she is ready to move back home beside Charles. They have her all set up, and Mae has secured someone to live in her home full time. Lorene doesn't have to clean or cook, just take care of her husband. Later that year, Mae moved back to West Palm Beach to her family and her job.

She misses living by her big pecan tree but accepts that she can never live there again. They had some fun times there over the years with her family, but now she must make a new life for herself again. She is now taking care of Webb, and her cleaning lady has left her, but she has her grandson Tommy's wife, Lori Ann, just down the driveway, who is as devoted to her as any of her daughters. When Lori Ann is around, she doesn't have to ask for help. Lori Ann is one of those people who knows what she needs before Lorene even realizes it herself.

Over the next few months she manages, but she is getting tired. The family in Georgia often comes to relieve her so she can go shopping or just get out of the house. She just thanks God for the good days and gets in a lot of reading instead of running around. The cold winter passes, and she thanks God again for a nice warm home where she has central heat and air. She often thinks of when she would have to gather wood to keep her home warm.

The year has passed, and the Florida bunch has all visited Lorene and the rest of the Georgia family now that the holidays are over. They are enjoying the cold weather and can maybe get some squirrel hunting in for a change. When all those boys get together on a cold morning you will get to hear the shots flying. They all have the young ones to teach how to respect the woods, the animals, and each other. All of the boys have to go for a hunting class and pass their gun-safety tests before they are turned loose. Of course occasionally one of the girls will join in. They have all been taught how to shoot a gun by their fathers, but they mostly just like to hit the little stores on Main Street and shop. They are all growing up so fast. She thinks, "The older you get, the faster time passes."

She is now having aides come in and help out with Webb through the summer and is beginning to get a good feel for who can be trusted overnight to give Webb the attention he needs. She is planning to get away at the end of the summer. Her granddaughter Debbie is getting married on October 19, 1985. They will then be Mr. and Mrs. Bradley Kent Gerhardt, and she wants to be part of this big wedding. Her grandson Nick is back from Germany, and she is looking forward to seeing him.

The hot summer is over, and they have survived it, thanks to good old air-conditioning. Webb's health is holding up, and he has become accustomed to having someone else take care of him, with the aides coming more often now. She has decided on whom to hire to spend the week with Webb while she goes to Orlando for Debbie's wedding. Of course, Charles will be right here. He is not big on going out of state for weddings. He will make sure his dad is well cared for and will be there every day.

Mr. and Mrs. Bradley Gerhardt

Lorene makes cake for Debbie and Brad

Jeanette is picking her up to stay at her house the week before the wedding. Of course she is the one to make her first granddaughter's wedding cake. The colors are burgundy wine and ivory. Every other layer will be white then red velvet cake, colored to match the bridesmaids' dresses. Her longtime friend Pearl Copeland is coming over to help make the sugar bells that will be around the cake, and are trimmed in wine colors to match. Each day she has an audience.

Al's brother Frankie and his wife, Ginger, is here in their winter home and just can't stay away from the baking. She gets all the delicate decorations made, and finally, the day of making the cake is here. She feels so rested, and with plenty of time, not having to rush has been such a blessing. She misses Webb but is glad to have a little distraction from being a caregiver. She is putting the cake together and using almond-flavored icing and raspberry filling between the layers. Honestly she has to admit this is one of the best cakes she has ever made, and if she, Jeanette, and Al can get it to the Langford Hotel where the reception is, she will be glad to get it set up and done. The reception is upstairs, thank God for elevators and that Debbie is having a candlelight ceremony. That gives her, Jeanette, and Al plenty of time to set up that cake for 250 people and have plenty of time to freshen up and rest before going to the church.

The wedding couldn't have been planned better. Jeanette was the monitor who stood by the door to tell the wedding party when to walk, and Nick and his new fiancée, Nusara, were taking care of the guestbook. Her granddaughter Michelina sung the most beautiful song, and her granddaughter Diane was the maid of honor. Of course the little ones, Brian and Shawna, were ring bearer and flower girl. She and Jan were ushered in and seated, with Pat walking that beautiful daughter down the aisle, and it was just beautiful. She then went over to the hotel for the reception, and they all partied until they were ready to throw them out. After all that, it was time for some good rest and relaxation.

After the wedding crowd thinned out, she had time to spend with everyone over at Jan's house. Pat had bypass surgery in August of 1981 and was doing remarkably well. She had such a nice vacation, and the weather was so beautiful, but now she was ready to get back to Webb. She wondered if he had a concept of time. She also wanted to be able to spend some time with her granddaughter Stacey's new baby, Christie Nichole who was born on February 4, 1985. It had been a very good year, after all.

Now with the holidays in full swing, things are happening with her large family in all parts of the country. The newlyweds in Winter Park are doing just fine in their little villa, which Debbie had bought before they were married for herself and Shawna, and they may outgrow it fast now that Debbie is expecting another child. Those great-grandchildren are growing more each year. Webb is still holding on and is healthy. He enjoys his little trips outside. She gets his lift and puts him in his wheelchair so that he can enjoy sitting outside on the deck in this fresh spring weather. She is certainly enjoying being next door to Charles's family. It is never boring. She has children in and out of the house daily, if only to grab a quick glass of iced tea. They all want to see their granddad every day and have become so attached to him. He always notices when they are around and will smile and act like he recognizes the ones he sees most.

The children all hunted Easter eggs and everyone had a big dinner over at Charles's house. "What will they ever do with all those eggs? Make egg salad, and make sure everyone who is married takes some to their house." It is now May, and Debbie has had another little girl, Jennifer Leigh, born on June 3, 1986. Now that their family is growing, Brad is adopting Shawna and they will all have the same last name by the fall. She will be Shawna Marie Gerhardt. Good for you, Brad.

Lorene's grandson David is now married to Sue, and they have no plans that she knows of to have a family. Besides, he plays with all the other nieces and nephews, and they all love David as if he were their daddy. They are both so attentive to her. They both work but always have time to check to see if she needs anything. With all the family going to the river for swimming and picnics, the summer is just rushing by. Gil's little family stops by often to visit now that they all live closer together.

Lorene has gotten very busy since her golden anniversary and is not only reading a lot of different books but also has started writing her memories of what her life was like for as far back as she can remember. She has a good start on it and is writing a little each day. She often talks about the old place; that is, where Grandpa Babe lived, and takes all her children who are interested to the old house over by Little River. They all like to walk down to where the river runs through the property and listen to her talk about how she and her brothers and sisters learned to swim right there.

Her son-in-law Pat is as interested as her children, and he drives her all over the old country roads and asks her to tell him about it. Even the grandchildren from Florida can go alone over the Bethel Hills, go visit Chitlin Switch where the old general store was, and then take a walk across Brice's dam. She has passed so many of her favorite childhood memories on to them. All the grandchildren love to stay with Grandma and work on the farm, but they don't want to go to Aunt Leona's if the peas are ready in the garden. They all hate to shell peas. The boys like to go hunt squirrels on the Okapilco Creek and around the Alman wash hole. They all also know that their great-granddaddy Jerry Hart was baptized in the water at the Alman wash hole. Grandma Furney told them. Of course all the children in the family have been with her to the lime sink and slid down those steep slopes when it was dry and full of leaves in the fall.

She just can't believe the New Year is here again and the children will all be graduating from high school. It seems she has at least one a year or there is a wedding for the older ones. May has just sneaked up on her. Jeanette's daughter Diane is having a big wedding in Orlando. She is off to Orlando again for another big wedding. The wedding gown has been pressed and is spread out over the entire closet. Jeanette will have her stay at the Sheraton Hotel with her good friend Pearl Copeland.

Al has walked his beautiful daughter down the aisle. What a great wedding with a huge wedding party. They have become Mr. and Mrs. Patrick Gassaway on May 2, 1987. She was married at the First United Methodist Church of Winter Park in Winter Park, Florida, which has a very long aisle. They have two flower girls. Her matron of honor is Debbie, with Shawna as the flower girl, and the ring bearer is Brian. That long aisle spread out with the wedding party was a sight to behold. They were just beautiful. Pat, Jan's husband, is upstairs videotaping the wedding, and we will all get to see it tomorrow. The very large reception was held at one of the new hotels in nearby Maitland, the Sheraton. The whole

Mr. and Mrs. Patrick and Diane Gassaway are married

family has showed up for this one, including Webb's younger sister Marie. Jan is having a big brunch for all of the family the morning after the wedding. We just have to find our way to her house from the hotel where we all slept. Her son Nick is coming to lead us all to her house.

Jan has made quite a spread, and we have eaten Brunch, and now we can watch the special video Pat has made for the newlyweds. They are off to honeymoon in Hawaii, so we get to see it first. It begins with their baby pictures and leads them up to the big day. This was a special video. Well, now it is time to say our good-byes and go back to Georgia and make sure Webb is OK. What a wonderful trip she has had, and what great memories.

Her son Vernon's oldest, Christopher Furney, class of 1987, is graduating from high school this June, and she is all excited for him. Not just because he is going away to college but also because he has been managing some of the rock-and-roll bands that come into Rockford to play at different events. If they haven't made enough money and can't afford a hotel room, good ol' Chris will even let them sleep in his dad's basement (and you thought your kids were loud). Well, he will be going to Colorado for college, and they will get a break. Chris is the artist in the family, and his creativity in photography has gotten him far. Good luck, Christopher.

Christopher Furney's high school graduation with Vern

Nichole Furney gets her master's degree four years later

Now back to the South, she has gotten to meet Nicky's fiancée at her granddaughter's wedding, and now Nick and Nusara will become Mr. and Mrs. Nicholas C. Acompora II on November 7, 1987. Their wedding is in the base chapel (her stepdad is in the navy) and is a little smaller, with only maybe 150 guests. Can you believe she was almost an hour late for her own wedding? Nusara's five-year-old son Marty is the ring bearer, and Shawna is the flower girl. The crowd was getting restless. They have a wonderful dinner and dance at Townsend's Fish House, which is their favorite restaurant in Orlando. The food was excellent, the music was great, and it was a good send-off to the Bahamas for them. Nusara has a son, Marty (the ring bearer), who was born September 20, 1982. Nick will adopt Marty as soon as they get married, so now Jan will get two new grandchildren this year. Also Lorene will get two more great-grands.

Lorene is pretty much into a regular routine taking care of Webb and making sure she goes out to get her shopping done as well as running over to have Mary Deas keep her hair looking nice. She writes as often as she can now with no interruptions. It seems the days just fly by, and she is getting more involved in the church activities since she now is right down the road from Hopewell, and they have so many things to get involved in.

There were times when Webb was in the hospital that she felt totally abandoned by her church. She has been a Southern Baptist all her life, and when she was in such need of someone to pray with, there was no one to minister her. Does a preacher abandon his flock? She has now found herself very comfortable with the people at Hopewell Church and has moved her letter there. The ladies in her inner circle always call if they need a dish to carry to someone who is ill or if there is a death in the community and they need dishes to carry over for the family. She cannot babysit for children, but she devotes as much time as she can for anyone who is elderly or a shut in, as Webb is. She enjoys their companionship as much as they do hers. She loves her church family and does love reading the Bible and going to Sunday school.

She can't wait to visit Jan's family when she gets the opportunity to go south again this year. They have gotten two new babies. Nick and Nusara have a new baby. Candice Nichole was born on May 3, 1988, and Debbie's little son, Zachary Kent, was born on July 19, 1988. Jan's son Brian is a big boy now and has been playing baseball since he was five. That keeps him and his dad, Pat, busy.

As much as she hates to admit it, Webb's body seems to be getting frail. He eats well but is so thin. They can only pray for him to be comfortable. Maybe he will perk up over the holidays with the children all coming and going. It was a big Thanksgiving, and the children who weren't here for Thanksgiving made sure they were here for Christmas. They are all aware he is not as well as he was. Thank God for Lori Ann. She always comes and helps her get ready for all that company.

Things are moving pretty fast this spring. Of course the children think Easter can't get here fast enough. We really have a bunch to go out and find the Easter eggs after church on Easter Sunday. Jan's household is a in a thither. Nick had subcontracted out the swimming pool to be built as he feels he knows who is best at each phase of the job. The kids can't wait. They are having Candice's first birthday party as a pool party in May. Jan is really nervous until she sees all seventeen of those crawlers have two parents each right on top of things. Candice had swimming lessons at six months as well as Debbie's baby Zack. Not one single mishap. Jan said she could actually relax. Nick had it all under control.

Lorene's ocean is really getting rocky again. She is trying to remain calm, but Webb has taken a turn for the worse. He needs twenty-four-hour care, and she has him in a nursing home. She is trying to prepare herself for the time that she knows will surely come. She and Charles have had the nurse come out around midnight to tell them his breathing is getting slow. Around one-thirty AM Webb died on May 22, 1989. She is relieved he can go and be with his Lord and finally have freedom from his old body, but she also is not sure about her feelings. They always say at least you have time to prepare, but she now knows it doesn't matter how long you have. You can never be prepared to separate from someone you have loved and spent the last fifty-six years of your life with, and shared the bad and all the good times with.

The call chain started, and one by one the children have all checked into Shoney's. They mostly just want to stay around her and Charles's house. All the arrangements have been made, and the obituary is in the paper for those who need the information. The night before the funeral, at the wake, Charles and Jeanette went over the plans again as she wanted to have the hearse ride by the house on the way to the church.

The next morning, the boys were all at Charles's house and were checking out the new puppies under the shed. Suddenly Jan's husband Pat falls flat on his face before anyone can catch him. After making sure he was conscious, Jan was called from the motel, where she was having breakfast. The plans they had made a long time ago went into action. They took Debbie's minivan with Vernon driving, Jeanette riding shotgun, and Jan with a pan of cold water to wipe Pat's face in the back. They were on their way to Valdosta. Don't wait for an ambulance, time is of the essence. When they got into the emergency room, Jeanette went with Pat to verbally explain while Jan got his paperwork in order. He was admitted to the hospital, then Vernon and Jeanette rushed back to be with Lorene and the rest of the family. They were just in time to get into line when the hearse went by the house. They arrived at the church right on schedule, and within a matter of minutes, the little church at Pleasant Hill was filled with people.

Little did they know the minister, Rev. Perry McClelland, Lorene had asked to preach at the funeral was not there. However, the preacher from Pleasant Hill was there and offered to preach the funeral. The family went inside, and when the services were over, they all walked together to the cemetery to say their last good-byes. While there, Lorene's minister showed up an hour late. She was just consumed with grief. When her minister, Rev. McClelland, apologized and explained that someone from Pleasant Hill had called him that morning and said the newspaper was wrong that the funeral would be an hour later, she just couldn't believe it. Can you believe she hadn't seen that preacher from Pleasant Hill in four years and he conveniently showed up for Webb's funeral? Then she was heartbroken.

Well, everyone survived, and Pat was released from the hospital in Valdosta a few days later. She did get to go see him with some of the other family members and would see him again in Orlando. He was transferred from Valdosta to Orlando Regional in Orlando and diagnosed with an arrhythmia problem. From there, his doctor had a jet come in from St. Petersburg with a cardiologist and nurse to transport him to Fort Lauderdale. He had to move fast to get Pat an internal defibrillator. Eventually Pat made it home, and now he had to learn how to live with a defibrillator in his chest.

Lorene is getting the things that have to be done after a death in order. There is little for her to do now, and she has decided to visit Jan and see if she can be of any help there. Of course she was needed. Not to take care of anyone, but just to be a companion to Pat and Brian. She never dreamed she would have so much fun. She took Brian to Mae's fabrics and let him pick out just which material he wanted, and Pat bought enough material for seven pairs of "jams." These were when the latest thing was the longer shorts that came down to your knees. Brian is now nine years old and was the most up-to-date kid in school. His grandma Furney was his hero, and she was loving every minute of it and was sure he had no idea how much she enjoyed sewing for him.

The time has passed quickly, and she keeps extending her vacation. She has found a common ground with Pat. They both love anything *National Geographic*, and sometimes Pat has a problem focusing on words. Now she loves to read, and he will sit and let her read to him for long periods of time. It was very therapeutic for them both. There is a bonus. Jeanette lives nearby, and the families are together a lot. She swims with the children, or another adult does, almost every day.

She is getting in a lot of aqua aerobics and can cook if she wants to, or not even have to worry about it. This is like a long vacation, and she is getting used to it. Vernon has sent an announcement. His daughter Nichole is graduating from high school. She will go away to college and get her BA degree and then go back for her master's degree. Nichole started working for Chrysler Corporation fresh out of college and worked her way up to being supervisor very quickly.

It is now the Fourth of July and Lorene is all lined up with the neighborhood children to watch the fireworks, which the older boys will shoot off. There are fireworks out over the lake and the ones right in front of the house, and you can see the ones from the navy base in the back. This is her first time away from home on the Fourth, and she loves it. After they all come in and she is ready for bed, Jan gets a phone call from her younger brother Louis, and he wants to speak with her. Louis tells her that her grandson David Furney has been in a motorcycle accident and is badly hurt. She is so worried for her son Charles's family who has always been there for her. When Jeanette gets the call from her, she tells her they will head back to Georgia the next day. Jan can't leave Pat, so the rest of the family will be with him. They are back in Georgia when the sad news happens. Charles's son David Furney died on July 6, 1989.

After David's death, Lorene decided to stay near home and near Charles's family. She knew how difficult it is to give up a child. She would be there while they were healing, and sure enough, when the children had a heavy heart, Grandma was always there to listen to them talk. She was wise enough to know they just needed someone to listen. It is now January, and the cold weather is moving into Georgia. She decides it is time to return to Florida. Jan and Jeanette have heated swimming pools, and she knows Pat likes to swim almost every day.

She is back at Jan's house, and unless it is just too chilly, she can keep healthy swimming in the pool. She is truly blessed to have such a big family in Orlando. Jan's house is always busy with a big Sunday dinner (Jan now has five grandchildren), and even though Jan is still working, the load isn't heavy. Jan has found a nice lady from her church who comes and keeps her house clean. Lorene and Pat do all the cooking, which they both love to do. Brian is now taking violin lessons, and she doesn't miss a concert, or one of his baseball games. She will spend about six months out of almost every year for the next few years at Jan's house and still maintain her home in Georgia. While in Orlando, she also has the opportunity to spend a lot of weekends at Jeanette's home. Jeanette is still working, but weekends are for family or everybody just getting together at one of the homes.

She will be returning to spend more time in Georgia. Charles's family has some bad news. Charles's wife, Shirley, has been diagnosed with breast cancer, and even though she had surgery, the prognosis isn't good. She was at the Hart family reunion in Kissimmee, Florida, when she mentioned she had discovered the lump to someone. She waited too long, it is growing. The whole immediate and extended families are praying for Shirley along with their many friends. She was the first and most beloved of the aunts in the family at that time. All the children and adults loved Aunt Shirley and her children. Aunt Shirley took care of the little nieces and nephews who visited her family from the time they were babies.

On May 13, 1992, Shirley Whittington Furney died. This was Charles's wife of nearly forty years. The sad family had to say good-bye to their loved one. One of the tearful children commented, "Now who will wash our muddy sneakers before our mom finds out we were playing in that clay ditch?" Lorene stayed home for a while to be with the family and with her neighborhood, who stuck so close to Charles's family. If any neighborhood was there for their neighbors, it was Hopewell Church community. She spent the rest of the summer with her Georgia family.

  She is back in Orlando and enjoying her home away from home. Pat is a little under the weather. He has just had another internal defibrillator installed. This is his third, and his doctor is concerned. He will see how this one works out. She is busy going to baseball games, and now Brian is showing his talent for music. Shawna is also playing the piano. She has been to all the concerts and just loves hearing all the classical music they play as well as the country. Candice will start violin lessons soon. Jeanette has to go out of town for a business trip to Punta Gorda. Lorene is going to go with her and stay at the hotel. They will be gone for a week and she will entertain herself while Jeanette goes to work each day.

Lorene visits Punta Gorda

This is just wonderful, having a day to myself in such a luxurious setting, she thinks, as she makes her way down the stairs to the swimming pool. There are only a few people there, so she finds herself a chair and then gets into the water. After a couple of laps across the pool, a young man gets in and greeted her. They struck up a conversation and found they shared a lot of common interests in books and writing. As they were having dinner later, she mentioned how nice this man was to Jeanette. The next day, she was excited to have a new friend down at the pool. As they were talking, he mentioned he was a writer and she was just amazed at her luck. She couldn't wait to tell Jeanette.

Of course, by now, Lorene was also doing some writing. The next day Jeanette wanted to know who this stranger was and made it her business to go down with her. Can you believe he was the author of one of her favorite books? Well, to say the least, she was in good company. They spent the next few days having lunch together and talking about authors and writing. When it was time to go shelling at Sanibel on Saturday, Jeanette was wondering if Lorene even wanted to go. Dumb thought, she was so excited to spend the day doing what she liked best walking on the beach and looking for the seashells.

Lorene is back at Jan's and gets some interesting news. Her son-in-law Pat is going on the heart transplant waiting list. Pat's heart has gone through three defibrillators and it is time, no more waiting. Her grandson Nick is going through his own rocky waters now. He and his wife are getting a divorce, and he has moved back home with his mom until they get their house settled. He was awarded custody of both children, and Pat will be the stay-at-home parent, so the children will always have someone home after school. He has promised his mom he will be there to care for the house and Brian when his dad gets the transplant. Candice is in kindergarten this year and going to a private Christian school with her brother Marty. Jan wants her dressed in little dresses, and they both have to look perfect when they go to school. Lorene is so happy she gets to hem all those new little dresses for Candice, and she thinks Candice is just beautiful in them.

Nick will be there for Brian if Jan has to leave for Gainesville in a hurry. Pat is going to the University of Florida Medical Center in Gainesville, Florida, for the heart transplant. Jan has a pager that will go off when they receive one. There is no cellular coverage here in the country outside of Moultrie, and she is plenty nervous when they visit for Thanksgiving. She leaves the hotel number as an alternative for the Transplant team. When the transplant happens, Jan will be in Gainesville for two months. Pat will be monitored for any rejection should that happen. When released, he will go into an apartment in Gainesville to recuperate.

This apartment must be free of bacteria and mold. Jan and Debbie start looking around and cannot find anything livable with two bedrooms that will accept a short-term lease in the area. Jan has looked at the recommendations, and one transplant family was washing the entire place down with bleach and water. Jan is in tears, and Debbie is consoling her when Aunt Jeanette calls. She asked them to let her try through her bank. She is vice president of First Union and feels they may be able to help. Sure enough, the Charlotte office has a short-term lease agreement with an apartment complex for executives who are transferred to that area. Jeanette got the wheels rolling. Now to get a heart.

Bike week comes and goes, and finally they get the call just before Easter. They have two hours to get to Gainesville. They're on their way. Before they even get to the turnpike, they get another call. A fifteen-year-old is already in the hospital, and it's a match for him. They are disappointed but happy to know the fifteen-year-old will get to live because he now has a new heart. It has been a few weeks, and Pat isn't feeling well so Jan takes him to the doctor, who tells her the nausea is probably the flu. When she returns to the car with the nausea medication, Pat is looking bad so she just drives him straight to the hospital.

He is admitted, and that night, he is complaining about a bitter taste in his mouth, and she and Jeanette discuss the situation and decide his body is starting to shut down. She calls Shands Hospital again. The next morning the cardiology unit she is working with advises her to call Shands and tell them they need to transport him as soon as they can. Finally they advise the hospital to clear a parking lot. The helicopter is on the way.

Pat is finally in Gainesville, ready and hooked up, and Jan is nearby at a motel when she hears the helicopter leave during the night. A few hours later, she gets the call. The transplant team is on its way back with a heart. On March 29, 1994, Jan's husband finally gets a new heart that gives him a normal life. Jeanette is there with her by then, as she has been with every crisis that has occurred since Pat's first heart attack fourteen years ago. Jan's children are all over the place, but they are now on their way to join their parents. What a celebration for all of Lorene's family and the knowledge that Jesus has been with them every step and has heard all their prayers.

After two months Pat is home and can receive visitors but must wear a mask. No children that aren't in the immediate family are to visit him. There are too many chances for a childhood illness. Lorene cannot wait to see him.

The excitement has dwindled, and everyone is getting back to normal. It won't stay that way for long. All the children except Jan and Pat are back in Georgia. Lorene is now eighty years old on November 29, 1994. What a celebration the children and all the grandchildren are celebrating with her extended family and friends. There is a big luncheon and birthday cake at Hopewell Church. She thinks it looks like half of Moultrie is there. Everybody is taking pictures, and children are running all over the place. Finally while they are still having their good time, she gets someone to just sneak her out to the house and let her catch a quick nap.

It has been a cold winter in Georgia, and everyone is ready to get out and about. Lorene is already thinking about what kind of dessert she will make for the Hart reunion this year. The Friday night dinner is usually for about seventy-five people. Not everyone comes in on Friday, and her youngest son, Jerale, will have an old-fashioned fish fry with the coleslaw, hush puppies, and the works, or Jan will make enough baked ziti casserole with meatballs and Italian sausage for the whole bunch. Saturday is the main feast, which is catered for 150 to 200 people. Everyone makes a dessert, which is a big thing because you get everybody's specialty.

After the big dinner it is time for the singing and dancing and the talent time for the little ones. This year there is a surprise performance by her fifteen-year-old grandson Brian Acompora. All of Grandpa Babe Hart's grandchildren are asked to sit in the front row for the entertainment. Lorene, Leona, Sarah, Effie, Eula Mae, Paul, Brannon, and Wilma and great-grandsons Charles, Gil, Neal, and Jerale have been selected. Grandpa Babe's great-great-grandson Brian will now play on Grandpa Babe's violin all the old familiar fiddle tunes they loved to dance to when they were youngsters. His 1847 violin has been restored by his mother, Jan, and this is the time to introduce it to the family again. Lorene has tears in her eyes as she remembers tapping her little toes as a small child to the music from her grandpa Babe playing the country tunes. The grandchildren will now dance again to those old favorites—Cripple Creek, Old Joe Clark, and Bile Them Cabbage Down.

Brian Acompora plays Grandpa Babe's violin

Then the rest of the family joins in dancing, and Brian plays "Down Yonder" for his Uncle Charles to lead off the round dancing. Lorene can't remember when she has had so much fun, and the party continues until well after midnight, and she has retired for the evening. After the "old folks" go to their cabins, the young ones pull out the guitars, banjos, and the fiddle and will sit around a campfire and play and sing until the sun comes up.

She is fussing around in the closets and is wondering, "What do I pick to wear this time?" Lorene now will be gone a couple of weeks. "Well, I'll just have to have Delores let me know what to bring." Her son Jerale has just picked up his new conversion van, and they are off on a road trip, north and west. She is full of excitement as they head off to their first destination, Rockford, Illinois, and will see Vernon in a few days. The road trip is so comfortable, and being in the van, she can actually see the countryside as they cruise on through Tennessee after a refreshing stay there overnight. Jerale and Delores will make sure they take breaks often and see all the sites as they travel on. As her children enjoy their visit in Rockford and Vern has showed them around his hometown, they are on their way even farther north. Next stop was Colorado Springs.

She is happy to see her grandson Sandy, who is stationed in Colorado Springs at the military base there. She is proud of the job he is doing, serving his country so far away from home. His next tour of duty will be in Germany. She just can't believe how beautiful it is, although she is a little nervous riding up and down those big hills. Little does she realize she is going to be in the mountains tomorrow? The Colorado mountains are something she had read about, and they are as beautiful and rugged as she expected.

Riding along, seeing the rugged countryside and those beautiful Aspen trees that go on forever. They are headed to Cripple Creek and have stopped at a place called Meadow Muffins to eat. She wonders where it got its name. However, the food is good. Now they are lost but having a wonderful time while they are. Oh, but the mountains are scary if she looks down, but as she looks up, she can see Pikes Peak, and the top is covered in snow. She had read that it is covered in snow even in the heat of summer. As they go through the tunnel on their way up, she is not so sure she likes this high altitude.

They are on their way back and are riding beside a very rough river that is so beautiful, like in the movies with people rafting on it. Then they are at the Royal Gorge. "Oh my goodness, I just can't believe this!" Lorene exclaims as she approaches that long suspended bridge. The cavern is so deep, and as she looks at the railroad tracks at the bottom running along beside the river, they look like a toy. No way will she walk out on that bridge. Just looking at it makes her scared.

As they start their trip south, she cannot believe how beautiful New Mexico is, and they are now headed for North Carolina. As they approach the Great Smokey Mountains, she sits back and relaxes, knowing she can enjoy the sights her ancestors saw. They migrated through that very rugged territory with oxen, carrying their personal possessions in a cart behind them. The Hart family ended up in Colquitt County, where they developed a community near where the Pleasant Hill Church stands today. As they come off the skyline drive, she is exhilarated to think she has completed the drive, and wishes her dear father could have enjoyed it with her. They are on their way back to Florida where they can rejoin their families and always remember that spectacular trip together.

The beautiful fall weather and the beauty of poplar trees in the branch behind her home, with their golden leaves, take her right into a mild winter. She will attend to her duties of visiting the nursing homes with a birthday cake, to celebrate with the seniors who have a birthday that month. She still has her Guys and Dolls luncheons and meetings to attend. The Sunday school classes are always a joy to her as well as attending the sermon. With all the things that are going on, she learns her granddaughter Charlotte, who lives next door with her dad, is having her an eighty-first birthday party right in front of the house.

Shoney's is full, with all her children here, and this time Jan can come even though Pat has to wear a mask. Charlotte has started the big pots of chili in her kitchen, and the birthday cake is all set up. There is a DJ that also sings, all set up on a flatbed truck trailer as a stage with music.

The good Lord has blessed her with another glorious birthday celebration filled with the joy of her big family around her. The music has started, and they have her start off the dancing with her children all joining in. To think her and Webb started all this so long ago, and the tradition has continued from the days at the Gene Mills dance hall. Who would have ever believed they would have so many dancers?

There's always more excitement. Jeanette and Al are having a fortieth wedding anniversary on December 22. Her children Jerry and Diane are having a surprise party. Jerry is having the food flown in with him from Texas. Dianne, Aunt Jan, and Aunt

Mae have to get the boys in a hustle to set the room up where Jeanette's neighbors are delivering them to a dance in a location they haven't been before. That was no surprise, but the party inside was. They never were so surprised, and they all had a grand time with a fifties' dance complete with poodle skirts, crinolines, and a jukebox. There was lots of fun and a great surprise.

Jeanette and Al's fortieth anniversary;
Al, Jeanette, Pat, Diane, and Jerry

Of course Lorene will also have a little time to visit Florida again when the cold of January 1996 moves in. She will visit her families in Orlando. She looks forward to going to Jeanette's now. The children have moved out, with Jerry living in Sarasota and Diane married. They can just relax around the pool and enjoy each other's company. When she goes to Jan's, she is not surprised to see Pat still has to wear a mask when they attend church. She has always attended Mass with them when she stays there. She likes that they can receive communion together every week. Brian is an altar boy, and she is so proud to look up and see him standing beside the priest as she receives communion. That is something she had missed in the Baptist church. She also has learned that they do not worship the Virgin Mary, and that God is in all their churches. They just never had communion very often in Pleasant Hill Church and not as often at Hopewell, as the Catholics enjoy Communion every week with each other.

She then goes further south to see her old friends and families in West Palm Beach. She just knows walking along the saltwater at the beach is good for her arthritis, and the waves rippling on shore is enough to make anyone appreciate the seashells that dot the coastline. Mae and Jerale are always so glad when she comes, and the children always have something they need to talk to Grandma about. She is happy to know Mae is continuing her Baptist faith here in West Palm Beach. Mae's family now goes to a Baptist church. They are all getting older, and with all of them married already, she wonders where the time went.

Now that Lorene is settled in for the summer, she gets busy with her own projects. She is involved with the Guys and Dolls at Hopewell and is busy going to different organizations teaching them how to build bluebird houses. She has her yard full of flowers that have to be watered, and if there is a group of her friends going out of town to go to a new restaurant or if there is a trip to Callaway gardens, she is with them. She is so busy you have to call early, or you won't catch her.

There is sadness in her heart she has had to give up another of her siblings. Her youngest sister Wilma, who was now living with her husband John in Orlando, has passed away. Her daughter Jeanette and Leona's oldest daughter Vara were there with John until the end and helped with the final arrangements. Vara appears to have everything worked out with Vanada for the final arrangements here in Georgia. Now Cristal is there, and Jan has just gotten back from the airport with her youngest son, Andrew. John and Cristal have decided to have her nephew Steve

Hart preach her funeral service at the little church, Pleasant Hill. There, Wilma as a young girl had first accepted Jesus Christ as her Savior when she went to church with her mother. Wilma's sons, Steve and Kenneth, with their families, are on their way to meet them in Georgia. Then everything starts breaking down.

Vara has just received the news from Vanada that the little church Cristal wants to have her service in is not available. Pleasant Hill Church has made plans to paint the inside this weekend. Well, it all worked out. The services were in the funeral home in Moultrie. You could hear a pin drop as Brian played his grandpa Babe's violin to the soft notes of "Ashokan Farewell" (Lorene's favorite from the soundtrack of the PBS series *The Civil War*). This was his tribute to a great Southern lady as the family entered the chapel. Her nephew Steve Hart preached at her funeral. She was buried next to her parents in Pleasant Hill Church Cemetery.

Later in the year, Lorene and her sisters were delighted to get an opportunity to go to North Carolina to see the fall foliage. They were there at the peak of the season, and she just loved seeing the maples in beautiful red colors and the poplars all dressed in gold. She would again enjoy being in the Great Smokey Mountains. Her sister Leona's daughters made arrangements for lodging, and they all had a great time.

She is again into a cold winter and is blessed to be in her warm home, where her grandchildren can come and go as they please. She has Charles's family as well as Gil's family to bring her anything she may need from the store if she doesn't want to go out. There is always someone there to keep her company, and she only has to walk next door if she chooses to visit someone. Charles also chooses to stay home in cold weather.

The spring has broken out in brilliant sunshine, and flowers are popping up all over the place. Charles's boys have raked up any leaves that have been left over, and it is just a good time to sit in the swing out front and think about the bountiful crops that will be in soon. She has enjoyed all the greens and is now tired of the cabbage. She is just ready to sit on the swing out front and shell peas and little baby butter beans.

Her brother Brannon has a little granddaughter Audrey, who is only about three years old, and they are enjoying spoiling her. Audrey's parents both work, and when he can get her over to Aunt Lorene's, she has a great time. While they sit on the swing and watch, she plays with the other children next door who have all kinds of toys in Charles's yard, and it seems there is always a puppy that one of his grandchildren has dragged over.

She has enjoyed going fishing with the family here in the ponds around the house. The fish may be bigger in Florida, but she still just likes to sit around with a cane pole and see if she can catch one here. Of course now that she is getting older the boys only want her to be where it is safe, and she won't fall into a hole of water off a dock. Gil worries the most when she is off fishing at her cousin Mary Lee Norman's. He says they are getting too old to be off fishing in that pond by themselves.

The hot summer has been a good one, and now that they are into fall, her heart has broken. Her brother Brannon was found dead in his home. He suffered a heart attack while he was making dinner. She is saying a sad farewell to another one of her siblings. She thanks God for the strength to keep her going. She will be eighty-three in November and still has fairly good health. Thank God her granddaughter Lori Ann lives down the road, and as always, she makes sure no one will happen up and find her house a mess.

Thanksgiving at Charles's house

Bonfire at Thanksgiving

Hayride at Thanksgiving

Thanksgiving is coming, and Lorene thinks the children will all be down again as they like to be here for dinner and celebrate her birthday at the same time. The ones who don't come for Thanksgiving just show up the weekend after, and they all have a big birthday bash for her. The younger children from out of state think they have to be here because Uncle Charles will always have a hayride and a huge bonfire.

Everyone in Georgia and Florida are excited. There is another wedding anniversary. Jan and Pat will be married for forty years on December 22 this year. This one won't be a surprise. Debbie and Nick will be having it at the golf clubhouse beside Debbie's house. The theme is Western. Grab your boots and grab your partner, there's gonna be a barbecue. She rides down with Charles and his family. There will be five generations at this party: Lorene, Charles, granddaughter Charlotte, great-grandson Robbie, and great-great-grandson McKenzie. What a celebration. There was a DJ to play any kind of music they wanted to hear, and of course, there were a lot of songs sung by Michelina, Mae's daughter, and Jan's granddaughters. Everybody wore their cowboy boots and jeans and had a good time.

Jan and Pat's fortieth wedding anniversary

Five generations; Lorene holding McKenzie Blaxton

Jan and Pat's fortieth wedding anniversary

It is finally late spring, and she is ready to hit the road again. She plans to go south. She will be at Jan's for a little while. Her last grandson, Brian, is graduating from high school. She remembers so well when his dad waited a year to have open-heart surgery and just wanted to see him start kindergarten. She would stand on the front porch with him when Brian would go to catch the bus and watch the pride in his eyes. Now thanks to God, he was graduating from high school. Brian A. Acompora, class of 1998, Winter Park High. It seems like only yesterday when his brother was graduating from the same school. Now for the graduation party. His friends are mostly a year behind him in school. Being an August baby, they put him a year ahead of the kids he plays baseball and the kids he played in the youth orchestra with. In a couple of months his proud parents will drop him at Saint Leo's College, near Tampa, with his little pickup truck he got as a graduation present, his microwave, little fridge, and TV—just like home.

Brian Acompora, class of 1998; Lorene, Brian, and Pat

Mr. and Mrs. Ron and Stacey Harvey are married

Lorene is visiting with Jeanette and discussing how much longer she can continue living alone. The children all feel she needs to be in an apartment where she can meet more people her age and have no responsibility for yard work or anything else that she can no longer do. She agrees she cannot fulfill the responsibilities physically, and they all agree she is fortunate to have a good, sharp mind and no illnesses. She can continue her church life at Hopewell and add some new pleasures to her life. OK, she's a little reluctant but agrees to move into Forrest Apartments, where she will have a cord to pull by her bed and one in the bathroom if she has an emergency. She also has a lifeline where she can push a button secured around her neck to get 911.

Well, Lorene is all moved in, and it is much better than she dreamed. She now belongs to the YMCA, which is only across the street, and she goes over at least four times a week for water aerobics. She has someone to help out with the housework once a week, and she has been very busy. She now has her old friends from the Guys and Dolls, the YMCA, and the service group always calling for a dish or a gift for a newlywed or a new baby. She still attends Sunday school and services on Sunday and prayer meetings on Wednesday nights. She looks forward to a rest in Florida every once and a while just so she can catch her breath. She's busy.

With all that's going on, she comes down with a serious case of bronchitis and ends up in the hospital in Thomasville, where she now has pneumonia and is really sick. She just can't believe it. Mae and Jeanette are there at the hospital, right behind her. They get a room at the nearby motel and are there when she needs them. She gets an allergic reaction to the medication and decides this is her turn to go. She just knows she is out of this world and on her way. Then she awakens and sees the same window that was in her hospital room. She is very unhappy and relates to Jan that she knew it was her time. Jan responded with "Well, Mom, if it was, why are you still here?" She thought about it for a minute.

"I guess maybe it wasn't my turn yet, I'll just have to see what it is he has in store for me." Several days later she returned to her little apartment, where she started setting out her gerbera daisies and little flowers in the area she had fixed up and then ran off to the YMCA for her water aerobics.

Now it is time to start getting the graduation cards again. She has Jason, Cindy, Bryan Furney, and Shawna who should be graduating this spring. Jason has won third place in the state for his architectural drawings. That should get him into a good college. Cindy is already enrolled at the nursing school in Tifton and can't wait to get going. Shawna has enrolled and has been accepted at the University of Central Florida in Orlando and will graduate from the same school as her mom. These great-grandchildren are not waiting for anybody. They are on the ball, and she is loving it.

Mr. and Mrs. Jason Furney are married

Mr. and Mrs. Patrick Canady with Lorene and Charles

Jennifer Gerhardt graduates from high school, and Shawna graduates from University of Central Florida

UF Graduate Program
Commencement
May 1, 2010

Zachary Gerhardt with a master's degree
from the University of Florida

Lorene is now enjoying her apartment and doesn't have a lot of responsibility. Now she has the laundry done when the house is cleaned. She can't change the sheets anyhow and is running out of air before she can do them. She has COPD but won't let it slow her down too much. You can count on her for a dish if someone calls from Hopewell, and she never misses a day swimming at the Y. Charles, Gil, and her grandchildren stop by every time they come into town. The rest of her family also stops by when they go shopping. Living in Moultrie isn't too bad.

The children have been at the hotel and are in town for their Aunt Effie and her family. Her husband, Durwood Crosby, has passed away, and they all want to support "Aunt Fluffy" and the rest of the family. He and Lorene's sister Effie also had a large family and, at one time, were farmers. Durwood left the farm also to find a better life for his family.

This is the big millennium year everyone is talking about, and Lorene is sure it won't affect her much as she doesn't have a computer and her needs are simple. So far she doesn't know what the fuss is about. She is still driving her car and getting to the places she needs to go. She has some really good friends she likes to see on a daily basis at the swimming pool over at the YMCA. Her granddaughter Lori Ann always manages to get her plenty of pecans and has them cracked before leaving them for her to shell. She is so grateful and knows that is one thing she won't run out of. Lori Ann and Tommy's son Jason, who graduated from high school last year, will be getting married soon. He is marrying his sweetheart from high school, who is also an architectural design student. Rebecca will work for the city of Moultrie while she is attending architectural design classes.

The peas and butter beans are now in, and Lorene is very busy getting her vegetables ready for the freezer. She only preserves figs and pears in jars now. It is just too much doing all that canning when she has such a nice big freezer. The children feel it is not necessary to get so much in the freezer, but old habits are hard to break. She wants to get everything finished up so she can go spend some time with Jeanette now that she has retired. They always go all over the place seeing different attractions, and maybe they will ride over to Winter Park to see the museum with the Tiffany glass collection in it. She will be back before Thanksgiving.

The big Thanksgiving feast will be at her son Gil's this year. Gil loves big dinners, and his wife, Betty, being from a very small family of four, hardly knows where to start. Jan and her family will come in the weekend before, and Jan will help Betty get the dinner ready. The boys are all hitting the woods, of course, to get in the hunting. Gil is not in the woods. He has decided he will help cook for the fifty-plus crowd of people coming for dinner. Lorene decides she will just make her corn bread dressing and then watch the rest work.

This big bunch has gotten too big for her to try to handle. While getting the tables set up, Jan said Gil appeared tired. She suggested he might want to see a doctor. He agreed. The whole crew shows up for the big dinner, and the house and the yards are full. The turkey and the corn bread dressing, which Lorene always makes herself—along with the yams, green beans, creamed onions, peas, cranberry sauce, and every kind of pie you can think of—was a big hit. After the crowd decided to clear out and the Florida bunch went back home, Gil came to spend some time with his mom. After tests that were done in Thomasville, he told her he has lung cancer.

Her world has been rocked upside down. She doesn't know how she can do this. She keeps her control and shares with him that he will need many prayers, and he needs to get his house in order. She is calm and confident on the outside, but her inside is just shattered. She will pray and ask all her friends to pray with her for her son and his family. Having started his married life later than the rest, his family is younger than the rest. She now knows it is in God's hands. She has told her children many times, "God can't help you if you don't give it to him. If you say you gave it to him but continue to hang on to it because you think you can fix it, he can't help you because you still haven't given it to him."

Gil is selling his little piece of property while he is well. Betty doesn't want to live in the country by herself. Lorene sees him as often as she can, and she even asks him for help with things she doesn't really need help with. She's trying to keep him busy. As time rolls on, she gets busy with her everyday things, like swimming, going away on little short trips but tries to stay close to home. The children are all coming in often now but not enough to become overwhelming for Gil. She has noticed he spends a lot of time with his brother Charles. They still are close brothers.

Charles's oldest son, Roger, has always been there to move her, cook for her, or anything he can do for his grandmother. Now she is asking him again to move her to a disabled apartment. She is only five feet tall and really needs a stove and sink she can reach. He is ready when the apartment is. She feels bad that Jeanette comes and has to clean up such a mess. She spends a week getting it cleaner than the Moultrie Hospital and making sure the plumbing, the wiring, and anything else is in order. This is a great day. Roger has moved her—for the last time, she hopes. He has taken his truck and moved her every time she has moved. She and Jeanette are real happy with the results. She has the window facing the garden in back covered with a solar tinting to cut down on the sunlight in the day, and the drapes are hung. It is just perfect, and she has enjoyed having Jeanette there.

Now Mae is on a visit and has brought a nice surprise. She has brought two of the prettiest pictures of cotton fields and the old houses in them. She doesn't know if they are valuable, but she has just fallen in love them. She agrees they are right where they should be. Mae always knows just what she likes and is always the one to make sure a special day doesn't pass without beautiful roses or whatever is appropriate for the occasion. She also has two beautiful pictures from Diane, which Jeanette has brought in. If this keeps up, she will have to get a larger apartment.

She hasn't said too much about her sister-in-law Melvin, but Webb's sisters have always said she was one of them. When they have a get-together, Webb's youngest sister, Marie, picks her up, and she is just one of the sisters. She now lives very close to Melvin's home. They see each other more than the others. Now Melvin doesn't drive, so when Lorene shops, she takes Melvin with her. They really love each other like sisters, and they will drive all the way to Thomasville just to save thirty-five cents on a bag of sugar. Really, Lorene just loves to go to Publix, and that is the closest one. They usually go out to eat on Friday nights. Now that Lorene lives in town, this is a treat for them both. Lorene always told Melvin she doesn't get out enough and socialize with other people, which is Lorene's thing. She never meets a stranger.

She knows everybody in the nursing homes and visits them often. If there is a luncheon anywhere in town and she is invited, she is there with a dish. She has a special friend Ruby Goodson from church and a special friend Rose from the Y. There are numerous others as well as Angie who would like her to just move in with them. All these people are her family of friends she likes to be with. Her children live all over the place, but she has friends that are near and dear.

Now Gil's cancer isn't getting any better, and he has had all the treatments, lost his hair and grown it back, but he won't let it get him down. His grandchildren are his life. Jami has always been his baby but is now growing up, and Haley and Jesse are right behind her. He tries to teach them all the things he knows he will not be there to teach them. He has so much to tell them and so little time. He will now have to depend on Carrie and Laran to finish this for him.

He has had yard sales and sold most of his farm equipment and has moved Betty into an apartment in town. They still have a lot of things in storage, but it will have to wait. Lorene knows he is tired and encourages him to rest. He sells the last of the fence posts and then decides it's time to rest. He goes into his room and crawls into bed. After about a week, Betty calls in the hospice and the family. She can't do this alone. The family will take turns. Jan and Mae will take the first week. After about five days, Jan needs to go home for more clothes and Mae will stay until she gets back. The day after Jan left, Mae knew she wouldn't get to go home for a break. Gilbert L. Furney died on September 4, 2002.

Can she possibly go through this again, Lorene is thinking. She takes time to compose herself and decides she is the one her children will be looking to for guidance. She puts on her best clothes, her makeup and puts her Bible under her arm. As long as God is with her, all things are possible.

The children have all been to the Keys for the lobster season and are still devastated with the big loss of Gil, "their biggest fisherman." When he was only ten years old, after paddling his daddy's boat out every day at Brice's Pond, he was given the name of "the little fisherman." Many of them have stayed home as long as they can to be with Lorene. She understands they all have jobs to go back to. Sadly they leave her in Georgia and try to move on with their lives and do whatever they can for Betty and their children.

Lorene gets right back into her regular routine of swimming every day and helping others when she can. She regularly reads her Moultrie paper, the *Reader's Digest* and, of course, her *National Geographic*. She always says, "A mind is too wonderful a thing to waste" and tries to keep hers active. She will be ready for the whole bunch when they come down for Thanksgiving again this year, and while they are here, she will celebrate her eighty-eighth birthday. Sometimes her mind can't help but wander back to the years when she and Webb were in their first little house by her mom and dad. There were just the two of them. Charles hadn't been born yet, and for the first time since they were married, they could actually just stand and hug each other and become intimate without worrying about someone interrupting them. They were just young people in love and enjoying just being together.

As the children started coming every two years, their concentration changed from just each other to the wonders of their children growing up. Somewhere in those years there were times that were really hard. Lorene let herself go, and Webb was out philandering and looking for the companionship he was not getting at home. These times were the times their love for one another paid off. She sure wasn't a quitter, and Webb always loved her for it. They may have had some bad times, but as their children grew, they had some great times that many people would cherish. When they moved back to Georgia and their children were all grown up, that young love was still there but in a more mature way? They no longer had to worry about buying a home or where the money for bills would come from. They still had health insurance and so many children and grandchildren that loved them dearly. Now in their old age, they could be intimate if they wanted to, and it didn't really matter to anyone but them. Their love for each other was still strong, and many were the days after Webb's death she just longed to be able to share her everyday experiences with him. Now she looked forward to that day again.

She hurries over to the YMCA for her exercise class and is so glad to be able to still get finished in time for the Guys and Dolls luncheon. Mary had fixed her hair yesterday, and all she had to do was get her makeup on, grab her covered dish, and go enjoy herself. She is thinking again that having a big bunch of kids is like having money in the bank. She has Mae making sure that her hair is done every week, and each one has something that they like to do for her because she is too hard to buy presents for. She has everything she could ever want. Her granddaughter Debbie always remembers to pay her dues at the YMCA every year in June before she can even pay them. She never has to worry about a magazine subscription; Jeanette and Cyndi take care of that, and her son Charles is there to share her life with anytime. He also has a house full of children and grandchildren of any age. He has just gotten a new one. His great-granddaughter Jaylin came into the world on February 4, 2003. Another little cotton top with those big blue eyes. A big family is the best.

All the families down south are getting ready to go to Cudjoe Key again. The boats are all ready, and it is already decided who will ride with who, so they can get the maximum lobster count for each boat. The first Tuesday night after they are there, they have a big fish-and-lobster feast. The girls will do the inside cooking, and the boys will put the lobster tails on the grill as well as the fish they want grilled. What a time. They always beg Lorene to come down, and she did for a while, but now it is just too hot in August and she doesn't care to get into all that excitement. She guesses that she and Webb must have gotten that started with all those fish fries when the kids were little. Of course now, all the kids who are big enough to steer a boat get to drive the boat so everyone else can fish or dive for lobsters. Webb would always buy the grandchildren their first fishing rod when she lived in Florida. That was always one of his biggest joys, along with helping them to pull in their first fish.

She is just getting ready to start plans for Thanksgiving. The kids are now getting their reservations at the new Hampton Inn. They are so excited. Shoney's has gone downhill, and lately they have stayed at the Holiday Inn. They are so glad that Wendy, who used to work at Shoney's, will be the manager at the new hotel. It is always nice to see a familiar face. She has known her sister Eula Mae was ill for some time. She has just learned she passed away on October 20, 2003. What a sad time for the family.

Now the holidays are over, and Jeanette has planned a wonderful trip for her and Melvin. It is spring, and they are going up to around Atlanta to see all the beautiful flowers and visit the Callaway Gardens. This will be a good time to just stay in a hotel and go see all the sights and eat out. Melvin is as excited as she is, and Jeanette makes sure they don't miss out on anything. What a wonderful getaway for a few days.

The heat of summer is upon Georgia. Lorene keeps mentioning the hurricanes that hit Florida while she was there, and she says this might be a bad year. It is now August, and it looks like she may be right. There are no plans to go catch lobster this year. The boys who are working for Palm Beach County are all on call. The storms are headed that way. Jeanette and Al sold their house last summer and moved into a condominium in the same complex as Mae, and they are happy to not have the burden of boarding up their home. West Palm Beach missed the bullet.

Jan and Pat's son Nick, owns a construction company, and has taken his men with the trucks and started with Jan's house first. They have boarded every employee's home up. If the storm hits Orlando, they won't have time to worry with their personal needs. They work for Fema and will be very busy.

It has been sixty years since a hurricane hit Orlando, but it came in fast and furious. Orlando took a direct hit. Lorene was very nervous because she could see on TV it was hitting Orlando. Jan's neighborhood, as well as many others, was devastated. The morning after, when it was safe, the boys headed for Jan's first. She had lost almost all the trees on her property, but the largest oak she had is now lying on the front of her house and she can't get the garage open, let alone get out. Jan has to be able to leave if necessary for medical reasons. Fortunately she had her Spanish tile roof replaced two years earlier. After the trees were removed, she just had to clean up. No major damage to her home.

However, her neighborhood was devastated by what looked like a small twister that came through. Her neighbors up and down the street had roof damage, and some of their ceilings were already falling in. It was very depressing for everybody. Lorene was worried about her son-in-law Pat. Last summer, when they were headed for Florida Keys, he was bitten by fire ants on the side of the turnpike. The wound had become very bad in spite of the doctors and the care he had received. He was diabetic, and the concern was for his new heart if they couldn't get the wound to heal.

All the destruction and seeing the swimming pool enclosure now lying inside the pool was depressing him.

Jan just left the windows boarded up, and three weeks after Hurricane Charlie, they had Frances headed their way. She got the call that they were leaving town and headed for Georgia. Jan had reserved five rooms at the Hampton Inn for her family and Nick's, plus rooms for his other employees' families. The boys were all still helping clean up from Charlie. When they finally got to her house eleven hours later, she went to the hotel with them because Moultrie would be getting gale force winds as it headed right up the state. What a little mini vacation they all had.

Most of the hotel was full of people fleeing the storm. The hotel treated them all so special, and the guests all formed a bond. They all enjoyed the company of each other during the stress of not knowing what was going on at home. Of course, with her being the only ninety-year-old there, they all treated her like royalty.

When the weather started getting bad in Moultrie, the Hampton Inn brought in food so the guests would not have to venture out. By now everybody knew who Lorene was, and they set her chair right in front of the television so she could hear the news while the children played up and down the hallways. She had her meals brought to her, she played with the small children, and when she was ready for a nap, she just went up to her room and took a nice nap with no noise. When they all started pulling out to go home after a few days, she felt like they were all a big family.

What a year. We have Thanksgiving coming, and all the family will be at the Hampton Inn again. This year after Thanksgiving they will celebrate her big ninetieth birthday on Friday. They have big plans, and they have decorated Maule's aircraft hangar so that you wouldn't even know it was a hangar. Mrs. Maule lets them dance there on Friday nights and said she would be delighted to have Charles's mother's party there. As usual there is the big immediate family and the even larger extended family and then all the friends in Moultrie. She is all excited and just can't believe her good fortune. The food is all set up on big buffet tables across the side of the room. The children are behind the table, serving their guests, and the grandchildren are serving the drinks and keeping the food line going.

Lorene's ninetieth birthday cake (Grannie Sweets)

Mae has a special cake made with her picture on it. It is a picture of her on her seventieth birthday, when she rode from Fort Lauderdale to West Palm Beach on the back of her son Jerale's motorcycle. The inscription reads "Granny Sweets." They have a big dinner and then a dance. A country band is here for music and brought some featured line dancers with them. Little did they know she had her own bunch of dancers? She gets to dance with Charles and then the rest of the boys. Everyone danced, down to the smallest toddler. Since it was a family event, there were no alcoholic beverages, and the adults brought all their children along. It just doesn't get better.

Lorene with siblings

Lorene's seventieth birthday with Jerale
from Fort Lauderdale to West Palm Beach

Lorene's ninetieth birthday

    She is finally settling down and getting back in her routine, when she hears that Pat's new treatments for the infection from the ant bite he received on his way to the Keys last summer isn't working. He has spent each afternoon for two months in a hyperbaric chamber. The infection has worsened and could get to the bone in his leg, which would cause his new heart to reject. Pat makes a quick decision and goes into the hospital a week after he was in Georgia. He will have his right leg amputated and be in rehabilitation until after Christmas. The surgery was successful and saved his life. She feels sad but knows he made the right decision.

    She is off to a good start for the new year. Thank God Jan's husband is healthy with his heart working fine. He is out of rehabilitation and is getting a new prosthesis. Moving forward, Lorene is trying to get her water aerobics as often as possible, but it is just too cold sometimes. She will do her exercises in the gym or at home. Her doctor is concerned because she is having some difficulty breathing. Can you believe it? As healthy as she thought she was, she has come down with pneumonia and is in the hospital for a few days. That surely took the wind out of her sails.

The children all rush over as usual, and everyone is telling her to slow down. Now she is using an inhaler, and she is worried he will put her on oxygen. If she slows down, that means she will soon be home bound. Phooey on that. You either use it or lose it. She can now get about and is driving back to Hopewell and shopping. She has filled her hummingbird feeders and hung them in the dogwood tree, and her lilies look beautiful. This didn't put too much of a dent in her social life.

She now has her sister Sarah living in the apartments near her. She has sold her big farm on Sarah Lane and is ready to live a more relaxed life. She is surprised to find that her sister doesn't have too many activities in her life, and gets busy trying to get her more socially active. Her sister sleeps late and can't get out of the house before eleven o'clock and doesn't like to swim, so that leaves her to find her own activities.

While Lorene is out of town visiting, she is gone for a month or so at a time. She is on her way to the condominium complex in West Palm Beach and has a scooter with her so she can get around easily between the units. Jeanette has gotten her a pass so she can use the bus for transportation, swim in any pool in the complex, attend movies in the afternoon, and go to all the live shows and dances in the theater. She was thinking seriously about moving into one of her daughter Mae's condos. She loves her children down south but misses her group of friends in Georgia as well as her sisters. She has decided after a couple of months that she will remain in her own little apartment with no one to tell her what to do, and when she should do it. Thank God she tried it before she turned over her own little place.

They will ask for a private dining room and all go to a restaurant in Thomasville this year for Thanksgiving dinner. They just don't have a house big enough for all of them, and if it was enough room to eat, there still wouldn't be enough bathrooms. When they go out for dinner, there are anywhere from forty to fifty of them. Lorene still thinks it is ridiculous for them to go to the Hampton Inn when they come home. She is sure she could find enough private homes for them to stay in. But she finally gets it. They all come home at the same time of year, so they can all wake up under the same roof. The lobby becomes their living room, and they have a hot breakfast to share with the others no matter who sleeps late. There are always so many teenagers you can't expect them to be ready when you are.

She just goes over and joins them and has a great time. After their big dinner, they will all go back and take a little nap before they head for the courthouse square. At six o'clock sharp, they will turn on the Christmas lights that are hung from the top of the courthouse and reaches over each street surrounding it, and everybody will go *ahhhhh*. The children will be so excited to see Santa in his sleigh, which is pulled by real live reindeer. Then everybody will hit the little shops to see what kind of treasure they will find. On the Friday after Thanksgiving, they will celebrate her birthday.

She has a great concern for Charles through the holidays. All the years working in the cotton mill while he was young then working in the mobile home factory putting in Sheetrock then the cotton gin has gotten his emphysema going crazy. He has a hard time breathing. By Christmas he is on oxygen for twenty-four hours a day. It doesn't look good. It is now so cold out, and Charles is home bound. She rides out to Culbertson as often as she can, and when she goes to Hopewell, she always stops by. If she has made a little food she knows he especially likes, she will bring it and share it with him. Their days are numbered, and she knows it. She just prays for him and also for herself.

It is getting warmer, and she is off to church at Hopewell and is sitting at the veteran's highway, waiting to make her left turn.

"Why do these people have to have such a line turning in here to go to church at the same time I am leaving? You would think the highway department would give them a longer turn lane." Then everything turns black. It sounds as if she can hear people murmuring. When she goes to focus her eyes, she can now hear them, and she is in the emergency room. There was a car coming when she pulled out, but she didn't see it as it was way back at the end of the row of cars that were winding their way onto Twenty-sixth Street. It T-boned her car. After two hours in the emergency room, she is discharged, so Roger can take her home. Well, nothing is that simple. Jeanette and Jerale are here at her house to stay the night and see how well she is. When Jeanette calls her doctor, he has a fit. He wants her back at the hospital.

The next morning she gets the battery of tests that show three hematomas to the head, two that are serious. There are bruises all over her body and her left leg is blackish purple from the thigh to the tip of her toes. When she is admitted to the hospital and gets into her room, here sits Mae and Jeanette.

She barely says hello, and she wants to know where her purse is. When she gets it, the first thing she does is look for her wallet. "Where is my driver's license?" She is now ninety-two years old and making sure she can still drive. She is looking at Jeanette distrusting. "Mom, the highway patrol took your license," replied Jeanette. She is not too happy and is already thinking how she can get it back. She later finds out her turbo-drive Chrysler has been totaled and her driving days are over.

She is in rehabilitation out at Cobblestone for around six weeks and manages the best she can to stay put. Fortunately she has a beautiful young lady for a roommate, Georgette, who is very intelligent and is from horse country around Okeechobee, Florida. She has been the rodeo circuit, and all her family are cow people and horse breeders. Georgette appreciates art and music. The scratches on her face are from the barbed wire she walked into at her sister's home where she lived. She is a sleepwalker, and now she will go to an assisted living, where she will not be able to walk off. How lucky could she be to have such a wonderful roommate?

Candice Acompora, high school graduate, class of 2006

While there, she finds out there are lots of people she knows. Mr. Jim Short was an attorney she knew and swam with her every day at the YMCA. His nice secretary had arranged a luncheon for all of them at the country club, just before they were admitted here. Also her old friend Della Mickles was down the hall from her.

Well, her time was finally up, and she was back safe and sound at home with no wheels. She would just have to make do. The grandchildren all picked her up, and of course, Lori Ann was always there any time she needed her. She is getting back into her routine and has had to tell the children she would not be able to take the trip to Orlando for the wedding. She just feels tired. Her grandson Nick Acompora is marrying a beautiful young lady from Chicago, Caryn Anderson. She is the single mother of a teenager, Mariah, and hopefully they will be strong enough to merge their families. All the family will be there for this big occasion.

Mr. Nicholas C. Acompora II marries Caryn Anderson

She was so shocked to see how poorly Charles was doing. He now needed twenty-four-hour care, and Roger and Charlotte had gotten him a room in the nursing home. He only lasted about three weeks. Charles W. Furney died on May 18, 2006. She walks out the door with her children to say good-bye to another of their own. She has lost a son, and they have lost a dear brother who was like a father to them as well. He was the one who cared and tended to them all. She can barely listen to the services. She just remembers, "No mother should have to outlive their children."

The hot summer is as hot as usual, but the days just fly by. She is keeping busy with the things she likes best and is spending a lot of time with her sisters. Things are not going well for her son-in-law who received the heart transplant in 1994. The heart is working great, but he is having other things going on.

Jeanette has brought her some tomato plants, and they are doing well along with her flowers, which she loves to take care of. All the children come in from out of town from time to time for their visits and make sure they don't all come at once. Mae and Gerald come up pretty often as the boys have hunting leases in north Georgia and like to stop by to say hello.

The children have already started getting their plans for Thanksgiving together. There are so many, they have to make sure their reservations are all in before the hotel gets booked up. They do really like to get together, and now that the grandchildren are married and are having children, the group just gets bigger.

The boys are having a big hunting trip up in Wisconsin, and Jeanette is planning a trip to Texas. They are going to Orlando to visit with Jan before they head out to different places. Jan's husband, Pat, has just been diagnosed with acute leukemia, and the prognosis is short term. He has grown up with all of them and is more like a brother, so they just want to visit while he is still in good spirits.

He is planning a big fishing trip with his son Nick, and they want to talk about it. He never got to go fishing. Two weeks after the diagnosis, Patrick A. Acompora Jr. died on October 24, 2006. His new heart held up good for thirteen and a half years. He just had other things in his body that broke down. The family showed up and was there to support Jan and her family, even the Belle Glade part of the extended family. Lorene was sad for their loss. She was the only mom he had for a while, and she loved him like a son. Somehow it won't be the same reading *National Geographic*. She was so glad she had all those children in Georgia to depend on. She rode down with Roger and his friend Jane and was glad to be able to be with Jan's family in their home.

It is now Thanksgiving, and although we lost two of our dear family, we have so much to be thankful for. We will all get together, and thank God for the many blessings he has bestowed on us. Lorene has noticed how her family squeezes closer when they have just gone through a tragedy and knows that is what family is all about. Stick together. She can truthfully know that her big bunch of Furneys stick together. This year she will spend Thanksgiving at Charles's house. The girls will all be there to help Charlotte, and it will be another bunch of turkey, corn bread dressing, yams, and since no one can make cracklin' bread like Charles always did, I guess we won't have any.

It is A glorious spring. Lorene's sister Sarah, who lives in the unit behind her, does not drive her car that much anymore. She has asked Jan to drive it around some to just keep the battery up. Jan is here for a visit and said she would drive it only if Sarah would go with her. They go to the vegetable stand for some tomatoes, and Jan picks up a little plant to take home with her. On the way back, she takes her for a drive around the "circle," Sarah is so excited to see all the beautiful azaleas, the dogwood in full bloom, and the beauty of one landscape prettier than the other. She exclaims she has never ridden over there before, and Jan just can't believe she has never seen all the beauty of her own neighborhood.

Her children come as often as they can now. Jan lives closer than the rest, so she tries to come often so the others don't have to make that seven-hour drive from West Palm Beach. They will go shopping or just go for a drive or to a restaurant, wherever she wants to go.

She wants to get out the clothes she will be taking for her next trip with Jerale. He is taking her to his hunting camp. He is so excited to share this with his mother. She, Jerale, Jeanette, and Mavis drive to up around Macon. She's not sure where she is but is shocked at the beauty of the place. It is not hunting season, and the boys always leave the camp in good shape. She is surprised to see that it is actually a house that was built by some of the hunters, the group that owns Duffey's restaurants in West Palm Beach. They even have parking places for their golf carts, and each place has an electric plug in for the occupants. They go inside and get their bags unpacked and are ready to hit the woods.

Jerale takes her on a quiet trip through the woods in the golf cart. There is no noise, and they can see the animals that are running around and the most beautiful birds out here in this wilderness. She can smell the mustiness of the moss and the leaves, hear the birds chirping, and everything is beautiful old trees, the whole place is green. They have to stop for a minute as she shows Jerale the difference between a wild plum tree and a mayhaw bush. He didn't know what a mayhaw bush looked like. It brings back such memories as she remembers going down by the river as a child with Grandpa Babe. He always knew where the mayhaw bushes were, and they would pick them for Grandma to make mayhaw jelly. She is now ninety-three years old and never dreamed she would ever see anything this beautiful again. Now to try out the dock that reaches out into the lake.

We have to catch some fish for dinner. She just can't believe as fast as she can get her hook in the water she catches a fish. They have enough for dinner, but she wants to keep fishing. She is having so much fun. Jerale just lets her continue fishing but is now taking them off the hook and releasing them. She wants to bring them home, but of course, they will not have a place to keep them until she goes home. They have gone inside and made dinner in a very comfortable kitchen. After dinner they bring their chairs down on the dock to enjoy a very pleasant sunset. They did eat out the next night. Everybody was too tired to cook after being in the woods all day. What a weekend she could never have imagined she would have at her age.

Lorene at Hunt Club with Jerale and the girls

She now has aides coming every day, and they walk with her. Walking, as well as her swimming, is keeping her in pretty good shape. She has a scooter and thought she would just drive it over to the YMCA every day, but it just didn't have what it takes to get her over the railroad tracks. Fortunately the county commissioner was coming by in his truck and brought her home. His helper rode the scooter the rest of the way. That's okay; Jan is bringing her a heavy-duty scooter that she can put in her Suburban when she takes her somewhere. She has an electronic lift that swings it right inside the back of the Suburban. It can go over railroad tracks.

It has been a beautiful fall, and everybody was home for a big Thanksgiving dinner and a big birthday cake for her ninety-third birthday. Now it is already time for the Christmas parade, and Jan is taking her downtown with her scooter so she can just scoot all over downtown. She is all bundled up and will watch Ms. Pat's dancers before the parade. Her great-great-granddaughter Callie (Charlotte's granddaughter) will be doing a little dance for her. She loves watching the children show off. Now we will see the parade. Each year she thinks it will be her last if it's just too cold, but the next year she's right back. This year, her granddaughter Stacey's husband, who is a policeman, has just the spot for them. Right beside his car, right in front of Friedlander's. Jan is off looking for the prized Moultrie Christmas ornament, and Lorene just sits and enjoys the parade with a good cup of hot cocoa.

The winter was cold this year, but she kept so busy it went fast. When she had some extra time, she would get out her tapes and just listen to some good old gospel or country music. Gil's wife, Betty, had gotten her a stereo.

Jerale and Delores celebrate their fortieth anniversary with a cruise

Jerale's family

The children have picked her up, and she is back in Florida again. It seems like they are all too busy to fish right now. Jerale and Jan are the only two left working, and Mae and Jeanette are just enjoying the beaches and the swimming pool with her. It seems they just want to go out to eat almost every meal, and she is quite happy if they would eat at home. However, she will just do what the crowd does. She gets her water aerobics in the pool there and will stay for a month or so then be on her way back to Georgia. The children in Georgia miss her and can't wait for Grandma Furney to get home.

It is now late spring, and we have lost another family member to a pancreas attack: her dear talented grandson from Illinois. Vern and Cyndi's son Christopher Vernon Furney died on May 16, 2008. The whole big Furney bunch is hurting, and many of them headed for the Hampton Inn in Rockford to support the family. He was a talented *Vogue* photographer and world traveler. He was involved at the time in the redevelopment of downtown Rockford with his dad Vern. He was the owner of a retro furniture store downtown. After the funeral, Jeanette and Jan waited a few weeks and returned to spend time with their brother Vern's family on July 4.

The cooler part of fall has gone. This Thanksgiving, we have a big treat. Not only will everybody wake up under the same roof at the Hampton Inn, but Wendy is also letting us use her conference room for dinner. We had the food catered, and all we did was set up the room, the steam trays, and go pick up the food. Everybody helped set up the food, and all forty-seven of us had a grand feast. The weather was in the seventies, and most of us dined out on the patio. After dinner Lorene had a big ninety-fourth birthday cake, a little nap, and then headed downtown for the lighting of the Christmas tree and turning on all the lights. Lorene is right there for the trip downtown on her scooter.

Lorene's ninety-fourth birthday

The great-grandchildren are a lot of fun now that they are all old enough to shop. The girls all want to go shop, and the boys are reluctant but usually will go and carry their bags for them as long as they don't have to wait for them to buy clothes. She loves watching the great-great-grandchildren's eyes all aglow when Santa rumbles down the street with his real reindeer again. It never changes, although the generation changes. She will let a tiny one sit on her lap on the scooter, while the others may be a little shy with Santa. This year they also get to ride ponies. Jerale's youngest grandson, Robert, is now five and is right there for everything his older cousins will do.

Lorene, Elizabeth, and Robert meeting Santa

During the last six months or so she tends to get lonely for her children. The remaining five have agreed to have at least one of the children visit once a month. She knows Jan can come down almost any weekend, and if she calls in time, she will just leave her job early and come for the weekend. She leaves clothes in the closet in case her mother calls, she can just leave from work. She is calling more often if she doesn't remember who is coming. She has been hospitalized for pneumonia and is now on oxygen twenty-four hours a day.

It is Vernon's month to be with her, and he will fly into the Sanford Airport, which is only a twenty-minute drive from Jan's home. Jan and her granddaughter Shawna will pick him up, and they will drive up to Moultrie.

Jan has reservations at the hotel, and Vern will stay with Lorene. They walk into the Hampton Inn around eleven PM. The night clerk Chris looks exasperated and says, "We are full because of the auto show at Spence Field." Jan gives him the reservation number only to find the reservation clerk gave her the wrong month, March. He promises her he will have a room tomorrow. They go to Lorene's apartment, and quietly Jan slips into bed with her. Shawna sleeps in a recliner, and Vern gets the couch. What a nice surprise she had when she woke up.

She is now fussing that she wants one of them to move in with her. Because of the economy, Jan finally is laid off from her job. Lorene is happy and thinks it is about time. Jan will be seventy this year. It is March when Jan pulls into the driveway. She can stay for about six weeks but will need to go home occasionally because she has a dog and a swimming pool that demands attention. She fell the first night Jan was there but no damage. She has had daily help for a while, but they cannot administer medication and Jan is so surprised to find out she now gets confused and doesn't recognize some of her medications. This happened so fast. Jan goes to the library when she needs to use the computer, and everything just snowballs. They need a family meeting.

She needs twenty-four-hour care. Jan stays until Jeanette can come relieve her. After the first week, Jeanette knows she is right, and they start to make the arrangements for a nursing home. Lorene knows she needs someone all the time and agrees to go, but she will choose the nursing home she likes. She is familiar with them all. Sunrise won out by a hand. At first Jeanette isn't happy, but afterward she sees how happy Lorene will be with being able to socialize and get the care she needs.

She knows so many people there and can take all her meals in the dining room. She's happy but is getting tired very easily. Now she has a constant flow of company and sits on the front porch every day to watch the bluebirds build a nest on the other side of the driveway. Later she will have the pleasure of watching them hatch and fly away. As the summer moves on, she will go for her therapy each day and meet her visitors in the living room out front, where she can talk without interruptions. Her sister-in-law Laura was already there, and then her sister Sarah also came into the nursing home. She was not lonely after all.

Al, Josh, and Jeanette at the high school graduation

    Thanksgiving is here already, and the Hampton Inn is hosting the big Furney bunch again this year. They will have the food in the business conference room again. Lorene is just hoping she can last through all this again. This time, when the children came to pick her up, she brought her sister Sarah with her for dinner, and they each can have a room for a nap later. After the big dinner, the place just filled up, and they sang "Happy Birthday." By now her sister Leona has arrived with her four daughters (the four Vs). She is so pleased to have all her family there and had so much fun she decided to skip the Christmas lights this year. She said good night, and she and Sarah headed back to their comfortable beds.

    Now Lorene is ninety-five years old and has gotten her wish to spend this Christmas at her son Charles's home. He has been dead for several years, but his daughter Charlotte, who now lives there, has gotten the family together to celebrate this holy day together with her. She is so grateful to God that she can join them at Christmas as she had for so many years. She had to leave early. Now that she is older, she just can't stay up for a long period of time and needs to retire early. The next two days she went to the dining room for her meals, but the rest of her time was spent in her small bed in the nursing home, where she could reflect on the many years she had spent on this earth.

Some of the first years were hard, but as the children got older, the lighter the load became. There was a time when she could not take her eight children, the big Furney bunch, to a lot of places she would have liked to. Now when people see the big Furney bunch, coming, with their big smiling faces and all the happy laughter, they are so happy to see them. She smiles at the thought of her eight children, twenty grandchildren, twenty-nine great-grandchildren, and sixteen great-great-grandchildren. She can't help but laugh at what she and Webb have created. All her children are property owners, they have managed to educate themselves, and all of them except one (and he is almost there) have retired from good jobs, and all are upstanding citizens in their communities. They have all accomplished what she set out for them to do, and she is so proud of them all.

Now it is time for her to rest before her final journey. She hears her daughter Jeanette coming down the hall with Flossie (her nurse). Flossie is telling Jeanette her mother is resting easy, just not eating much. Of course Jeanette has her eyes full of concern and tries to give her mom a little chicken soup. Jeanette stays for a few hours and then is ready to go to her hotel room. She has just completed a seven-hour drive just to see her mother. Lorene knows Jesus is coming to get her soon and hopes the other children will not feel guilty about not seeing her. She has seen each of them recently. Now she just needs a little nap, and she is sure this time, when she opens her eyes again, she will be able to *look upon the face of God and feel his presence.* She closes her eyes and drifts off.

On New Year's Eve in 2009, her family and friends have gathered again. Her grandson Brian has composed himself well enough to play with a long bow the soft notes of "Ashokan Farewell" on her grandfather's violin, which Lorene had requested he play at her funeral. This is his greatest tribute to a great Southern lady, his grandma Furney.

Lorene Hart Furney died on December 27, 2009.

Lorene with children, 1989

CPSIA information can be obtained at www.ICGtesting.com
Printed in the USA
LVOW040323090812

293597LV00001B/9/P

9 781477 145029